CHASING
THE BEAR

CHASING
THE BEAR

HOW BEAR BRYANT AND NICK SABAN MADE

ALABAMA THE GREATEST COLLEGE

FOOTBALL PROGRAM OF ALL TIME

LARS ANDERSON

GRAND CENTRAL
PUBLISHING

NEW YORK   BOSTON

Grand Central Publishing
Hachette Book Group
1290 Avenue of the Americas, New York, NY 10104
grandcentralpublishing.com
twitter.com/grandcentralpub

First Edition: September 2019

Grand Central Publishing is a division of Hachette Book Group, Inc. The Grand Central Publishing name and logo is a trademark of Hachette Book Group, Inc.

The publisher is not responsible for websites (or their content) that are not owned by the publisher.

The Hachette Speakers Bureau provides a wide range of authors for speaking events. To find out more, go to www.hachettespeakersbureau.com or call (866) 376-6591.

Library of Congress Cataloging-in-Publication Data has been applied for.

ISBNs: 978-1-5387-1648-9 (hardcover), 978-1-5387-1649-6 (ebook)

Printed in the United States of America

LSC-C

10 9 8 7 6 5 4 3 2 1

For my beautiful twin girls, Autumn Kaye Anderson and Farrah Rose Anderson: Know that Daddy loves you, always.

Contents

CONTENTS

CHASING
THE BEAR

CHAPTER 1

Bryant and Saban: On the Same Team at Last

PAST AND PRESENT

The grandson rode in the car behind the long white hearse on that cold January day in 1983. Looking out the window as a twenty-year-old, he saw thousands of fans on Interstate 20/59 stop their cars and pickup trucks and 18-wheelers to watch the funeral procession of three hundred vehicles roll by, their headlights aglow in the gray winter afternoon. At overpasses the grandson spotted businessmen with their fedoras placed over their hearts and farmers in overalls with tears rolling down their cheeks. There were hundreds and hundreds of children, too, wearing Crimson Tide jackets and gazing in wonder at the spectacle.

All along the fifty-five-mile route from Tuscaloosa's First United Methodist Church to Birmingham, where the graveside service would be held at Elmwood Cemetery, he witnessed thousands of mourners standing at the side of the road, their faces frozen, just there to watch, to feel, to witness history and the South's longest farewell. That was when it really hit Marc Bryant Tyson: His grandfather, Paul "Bear" Bryant, who had died two days earlier at the age of sixty-nine, might have been the most revered figure in the history of Alabama.

"The love I saw that day of the funeral for my grandfather shocked me," Tyson said. "It was like the entire state had lost a member of their own family. It took my breath away. I had no idea. I mean, *no* idea."

The grandson is fifty-six years old now, and he has a son of his own: Paul William Bryant Tyson. Marc began taking Paul to Alabama games when his boy was four years old in 2004. Sitting in their seats in the front row of the south end zone at Bryant-Denny Stadium, surround by fans in black-and-white houndstooth hats, the father and son would see the image of the Bear appear on the video boards, and then his gravelly, pack-a-day voice would rumble down from grandstands over the PA system, like God shouting from the heavens in a Southern drawl: *I ain't never been nothin' but a winner*, causing the crowd to erupt in a kind of rapture.

Through the years Marc kept bringing his son to games, pausing at the bronzed statue of Bear Bryant outside of the stadium and sharing stories about Paul's great-grandfather. Tales about how Marc and Papa—Marc's name for Bryant—used to fish together in ponds around Tuscaloosa, with Bear using a cane pole, a red-and-white bobber, and crickets for bait, trying to catch blue gill bream that weighed a half pound—his favorite food, even more than steak. How Bryant used to let him climb the thirty-three steps to the top of his iron tower during practice and watch the Tide players with him, the Bear with a bullhorn in hand, eyeing his players in combat. How Marc stood on the sideline during games and would greet his granddaddy after the final whistle on the field, where Bryant would put his arm around his grandson and together the two would walk through the growing afternoon shadows toward the dressing room.

How at nights after games Marc would tune the radio in Bryant's den to a game that featured another Southeastern Conference team, the crackling play-by-play filling up the room as Bryant ate dinner on a rickety card table tray. And how Bryant had attended Marc's first high school football game, which he played in Brookstown, Georgia, when he was in the eleventh grade. Not wanting to make his grandson nervous, Bryant had planned to sneak into the game, sit in a corner of the grandstands, and act like he was reading a newspaper, holding it open just beneath his eyes. He was discovered by admiring fans, but when Marc saw his grandfather it filled him with the one thing that Bryant always instilled in his players: confidence.

Young Paul was hypnotized by all these stories about the man he never met. He soon grew fascinated by another Alabama coach, one whose coaching career overlapped his great-grandfather's by ten years, but a coach that Bear Bryant never faced on the field: Nick Saban. In November 2009—Saban's third season in Tuscaloosa—Marc and Paul were in their Row 1 seats inside Bryant-Denny Stadium at the beginning of the fourth quarter against Louisiana State University. Trailing the Tigers 15–13, an older Crimson Tide fan recognized nine-year-old Paul and bent over and kissed him on the forehead for good luck. A moment later, Alabama wide receiver Julio Jones caught a pass and blazed down the sideline to give the Tide a lead they would never surrender. The affectionate fan rejoiced.

Over the next few years Paul rarely missed attending Alabama games, traveling to see his Tide play in season openers, conference games, SEC title games, and national championship games. He met Nick Saban at various functions where the coach was speaking, and the two talked a few more times in Saban's office on the second floor of the Mal Moore Athletic Facility, a redbrick structure on Paul W. Bryant Drive. The sight of the five-eight, 180-pound Saban always held the boy's eyes, and the coach's words left him thunderstruck after every interaction. Paul imagined that was how his great-grandfather made his fans feel.

By the time he was a junior in high school in 2017, the great-grandson of the Bear had grown into a six-four, 210-pound quarterback at Hewitt-Trussville High outside of Birmingham. In December 2017 Saban invited Paul to Tuscaloosa for a practice. Standing on the sideline as his Crimson Tide players warmed up, Saban told Paul, "Every coach I have talked to on our staff wants you to play for Alabama. This isn't because of your great-grandfather. This is because of you and the player we believe you can become." Paul, who grew up with a bust of his great-grandfather in his bedroom, couldn't suppress his smile. Saban shook his hand and said, "Now you think about it. I've got to get back to practice." And off Saban jogged.

On April 5, 2018, Marc and his son drove on Interstate 20/59 from Birmingham to Tuscaloosa—the same ribbon of road the Bear's funeral procession had traversed in the opposite direction thirty-five years earlier. Father and son then walked into Saban's office. "We need you, Paul," said Saban, seated close to a coffee table that had four national championship rings sitting on it, their diamonds sparkling in the soft office light. "We want you to be a leader of this recruiting class." Then, the great-grandson of the Bear made it official: He turned down scholarship offers from Notre Dame, Michigan, and LSU, and committed to Alabama.

In December 2018, Paul enrolled for classes and immediately began practicing with the Crimson Tide, who were preparing for the College Football Playoff. Saban was on his personal quest to win his record seventh national title—one more than the Bear. On the practice field, just a few blocks from Bryant-Denny Stadium, the great-grandson started flinging the football around as Saban intently watched.

On Paul's first night on campus, Marc helped his son move into Paul W. Bryant Hall. As they unpacked suitcases in the dorm named after Paul's great-grandfather—four decades earlier, Marc had eaten meals with Papa in the brick colonial building known as "the Bryant Hilton"—father and son marveled at how the past was meeting the present. Together, their dreams stirred. For the first time, a Bryant and Nick Saban were on the same team.

The DNA of the Bear was back at Bama.

CHAPTER 2

Mamma Called

1958

He drove his white Cadillac through the winter afternoon, passing farmhouses and shacks in the Alabama countryside, winding through flatland cotton fields and woods of southern pines. It was January 30, 1958. Two days earlier Paul "Bear" Bryant had loaded his life and his family—wife, Mary Harmon; son, Paul Jr.; and their dachshund, Doc—into the car and rolled out of College Station, Texas, and headed 650 miles east for their new home: Tuscaloosa, Alabama. Bryant had been successful in his four years as the head coach of Texas A&M, transforming a team that went 1-9 his first season to one that compiled a 17-3-1 record during his final two years. Now he was about to return to the birthplace of his college football career.

For several months, Crimson Tide fans had sent Bryant hundreds of letters and telegrams, pleading for him to return to Tuscaloosa, where the Tide program under coach J. B. "Ears" Whitworth had fallen into an abyss. Starting in 1955, Whitworth began his tenure with fourteen straight losses. He benched future Green Bay Packers quarterback Bart Starr for most of his senior season in '55 and by the end of the '57 campaign—the low tide of Alabama football—Whitworth had an overall record of 4-24-2, prompting the school to let him go. In some of the missives to Bryant, grade school and high school boys promised to play for him if he would come home to Alabama, where Bryant had been an end on the Tide team from 1933 to 1935.

Bryant initially resisted the overtures, believing he was on the path to winning a national championship in College Station. The first training camp he held as A&M's coach was in the small Hill County town of Junction, where the school had a 411-acre adjunct campus. Bryant felt his boys needed to be "toughed up," so he put them through a brutal ten-day regime. Practices began before dawn, and the days wouldn't end until meetings concluded at 11 p.m. Junction was in the grip of a drought and a heat wave—each day the temperature topped more than one hundred degrees under the fireball sun—and Bryant was a ruthless dictator, working his players on the parched Texas turf to the point of near collapse, rarely allowing water breaks. Each morning fewer and fewer players showed up for the start of practice, but this was Bryant's hope: He wanted only the strongest and roughest guys to remain on the roster, his brand of Darwinian football. The survivors of this camp became known throughout the region as "the Junction Boys."

Bryant adored those players who stuck with him. But on December 3, 1957, he called a press conference at the Shamrock Hotel in Houston. Sitting in front of a microphone and dozens of newspapermen who puffed on Pall Malls and Lucky Strikes, Bryant explained that the decision to return to Alabama was the hardest one he ever made. "The only reason I'm going back," he said, "is because my school called me." He later explained in his hallmark folksy style, "Momma called. And when Momma calls, you just have to come runnin'."

Now the miles on his Caddy odometer rolled over and over as Bryant and his family entered the city limits of Tuscaloosa on a January afternoon in 1958. From behind the wheel, the coach spotted a billboard and told his wife to look up. They saw: "Welcome Home Bear and Mary Harmon."

Bryant glanced at his wife, an Alabama native who was shining with happiness. "All my life," she said, "*all* my life, I've wanted to come back here to live."

Bryant was forty-four years old, stood six foot four with wide shoulders, had an equally wide smile, and was still country strong—he could grab a defensive player by the jersey in practice and toss him aside without much effort, as if he were nothing more than a water boy. He spoke in a rumble and his laugh could fill up a room. He had a hair-trigger temper and fined anyone who cursed on the practice field $5—a pot to which he often contributed himself after an R-rated word flew from his lips.

Bryant had met Mary Harmon Black at the University of Alabama in 1934, when Bryant was on the football team and president of the on-campus A-club, an organization for athletes. Bryant had helped the Tide win a national championship that season, earning second-team all-SEC honors as an end. He played his senior year, 1935, with a partially broken leg. Legendary sportswriter Grantland Rice told a friend that Bryant would have been an All-American if he hadn't gotten hurt.

The summer before his last year in college, Bryant and Mary Harmon drove south to the small town of Ozark, Alabama. A campus beauty queen who came from a wealthy Birmingham family, Harmon fell hard for the handsome and charismatic Bryant. The pair tied the knot in Ozark, though they kept it a secret because Bryant feared that his coach, Frank Thomas—who didn't like his players to wed—would take away his scholarship if he found out.

Bryant and his wife had visited Tuscaloosa in late December 1957. They checked into the Hotel Stafford, the grandest accommodation in town, where local families often enjoyed multicourse Sunday lunches. On New Year's Eve the Bryants attended a dinner dance at the Tuscaloosa Country Club, where Bryant shook every hand that was thrust at him, patted backs and worked the room, sharing anecdotes from his playing days and telling everyone how happy he was to be back—and how much work needed to be done.

Now having moved to Tuscaloosa and living in the Stafford in late January 1958—the Bryants stayed there for several months while house hunting—Bryant was back in his Caddy and driving through the predawn darkness. He arrived at his office at 5:30 a.m., slid behind his desk, and sat in his chair. Alone in the building, alone in the quiet, alone with his thoughts, he was overcome with a familiar feeling that always seized him when he contemplated his football team:

He worried like hell.

Before Bryant was introduced as head coach in Tuscaloosa, he slipped into Friedman Hall, a two-story dormitory where the football players lived. Bryant wanted to look over his about-to-be players without their knowing he was even on campus. "Coach Bryant walks in and sees players smoking cigarettes and cigars, and there are liquor bottles and beer bottles all over the place," said Bill Oliver, one of Bryant's first recruits at Alabama, who also coached with Bryant from 1971 to 1979. "He had a passkey, which unlocked the doors to both floors. He looked in the rooms and saw how out of shape the players were. He said to everyone, 'Y'all have a nice day.' No one recognized him."

Bryant had a detailed five-year plan to build Alabama into a national title winner, one that involved aggressive recruiting, player conditioning, style of play, and even the type and extent of media attention he wanted to cultivate. At his introductory press conference a reporter from the *Birmingham News* stated, "Coach, the alumni are expecting your team to go undefeated next season."

"The hell you say," Bryant quickly groused. "I'm an alumni, and I don't expect us to go undefeated."

Bryant knew that the task ahead of him was daunting. In Alabama's final game of the '57 season, Auburn had drilled the Tide 40–0 as the Tigers marched to the Associated Press national title. That loss to Auburn featured a microcosm of all the ills that infected the Alabama program: a lack of talented players, undisciplined play, poor coaching, and a who-really-gives-a-damn attitude that was evident in the actions and on the faces of the players, the coaches, and even the training staff. Whitworth's contract expired at midnight after the Auburn game, and he asked that it not be renewed. He knew he had failed at Alabama. With moist eyes, he told reporters in the locker room that he was going to do some hunting and fishing in Oklahoma. "Then I'm going to sit down," he said, "and do some serious thinking about my future."

Less than two weeks later, Bryant held his first meeting with his players on December 9, 1957. Though he still had one more game to coach for Texas A&M, he wanted to issue a warning of the storm that was about to blow into Tuscaloosa. He pinned a note on the bulletin board in Friedman Hall that announced there would be a team meeting at 1:20 p.m. in the basement of the hall in a room that was filled with high school–style wooden desks.

Bryant entered through the basement door and stomped to the front of the room. Hands on hips, in silence, Bryant looked at his players. His square-jaw glare cast an oh-my-God pall over the faces of the players: This was the man who had inspected their dorm days earlier. They froze, execution chamber silent. Bryant thrust his hands in his pockets and rattled his loose change and keys—always a signal that he was about to say something of importance. They felt the heat of Bryant's mere presence, of his natural-born intensity, a characteristic that thousands would witness over the next quarter century in Tuscaloosa and around the country.

"Men, y'all don't know who I am and I don't know who you are," he said. "We are going to have spring practice in a little bit. Some of you after spring practice is over I'll know. Some of you I won't know. And if I don't know you, that means you don't matter anyway. I don't want to hear anything about past coaches. The whole problem is right here in this room. And for those who can stay, we will fix it. Yes, we will fix it."

A few minutes later, four late-arriving players pushed open the door to the meeting room. Bryant immediately shifted his eyes in their direction and stopped speaking. A momentary silence was broken by a loud and forceful "Get out! Get out!" Bryant then looked at an assistant and told him to lock the doors. "There will be no interruptions," he said.

During his talk, Bryant didn't focus only on football. He laid out how he wanted his players to behave, from how they should write letters to their mammas and papas on a regular basis to the respect they should show their elders to how important it was to never act like they were better than anyone else simply because they played football. "If you're not committed to winning ball games, to make your grades, go ahead and get your stuff and move out of the dorm, because it's going to show," Bryant said. "You can have all the God-given ability in the world, but if you don't hustle, you won't play. We're going to start somebody in your place."

The meeting lasted twenty-three minutes. Bryant then left to fly back to College Station to coach his final game at Texas A&M, a matchup in the Gator Bowl against Tennessee. The Aggie alumni were furious that Bryant—who had seven years remaining on his contract with A&M—was abandoning their school, and his players were listless, suffering a 3–0 loss to the Volunteers. Two days later, Bryant and his family were on their way to Tuscaloosa; the Texas oil fields disappeared in the rearview mirror.

Bryant met with each player in his office. "Everyone was scared for our one-on-one meetings," said Marlin "Scooter" Dyess, a running back and defensive back on the team. "The first one to go over and see Coach Bryant was a big lineman. Coach asked, 'Are you in a fraternity?' He said, 'Yes, sir.' Coach then asked, 'You have a car?' It turned out he did. Then Coach asked, 'Do you have a girlfriend?' The lineman said, 'Yes sir.' Then Coach Bryant replied, 'Son, I don't think you're going to have time to play football.' Of course, the lineman relayed all of this information to us, and so we all knew not to tell Coach Bryant if we were in a frat or had a car or had a girlfriend."

In these meetings Bryant also asked each young man about his brothers and sisters, about his parents, about his dreams for the future. He quizzed them on what they wanted to do with their lives once football was over, and he wanted to know what their motivations were—who were they playing for and why football meant so much to them. He wanted to know what made each player tick.

On January 10 he called another team meeting. "We are going to do two things," Bryant said. "We are going to learn to play football, and we are going to get up and go to class like our mammas and papas expect us to. And we are going to win. Ten years from now, you are going to be married with a family, your wife might be sick, your kids might be sick, you might be sick, but you will get your butt up and go to work. That's what I'm going to do for you. I'm going to teach you how to do things you don't feel like doing."

Bryant hired a staff of nine assistants, chosen largely for their skill in recruiting and ability to sweet-talk parents and players into believing that Alabama was the only school for them. He redid the football offices, hired a "nice-looking brunette" to receive callers in the reception area, and put up a sign that read: "Winning Isn't Everything, But It Beats Anything That Comes in Second."

He installed nine air-conditioning units in the renovated football headquarters, which now featured modern furniture, fluorescent lighting, and new floors of inlaid tile.

Within days of Bryant announcing he was returning to Tuscaloosa, several top in-state recruits committed to Alabama, including a trio of All-City players from Montgomery—Jimmy Sharpe, Cliff Russell, and Carl Hopson. Bryant also hit the recruiting trail, driving around the South in search of players. In the homes of prospects, Bryant would take off his brown fedora, shake hands with mammas and papas, and then sometimes offer to make coffee. A smile—equal parts welcoming and disarming—continually radiated from his face. He would describe how he would take care of the parents' child once he was in Tuscaloosa, how he'd look after him and make sure he was attending to his studies. He also promised to infuse their child's life with discipline and resolve. No boys in America, he vowed, would be tougher than his players.

Bryant was a charmer in these living rooms. Leaning on his own experience of growing up poor in rural Arkansas, he could talk about crops with farming families and working on cars with fathers who got their fingers dirty for a living. He wouldn't turn down a mason jar if it was offered—he didn't mind a nip of moonshine—and he could discuss what it was like to make it through hard times. He could connect to all types of families, emphasizing the common traits he shared with them. His ability to empathize and engage endeared him on every in-home recruiting visit.

Bryant quickly developed one of the most thorough recruiting operations in college football. First, the staff compared notes on a prospective recruit, discussing minute details such as whether the player had flexibility in his ankles and knees and how he reacted when he was beaten on a play. If Bryant believed the prospect possessed enough talent to play at Alabama, he and his staff would then dig into his background, talking to his parents, his high school teachers, his guidance counselors, his mentors, his friends, even his neighbors. Bryant believed that he could mold a high school athlete with great character into an elite player, because that player would listen to his coaches and endure the pain of his practices. To Bryant, character—and proper temperament—mattered as much as raw talent.

In his first months on the job Bryant met with high school coaches across Alabama, trying to win over each one and convince them that a new day had dawned in Tuscaloosa. Bryant viewed his relationship with state high school coaches as vital as anything else in his role as Alabama's head coach: If he got the high school coaches on his side, Bryant believed that they in turn would convince their star players to attend Alabama.

"When I sat in Coach Bryant's office on my recruiting visit he was very direct in saying, 'We're going to get Alabama back where we belong. We've won Rose Bowls and national championships. And through hard work, that's the level we're going to get back to,'" recalled Bill Battle, a native of Birmingham who played end at Alabama from 1960 to 1962. "Coach Bryant also said he needed the best high school players in the state to come to Alabama. He believed that there was enough talent in the state to accomplish all the goals he had."

Upon Bryant's arrival, football became a year-round activity for the players—a first for the team in Tuscaloosa. Before spring practice began in March, he implemented a tortuous off-season conditioning program. In a gym on the top floor of Little Hall—named after William Gray Little, who introduced football to Alabama in 1892—players would work in small groups, moving between running stations, wrestling drills, and exercise routines. These off-season workouts were rare in college football at the time, and Bryant's winter program was more strenuous than most teams' spring practices. Players hit blocking sleds that were pushed against a wall, hitting them until their shoulders ached and they had trouble lifting their arms. And they did what was called a grass drill—dropping to the floor and rising as quickly as possible, over and over. Bryant lined the stuffy gym with trash cans that reeked with vomit after every training session.

For the players, though, the real struggle began with Bryant's first spring practice in Tuscaloosa. It was every bit as intense as his infamous Junction practice in Texas: From dawn until well past dark, the players were either on the field, in meetings, or studying film until they collapsed into their beds at 11 p.m. The Southern heat wasn't as scorching as it had been in Junction, but the players were rarely allowed water breaks and were given salt tablets to prevent cramps. But the tablets only deepened their thirst, and the desperate-for-water players were driven to sucking on sweat-soaked towels, hoping to find any kind of relief. After practice, players would stand under the shower heads with their mouths agape and eyes closed, as if they'd finally found a water hole in the desert.

About two dozen players quit the Alabama football team that spring. Some thought Bryant had lost his mind and was intent on inflicting cruel and unusual punishment. Players were expected to hop up as soon as they hit the ground in a drill or a scrimmage.

One time a player was slow to rise, causing Bryant to yell, "Nobody makes money on their ass except a prostitute!"

Some players simply couldn't endure the misery of these practices. But Bryant had his reasons for putting his boys through nearly two weeks of waking hell: He wanted to rid the program of players who didn't have the deep-seated desire to play for the Tide. The coach preferred players to quit in the spring rather than during a game, and he needed to find out who had the toughness, grit, and fortitude to deserve an Alabama football uniform in the fall.

Bryant said that he had inherited a fat, bloated, lazy, uncommitted team when he arrived in Tuscaloosa—football sins that needed to be washed away that spring. And washing away he was.

€   €   €

Before the spring semester ended and summer vacation began, Bryant summoned each remaining player on the roster to his office. He then gave him a detailed summer workout plan. Most were designed to increase their quickness. Bryant believed that the key to the future success of Alabama was to have the quickest team in America, and he demanded that each of his boys work hard in the summer on their own to improve their speed.

Right guard Billy Rains, who had played at 210 pounds the previous year, was told by coaches that he needed to get his weight down to 192 by the start of fall practice. Fearing what would happen if he didn't make that weight, Rains spent the summer at his home in Moulton, Alabama, on the high school field running and riding a bike every day. Like most of Bryant's boys who had survived the first six months in Tuscaloosa, Rains didn't want to disappoint his new coach. So he worked harder than ever before at home. Even as the last glimmers of sunlight shot across his high school field, friends could see the silhouette of Rains, running and grinding through the summer twilight.

Bryant penned a letter to his players on July 15, laying out what they could expect when they returned to campus for the beginning of practice on August 30. "You must report in good shape because our plans call for real hard work the first two weeks of practice," Bryant wrote. "After that, we hope to simply sharpen up and rest up for each game. Anyone failing to report in good physical condition would throw our plans out of kilter, so if you cannot report in good shape, please don't report at all."

Bryant also handwrote notes to many of the letters. To one player he wrote, "Come in racehorse condition."

Late that summer, in the meeting room at Friedman Hall, Bryant spoke to his incoming freshmen class—his first class of recruits, which totaled about one hundred and included players who were trying to walk on. Bryant had constructed winning programs at Maryland (in his one season as coach he led the Terrapins to a 6-2-1 record), Kentucky (over eight seasons the Wildcats finished in the Top 20 five times under Bryant), and Texas A&M (after finishing 1-9 in his first season, the Aggies went 8-3 in his fourth and final year in College Station). His history for authoring quick turnarounds was the message his assistants sold to recruits and their families as they fanned across Alabama and nearby states to entice blue-chip prospects to Tuscaloosa.

Bryant believed that these incoming freshmen would be the backbone of his program, the players who would eventually make the plays to lead Alabama to its first national championship since 1941—the year America entered World War II. It had been seventeen autumns since the Tide had last been named the best team in the country. Most of the young faces in this room were only knee-high when coach Frank Thomas guided Alabama to a 9-2 record and a victory in the Cotton Bowl over Texas A&M, prompting the Houlgate System (a mathematical system used between 1929 and 1958 and that is now recognized by the NCAA in its Football Subdivision record book) to name the Crimson Tide its national champion. These young players in the room didn't know what Alabama was capable of.

"What are you doing here?" Bryant asked his freshman players, who at the time weren't eligible to play. For several seconds Bryant eyed his young players in silence. "What are you doing here?" he asked again. Again, Bryant looked into the eyes of his boys, moving from one to the next, slowly. The room remained quiet.

"Tell me why you're here," he said, his voice rising. "If you're not here to win a national championship, you're in the wrong place." Bryant then described in detail how Alabama would accomplish that goal. The players hung on his every syllable, as if the words were thundering down from the clouds.

"Look around at the guys sitting next to you," Bryant said. "Chances are, four years from now, there's probably going to be no more than a double handful of you left... But if you work hard and do the things I ask you to do, you can be national champions by the time you're seniors."

During camp Bryant maintained a meticulous schedule. At 6:00 a.m. he held a staff meeting, reviewing every detail of the upcoming practice and what he wanted to accomplish. At 7:25 he presided over a team meeting. By 9:00, the players and coaches were on the field. For two hours, the players ran from drill to drill—no walking was allowed. He again met with his coaches at 11:15 to go over the afternoon practice session, which began at 3:30. The players, exhausted after four more hours of practice, ate dinner at 7:00 while Bryant met with his staff at 7:30 to plan the next day's practices. One assistant calculated that he made about eleven cents an hour during camp.

"The varsity players could hardly walk after practice," said Bill Oliver, who was a freshman in 1958. "Coach Bryant and the staff worked the heck out of them. It took every bit of courage they had just to make it out onto that field. Everyone absolutely dreaded practice."

The message was clear: Players either played with passion and intensity for Bryant at all times—no matter the circumstances, no matter the place—or they wouldn't be around for long. A reporter from the Associated Press quoted Bryant as saying, "The riff-raff are fast eliminating themselves."

Later in the fall, Bryant and a friend bumped into one of the "riff-raff" players who had left the team and was now working at a hotel in Tuscaloosa as a bellman. "Hello Coach," the player said. Bryant didn't bother to acknowledge the player. When Bryant's friend asked why he didn't even say hello, Bryant sternly replied, "He's a quitter. Hell, I wouldn't let him carry my suitcase in here. If I was supposed to be on the fifth floor, he'd be liable to leave it on the second."

Mamma Called

●　　●　　●

By the start of the 1958 season, because of the hard practices, the roster had been whittled to forty-six players who were eligible to play, only seventeen more than had survived the Junction training camp in Texas. But Bryant liked the players who stuck it out—they had the mettle and tenacity he was looking for. He knew he didn't have the talent he needed to compete for an SEC title, but a standard for toughness was being established. The Bear's own DNA was beginning to flow into the Alabama program.

Bryant described the kind of game his team would play in 1958 as "garbage football," featuring quick kicks on second and third down and trick plays to try to fool the defense. "Coach Bryant felt like he had a much better defense than offense," said Scooter Dyess. "So the quick kick allowed him to pin the opposing offense deep in its own territory and then he'd let them make a mistake, like fumble the ball or throw an interception, and then our offense could capitalize on the short field. This was smart coaching because we didn't have the caliber of players that most of the teams had that we faced."

Alabama opened the season at Ladd Stadium in Mobile against LSU and its star player, Billy Cannon, a running back who would win the Heisman Trophy three months later. Before the game, a heavy rain fell on Mobile for two days. Still, more than thirty-four thousand fans filled the wooden bleachers to see Bryant prowl the soggy sideline for the first time as the Tide's coach.

Bryant often ordered his offense to quick kick when they faced a second- or third-and-long—the center would snap the ball to a back who would then punt the ball to the unsuspecting LSU defense, which didn't have a returner back deep. On several quick kicks the ball bounced deep into Tiger territory.

Then midway through the first quarter a loud snapping sound emanated from the north end zone. Bryant and everyone else turned to look: A temporary wooden grandstand, holding more than 1,400 people, collapsed. Screams echoed across the field. Officials quickly stopped the game. Players and other fans rushed to pull fans from the wooden heap. Ambulances drove onto the field. No one was killed, but more than sixty were injured and twenty-five were hospitalized. Only minutes into the Bear Bryant era it was as if unnatural acts were already occurring.

Once order was restored, Alabama kicked a field goal to take a 3–0 lead at halftime over the eventual 1958 national champions. In the locker room, the players sipped glass bottles of Coca-Cola in their mud-stained uniforms as Bryant spoke. "Everybody listen now," Bryant said. "It's the most important thirty minutes of your life. Everybody needs to decide what he's going to do. If we fumble the first play, are you going to give up? Or are you going to hold? You've come this far—give it your best. Give it your very best."

The Tide players charged out onto the field. But the team was still young, still learning the ways of Bryant and his staff. LSU rallied behind Cannon and won 13–3. The Tigers had outgained the Tide 262 yards to 100. Alabama attempted three passes and failed to complete a single one. But the game stayed close for one reason: the quick kick.

Throughout the season fans were often perplexed by Bryant's use of the quick kick. Once, when Alabama quick kicked on a second-and-one from its own 24-yard line against Mississippi State, Winston "Red" Blount, an Alabama athletic board member and future postmaster general of the United States, wailed, "How you gonna win kicking all the time?" After another quick kick later in the game, he screamed, "Hell's bells! We done hired ourselves an idiot." But Bryant's strategy was clear: He hoped to keep games close by pinning his opponent deep in their own territory with the quick kick. It started working by season's end; Alabama won three of their last five games to finish 5-4-1. The Tide wasn't invited to a bowl game—the only time in Bryant's twenty-five years in Tuscaloosa his team wouldn't play in the postseason.

During the season Lee Roy Jordan—a high school lineman from Excel, Alabama, who would become a mainstay of the Alabama D—visited Bryant in his office. The couch across from Bryant's desk had shortened legs, and the springs in the seat cushions had been removed, causing Jordon to drop like an anchor when he sat down. "When I looked up at Coach Bryant behind his desk it was like he was sitting on a pyramid from my perspective on the couch," Jordan said. "It seemed like that desk and his chair were lifted four feet in the air. He was obviously in charge. I knew how hard it was to play for him, but I grew up on a farm and it required hard work. Most of us on the team back then were from farms and we liked to work. Coach Bryant told me, 'I'm going to offer you a scholarship.' I said, 'Yes, sir, I'm coming to Alabama.' And that was it. He was a winner—I could just feel that in his office—and I wanted to be a part of that."

Late in the season Bill Battle, then a junior in high school in Birmingham, sat on the bench during a game—a common practice for recruits visiting the school at the time. He sat next to Billy Neighbors, a high school senior recruit on a visit. Battle asked Neighbors, "Is Coach Bryant as tough as everyone says he is?"

Neighbors, a native of Northport, Alabama, told Battle, "I don't care if Hitler is coaching Alabama. If you're a good high school player from this state, you are coming to Alabama. You hear me?"

Battle soon committed to Bryant and the Tide.

🏈   🏈   🏈

During the season the Bryant family—Mary Harmon and Paul Jr.—moved into a brick house on Lakeshore Drive. Bryant liked how sturdy it looked. The previous coach, Ears Whitworth, had rented a house during his stay in Tuscaloosa. Bryant wanted to show fans and players that he was planting roots and had no intention of leaving the job anytime soon.

Shaded by pine and oak trees, the eight-room house featured an expansive game room, which was where the Bryants would throw parties for as many as three hundred guests and entertain recruits visiting the school. Mary Harmon was Bear's ultimate recruiting closer. Charming, elegant, and sociable, she would assure the mammas and papas of prospective players that their child would be taken care of if they chose to play for her husband. She would tell them that their boy would be a part of the Bryant family.

Slowly, Bear Bryant was putting his house in order in Tuscaloosa.

CHAPTER 3

The Secret Mission

2007

The private jet rolled down the runaway at Tuscaloosa Regional Airport, gaining speed and lifting into the low-slung underbelly of gray clouds. It rose steadily through the thin winter air and sleet and finally broke into the blue yonder at ten thousand feet. Back in the cabin, a sixty-seven-year-old man with silver hair sat in a leather seat, knowing he was embarking on a critical secret mission—the most important of his career at the University of Alabama.

It was New Year's Day, 2007—nearly four weeks short of the twenty-four-year anniversary of Bear Bryant's death in 1983—and Mal Moore was desperate. A month had passed since Moore, the Alabama athletic director since 1999, had fired Mike Shula after the Crimson Tide lost to Auburn for the fifth consecutive year, finishing the 2006 season 6-6. Over the ensuing month Moore's search for a new coach had been a bust. He tried to lure South

Carolina coach Steve Spurrier into taking the helm at Alabama, but his advances were rebuffed. He thought he had a done deal after meeting with West Virginia coach Rich Rodriguez—several media outlets reported he would be the next coach in Tuscaloosa—but at the last hour Rodriguez chose to stay with the Mountaineers.

The high-profile rebukes were embarrassing PR setbacks to Moore—some football staffers tagged him "Malfunction Moore"—and he was mocked countrywide for his inability to find someone, anyone, to take over the once proud Crimson Tide program. But he wasn't a quitter. Once a backup quarterback on Bear Bryant's 1961 national title team and a former assistant coach under him, Moore was now clandestinely in pursuit of the one person he believed could be a modern-day Bear:

Nick Saban.

During Moore's search, interim head coach Joe Kines led the Alabama program. The defensive coordinator on Shula's staff, Kines prepared his team to face Oklahoma State in the Independence Bowl. When news broke that Rich Rodriguez had turned down the job, the Crimson Tide players had just finished a practice and were in the locker room. With wet eyes, Kines told his players to gather around him. He told them not to worry about this low-tide moment. "Y'all don't concern yourself with the coaching search and what is going on with Rich Rod," he said. "I can promise you this much: We're going to get somebody good for y'all."

Days later, the team flew to Shreveport, Louisiana, to continue its bowl preparation. On the night of December 27, freshman quarterback Greg McElroy went to dinner with a few other fresh-men players and their families at the Superior Grill restaurant. McElroy's father, also named Greg, worked in the front office of the Dallas Cowboys and midway through the dinner he mentioned, "There is some buzz about Nick Saban coming to Alabama."

The players were shocked and questioned his information. The elder McElroy then mentioned that he had spoken to "someone in the know" and said, "It's more realistic than you might think."

The younger McElroy left the restaurant that evening with one question swirling in his head: Could this really happen?

●　　●　　●

For more than a generation, Alabama had been looking for an heir to the Bear. Except for Gene Stallings, who won a national title in 1992 and spent seven years in Tuscaloosa, no coach had lasted more than four seasons at Alabama since Bryant retired in 1982 as the winningest coach in college football history with an overall record of 323-85-17. Bryant had made the job sacred, and his long shadow haunted those who followed him.

Bryant's successor was Ray Perkins, who was beloved because he was a wideout on Bryant's 1964 and '65 national title teams. But then Perkins removed the legendary thirty-three-step tower from which Bryant, armed with a bullhorn, would watch practice. Perkins preferred to be on the field with his players; he considered the tower a distraction, so he had it hauled away on a flatbed trailer and stored behind a warehouse in a storage yard, where it was left to rust. Casting aside that iconic feature was viewed in Tuscaloosa as an insult to Bryant, akin to removing a stairway to football heaven. Perkins was never forgiven. He left after amassing a 32-15-1 record.

Then Bill Curry was hired from Georgia Tech, but he didn't have any connection to Bryant or Alabama—facts he was reminded of almost every day in his three years in Tuscaloosa. After failing to beat Auburn in three seasons, Curry was unwilling to stay in a place where he believed he would never be accepted. He left Alabama after compiling a 10-1 record in the 1989 regular season for what he deemed to be a better job: head coach at Kentucky.

Stallings, a former Bryant player (at Texas A&M from '54 to '56) and Bryant assistant at Alabama, became head coach in 1990 and won the '92 national title, but then, for the better part of the next quarter century, the once powerful program descended into mediocrity. In 1997 Mike DuBose replaced Stallings, who retired, but Dubose's four-year tenure was marred by a sexual harassment scandal with a former secretary (that the university settled) and an NCAA investigation involving booster Logan Young and the recruitment of a defensive tackle from Memphis named Albert Means (that eventually led the NCAA to put Alabama on probation for five years). DuBose resigned after Alabama lost to Auburn in November 2000 to finish the season at 3-8, the school's worst record in more than forty years. Dennis Franchione was then hired in 2001 from Texas Christian University; after two forgettable seasons, he left for Texas A&M. In 2003 Mike Price was brought in from Washington State, but before he ever coached a game, he was fired when it was revealed that he had spent a boozy wild night at a strip club in Florida, a sin that will take down any Alabama coach who has yet to win a game.

Needing a coach with a wholesome-as-milk image, Mal Moore

in May 2003 tabbed Mike Shula, a Crimson Tide quarterback in the 1980s and a son of NFL coaching legend Don Shula. But Shula never returned the football program to the rarefied heights reached by the Bear. During his tenure Alabama was still recovering from the NCAA sanctions imposed in 2002 that included five years' probation, scholarship reductions, and a two-year bowl ban. The fresh-faced Shula often seemed overwhelmed and skittish on the sideline. Perhaps Shula would have lasted longer and been more successful if he had convinced a future Heisman-winning quarterback to sign with the Tide in December 2005. Shula spent dozens of hours with the rising star, but at the last minute Tim Tebow opted for Florida. Shula never landed a marquee, program-changing recruit. Though he was well liked as a person in Tuscaloosa, Shula was dismissed after four seasons and a 26-23 record.

Now, flying at about 490 mph and nearing South Florida, Moore knew he needed to make the hire of his life or perhaps lose his own job. Alabama fans were out of patience. Moore understood that if he didn't entice Nick Saban, the coach of the Miami Dolphins, to move to Tuscaloosa, he might as well not return himself. Moore even told the pilots that if Saban wasn't on the private jet with him on the return flight, they should just take him to Cuba so he would never been seen or heard from again. That, Moore figured, would be a better option than facing the growing anger in Tuscaloosa.

●   ●   ●

Mal Moore didn't know Saban well, but he had a unique connection to the Miami coach. Moore's nephew, Chuck Moore, was a homebuilder in north Georgia, near Lake Burton, a 2,775-acre reservoir with sixty-two miles of shoreline in Rabun County. When Saban was coaching LSU in the early 2000s, he remodeled his vacation house on Lake Burton and asked Chuck Moore to lead the project. Chuck Moore was astonished at how Saban constantly talked to his team of builders and offered words of encouragement. Saban frequently consulted with Moore, reviewing plans, asking questions, tweaking designs. Moore eventually told his uncle Mal that he would love this guy named Nick Saban, because he was just like Mal's old coach Bear Bryant in his attention to detail and ability to motivate.

Moore had called his nephew during his coaching search and asked him if he thought Saban would ever consider coaching at Alabama. "Uncle Mal, when Nick was at LSU, he and I would talk football all the time," Chuck Moore said. "He didn't even know I was your nephew. One day I told Coach Saban that you were my uncle, and he asked about your career. I told him how you'd been a part of all those championship teams at Alabama...I asked him if he'd ever be interested in coaching at Alabama, and he said he had a great job, but Alabama would be a place that he would love to coach one day if he were in the job market."

As far back as November 27, 2006—more than a month before Mal Moore flew to Florida—rumors had circulated in the media that Alabama wanted to hire Saban, whose agent, Jimmy Sexton, had been contacted by Crimson Tide officials shortly after Shula had been fired. Two weeks later Saban was asked by a reporter about Alabama during a press conference. "I'm flattered that they may be interested in me, but it never really progressed, because we never let it progress," he said. Then, on December 21, Saban uttered the statement that he would regret for years. "I guess I have to say it," he said. *"I'm not going to be the coach at Alabama...I don't control what people say. I don't control what people put on dot-com or anything else. So I'm just telling you there's no significance, in my opinion, about this, about me, about any interest that I have in anything other than being the coach here [in Miami]."*

Most certainly, Saban was in an awkward position. The NFL regular season wasn't over and, though Miami's season had spiraled downward and the Dolphins would lose their final three games to finish 6-10, Saban was still fighting to win games. In spite of the losing streak, Saban's singular focus was on the Dolphins—all of those close to him say that—and he didn't want the possibility of him leaving for Tuscaloosa to shake his players' belief in him.

Even though Miami's 2006 season had been a failure, Saban had enjoyed a measure of success with the team. In 2005, his first year as an NFL head coach, Miami limped to a 3-7 start. He treated players like they were in college, not allowing them to wear hats in meetings and timing them in the 40-yard dash in training camp to determine who was and wasn't in shape. At first the players didn't respond to his heavy-handedness, but the Dolphins won their final seven games to finish 9-7. They missed the playoffs, yet Miami appeared to be a team on the rise.

In the off-season Saban believed he'd found the player who could guide the 'Fins to the Super Bowl. Free agent quarterback Drew Brees was brought in for a tryout and Saban wanted to sign him, but the Dolphins medical staff intervened. Brees, coming off major shoulder surgery to his throwing arm, flunked the physical administered by the team's doctors. Miami then traded a second-round pick for quarterback Daunte Culpepper, who began the 2006 season as the team's starter but was benched after four games. Failing to land Brees, who went on to become the MVP of Super Bowl XLIV in 2010, would turn out to be the defining hour of Saban's tenure in Miami. He had been promised full control of personnel when owner Wayne Huizenga hired him away from LSU, but at this fork-in-the-road moment in franchise history, Saban was overruled.

When Moore landed in South Florida early on the morning of Monday, January 1, 2007, he had to keep his trip a secret because of Saban's public statements about not leaving the Dolphins. Moore had wanted to sit down with Saban during the NFL season, but Saban told his agent, Sexton, that he wouldn't contemplate another position until after the season was over. So now Moore, who didn't have a scheduled appointment with Saban, waited. For several hours, as late morning bled into late afternoon, Moore called Saban multiple times, but he didn't answer. Frustrated, Moore thought his chances were doomed, that the savior he sought would not become Alabama's head coach. He checked into a Fort Lauderdale hotel and continued to wait. Then, late at night, Saban returned his call. Moore spoke with Saban and wife, Terry, for an hour, selling the couple on the University of Alabama and life in Tuscaloosa. Near the end of their conversation, Saban finally lowered his usual protective demeanor, hesitantly admitting to Moore that he was frustrated with the Dolphins and tired of coaching professional players.

Moore, who had spent four years in the NFL as an assistant coach, sympathized. "Nobody comes to see you," Moore said. "No one calls you. No one talks about the team. And the wife doesn't do anything. If you want a quarterback, you trade for one or you buy one. Same with a defensive end. You don't recruit."

At the end of their conversation, Saban said he'd call Moore the next day and they could meet for lunch. That night Saban phoned Gene Stallings, whom he'd known for several years. Stallings taught at Saban's coaching clinic when Saban was at Michigan State in the late 1990s and the two had kept in contact. Saban wanted to know the intimate details of the Alabama program and Tuscaloosa. After speaking with the former Tide coach, both Saban and his wife grew more intrigued with the idea of moving to Alabama.

By noon the following day, however, Moore had yet to hear from Saban. Certain his mission had failed, Moore packed his bag and asked the driver of the hired Mercedes sedan to take him to the airport. But on his way to the hangar where the private jet was parked, Moore's phone rang. It was Sexton, who told Moore that the Sabans needed a few more hours to think about coaching at Alabama and that Moore should wait another day in South Florida. Moore followed Sexton's instructions and checked into another hotel, one closer to Saban's home in Fort Lauderdale. Throughout the day University of Alabama president Robert Witt repeatedly called Moore for updates; Moore, who still hadn't personally met with Saban, merely said negotiations were stuck in a holding pattern. Even though a dozen other coaches had expressed interest in the Alabama job, Moore was willing to wait for Saban—at least another day.

Saban met with Huizenga about the time Moore was speaking with Witt. The Dolphins owner wanted Saban to stay in Miami, but Huizenga ultimately said that Saban needed to do what was best for himself and his family. By this time Moore was losing patience. He drove to Saban's house. When Moore approached the sprawling mansion, he saw TV crews set up nearby and a helicopter hovering overhead. Undaunted, as one within a few feet of his prey, he knocked on the door. For over an hour he met not with Nick but Terry Saban—it was a stroke of luck for Moore that Nick was still at the Dolphins' headquarters.

Moore knew that Terry was the key to hiring Saban. She was his confidant and most trusted advisor and had played a vital role in her husband's success. Moore turned on his extensive Southern charm, sweet-talking her in his honey-dripping drawl. Moore explained that unlike in the NFL, where coaches' wives play little or no role in the community, Terry could be a prominent figure in Tuscaloosa if she desired and would have a platform to help others. Moore also emphasized that the Sabans—including daughter Kristen and son Nicholas—would enjoy Tuscaloosa, a kind of football Mayberry. The vision Moore laid out made the move, and the coaching job, even more tantalizing for Terry.

Moore, a member of Bear Bryant's first recruiting class in 1958, continued his sales pitch, waxing poetic about the high quality of life on the banks of the Black Warrior River in Tuscaloosa, its friendly community, its legendary football program, and its fans, so desperate for a winner. As Moore went on and on about why her husband would be perfect for the job, the phone rang. It was Saban. "I don't think I'm even going to talk to [Moore] tonight," Saban told Terry. But then his wife said, "Oh, Mal's already here. We've been talking for over an hour."

Saban soon arrived. He told Moore, "Mal, when I go to work I feel like I'm working at a damn factory. I never see a soul." After about an hour Moore rose to leave—still without an answer from Saban—and he said he would be flying back to Tuscaloosa the next day. As she walked him to the door, Terry Saban grabbed Moore's arm. She had made her decision—she wanted her husband to take the Alabama job. "We've got to get him on that plane tomorrow," she told Moore.

The next morning, with the media still camped outside of his house, Saban was unable to drive to the Dolphins facility without detection. He called the team headquarters. From a speakerphone, his voice thick with emotion, Saban told the staff he was leaving. Moore arrived at Saban's house later that morning, and Saban told Moore that he was accepting the job. "We need to get out of here as soon as possible," Moore said, smiling widely.

Moore had the driver back the Mercedes into Saban's garage, not wanting the cameras on the ground or aboard the helicopters to see who was about to enter the car. Terry, daughter Kristen, and one of Kristen's friends—all holding hastily packed bags—squeezed into the back seat, their bags on their laps. Moore perched atop the front-seat center console, and Saban jammed himself next to his new athletic director. The driver pulled out of the garage and the six of them charged to the airport, with multiple helicopters following the sedan.

After the car parked outside the private terminal, Moore, Saban, and the rest of the group walked toward the plane. An airport worker who had grown up in Alabama ran to Moore and excitedly said, "Roll Tide! Coach Moore, you got us our man!" Moore called his nephew in Georgia, telling him the news and thanking him, saying he didn't think he ever would have reeled in Nick Saban without his help.

●   ●   ●

Above the clouds, the jet cruising toward Tuscaloosa, Saban sat across from his new boss. Their eyes meeting, Saban said, "Mal, you must think I'm a helluva good coach, don't you?"

"Damn, Nick," Moore replied, "I wouldn't have spent so many sleepless nights if I didn't think you were the man for the job."

"There are a lot of good coaches out there, but I know how to recruit and get difference makers," Saban said. "I can't coach without great players."

"Nick," said Moore, "that's the best thing I've heard you say."

At that moment Moore believed—with all his heart—that he had finally captured the heir to the Bear.

●   ●   ●

Word traveled at warp speed, as if pushed by a winter gale. By 11 a.m. CST on January 3, 2007, fans in Tuscaloosa began arriving at the Tuscaloosa Regional Airport, standing in the Bama Air terminal that was used by private planes. The crowd swelled to three hundred by early afternoon. From then on most craned their necks skyward, anxiously scanning the dull gray expanse, as if looking for the Maker himself to appear. Then, at 3:45 p.m., the private jet carrying Saban and company touched down. When the plane door opened, Terry Saban stepped off first, waving to the crowd with a surprised, oh-my-heavens look on her face. Then Saban appeared, outfitted in a gray suit, lavender shirt, and no tie, and walked over to the fans, who were chanting, "Roll Tide! Roll Tide! Roll Tide!"

Saban signed autographs as he walked though the narrow terminal, telling fans that he was "happy to be here." One female yelled, "Thank you, Jesus! Thank you, Nick Saban!" A fan held a sign that read, "We've Been Saban Our Hearts for You!" A blond woman in a Crimson Tide football jersey kissed him on the face—she would be charged with DUI later that night—while others patted him on the back. Reporters circled Terry Saban. "In the end our hearts craved the college tradition," she said. "It took us a long time to get out of there, we're glad to be here." Left unsaid was that the Sabans had yet to spend extensive time in Tuscaloosa—T-Town, as they would later hear it be called—other than when Saban, as LSU's coach, was in the college town for away games and for off-season coaching clinics.

The Sabans climbed into a crimson-colored Chevrolet Tahoe, one of five in the cavalcade of cars that motored away from the airport and slowly snaked its way to the campus football complex. But the fans wanted more. Some ran alongside Saban's SUV, overjoyed, in a fever, trying to catch one more glimpse of the man they considered to be their football savior. The Sabans had never experienced anything akin to this; when they flew into Baton Rogue after being hired away from Michigan State in 2000, one person met them at the airport—the LSU equipment manager. But now, after being on the ground in Alabama for only a few minutes—and even though the college students were on winter break—they already knew: From this day forward in Tuscaloosa, the entire landscape of their lives would be public property.

The next day, in a large conference room on the second floor of the Mal Moore Athletic Facility teeming with television cameras and nearly a hundred reporters, Saban stepped up to a podium. He wore a gray suit, white shirt, and red tie. Cameras clicked and flashed in his face before he uttered his first word—his vision for the Crimson Tide. "Everybody should take the attitude that we're working to be a champion, that we want to be a champion in everything we do," said Saban. "Every choice, every decision, everything that we do every day, we want to be a champion. Everyone take ownership for what they need to do relative to their role, whatever it is, whether it's being a fan, a booster, be a good one. Any kind of supporter that you are for this team, everyone take ownership that we support each other so we can have the best possible football program that Alabama has ever had."

Saban continued to speak, but print reporters looked down at their notepads and frantically scribbled those last words, realizing Saban had spoon-fed them the lead to their upcoming news copy: *We can have the best possible football program that Alabama has ever had.*

"When we won the championship at LSU in 2003, the players developed their goals for the team. I thought it was interesting that that was the first team I ever coached that didn't have a goal that was result oriented, like go to a New Year's Day bowl game, win the SEC championship... We're not going to talk about what we're going to accomplish; we're going to talk about how we're going to do it...

"We want a big, physical, aggressive football team that is

relentless in the competitive spirit we go out and play with week in and week out. What I would like for every football team to do that we play is to sit there and say, 'I hate playing against these guys. I hate playing them. Their effort, their toughness, relentless resiliency, go out every play and focus, play the next play, compete for sixty minutes, I can't handle that.' That's the kind of football team we want...

"What I realized in the last two years is that we love college coaching because of the ability it gives you to affect people, young people in their development, their character, their attitude... My commitment to the [Dolphins], and it was premature not to stay there, all right, but I knew, [owner] Wayne [Huizenga] and I talked about this, that my heart was to go back to college."

Saban was asked a final question by a local reporter: *What would it mean for you to have a statue on the Walk of Champions and how soon can we expect it?*

"We're going to work very hard to [win a national title], but we're going to stay focused on the process of what it takes to do it," Saban said. "I can't make any predictions, nor will I ever, about when something's going to happen. I like to keep working on it, making it better, making it better than everybody else has, then all of a sudden you have a chance to do that."

After talking to the media forty-five minutes and taking about a dozen questions, Saban eventually walked into his office, shut the door, and slid behind his new desk. Then he did the one thing he always does:

He worried like hell.

For the previous four seasons, Mike Shula had treated his Alabama players like pros, not adolescents in need of discipline. Shula, who had spent fifteen years coaching in the NFL before arriving in Tuscaloosa, expected responsibility and accountability, but he didn't necessarily demand it. A devout Christian, he rarely cursed or raised his voice. After one of the few times he did yell he apologized minutes later. "He wasn't exactly feared," said one former player. "He was one of the nicest guys you'd ever meet, but players knew they could get away with a lot. There just wasn't much discipline—and it showed on game days."

"Coach Shula was a hands-off, pro-style coach and he wasn't a guy who would crush you if you did anything wrong," said Greg McElroy, a freshman on the 2006 team. "No one was happy with the lack of progress we made in his final season. I remember after we lost to Mississippi State at home [24–16] and everyone was sitting in the locker room asking, 'What just happened?' Still, I never thought Shula was going to be fired. And to this day, I don't think he would have been let go if there hadn't been some sort of communication behind the scenes between Jimmy Sexton [Saban's agent] and Alabama in which Jimmy said that Nick was interested. I don't have proof of that, but I believe it."

A few days after Saban held his introductory press conference he ambled into the team meeting and spoke to his players for the first time. When Shula addressed the team, players always were talking when he entered the room; now no one said a word as Saban strode toward a podium. With a note card in his hands, Saban looked up—and what he saw disgusted him. Players were sprawled out in their wooden chairs, slumped like teenagers at a movie theater. "One of the first things I need you guys to do is sit up in your chairs," Saban said, uttering his first words to his team.

The players quickly straightened up. The room fell quiet. The coach had their attention. Saban eventually handed out an itinerary that laid out a detailed minute-by-minute schedule of what the players were to do each day during winter conditioning, also known as "the Fourth Quarter Program." The players were given a dress code for the workouts: team-issued shirt, shorts, socks, and shoes. If a player violated the code, which included tucking in your shirt, then everyone had to leave the Hank Crisp indoor practice facility and return to the locker room to help that player get appropriately dressed. The message from Saban was clear: In his world—a regime, actually—little things mattered as much as big things.

"We were all really anxious and nervous before that first meeting," McElroy said. "He walked in and he had such a presence. It was like a four-star general walking in and we are his guys at basic training. And after that first meeting, he reassigned our seats and gave us a seating chart. That was the first indication that he was going to readjust everything and he was going to be an extreme micromanager, which was the opposite of Coach Shula."

Under Shula, the winter conditioning program lasted four weeks; under Saban, it would last six and would be as psychologically grinding as it would be physically taxing. "Those six weeks were pure hell, but Coach Saban had to change the mind-set of the players and mind-set of how we worked," McElroy said. "With Coach Shula, we had done light weight training and mobility work in the winter. With Coach Saban we were maxing out in our lifting and going super heavy. He just killed us. He wanted to see who could handle it mentally."

In spring practice, Saban had another message for his players: Practices would not be for the faint of heart. Saban, for example, instructed offensive line coach Joe Pendry to light into McElroy, then a backup, for a variety of QB transgressions—holding on to the ball too long, forcing a pass into coverage, not making the correct read. Pendry would scream so loud that the entire team would hear. But there was plan behind this verbal assault: Saban wanted to prepare McElroy for the pressure he would face—especially in the fourth quarter of SEC games—when he became the starting quarterback in 2009.

From every corner of the state, they came. RVs and campers and pickup trucks and BMWs trekked into Tuscaloosa three days before the big game in April. Once the tailgating tents were set up near the stadium, the grills were fired and the barbecues commenced throughout the campus. It was just a matter of a couple sunrises and sunsets before the Alabama faithful would enter their church, Bryant-Denny Stadium, to revel in the promise that loomed large in their imaginations and hopes. In the hours before the A-Day game, the name given to Alabama's spring game, it was a time for Tide fans to dream—to dream of the resurrection of the Bear in the form and potential of Nick Saban.

For four months Saban had been hard at work, having signed an eight-year, $32 million contract with Alabama, making him one of the highest-paid coaches in either college football or the NFL. His contract featured several plums that were the envy of college coaches across America: two cars, a country club membership, and twenty-five hours of private use of the university's jet. The Tide was already seeing a return on its investment. Though he had only a month to shore up his 2007 recruiting class, Saban cobbled together a group that was ranked tenth best in the nation by Rivals.com, confirming to the Crimson-clad masses that their Caesar had arrived.

They got their first look at him on April 21, 2007, a sunny spring afternoon that had all the trappings of a game day. The quad in the heart of campus—an expanse of lush green and oaks above the buried remains of several dorms that burned during the Civil War—teemed with excited, exhilarated, expectant fans. Virtually every parking lot within two miles of Bryant-Denny was full as kickoff to this glorified practice approached. Wearing T-shirts that read "Sabanation" and "Got Nick?" the fans kept coming in droves, pushing through the gates and rushing to find the best seats. The attendance record for an SEC spring game had been set in 1986 at Tennessee with seventy-three thousand, but that mark was shattered in Tuscaloosa thirty minutes before kickoff.

When the fifty-five-year-old Saban jogged onto the field for the first time, the crowd roared; it seemed like the sky had ruptured in a rolling, rumbling thunderclap. The sound was so powerful that it could be heard for blocks and blocks, where many fans who had been turned away from the packed stadium stood outside of apartments, fraternity houses, and academic buildings. The players were in awe as they jogged back to the locker room after warm-ups; many gazed up and up and up into the stands, unable to comprehend that every available seat had been occupied fifteen minutes before kickoff. Fans even stood on the ramps and squatted in the aisles to see what they had come to see.

About seven minutes before kickoff Saban again appeared on the field. Dressed in a gray suit, white shirt, and crimson tie, Saban stood twenty yards behind the offensive line, watching, clapping, shouting instructions, critiquing. The White team beat the Crimson squad 20–13, but that wasn't important to all those who had traveled so far—some even in private jets—to witness a scrimmage. This was the start of something in Tuscaloosa. The crowd of 92,138 was the largest in college football history ever to attend a spring game.

● ● ●

During his first summer conditioning camp in Tuscaloosa, Saban was firm with his players. He banned the word "hot" from their lexicon as the team worked out under the tar-bubbling Southern sun. Even in temperatures as high as 105 degrees, Saban ran his players hard. Every Monday they endured anywhere from sixteen to thirty-two full field sprints. Each player was timed, and if one ran too slow the entire team would restart. Players weren't allowed to bend over to catch their breath—if one did, then everyone had to keep running. Like Bryant many years before him, Saban was trying to create a culture of toughness and perseverance.

"Those summer workouts were unlike anything I'd ever been through," said McElroy. "We'd lift before we ran and there were days our legs would be dead even before we went out to the practice field for our sprints. Guys would get taken off the field because they couldn't make it and go straight to the training room for IVs. By the end of the summer we had been grinded down. But it was all about creating a new mind-set at Alabama."

The Secret Mission

Once preseason practice started, Saban jogged around the field from position group to position group, preaching fundamentals. He critiqued the footwork of his quarterbacks, taught offensive linemen the blocking techniques he wanted them to master, coached the defensive backs how to play the ball when it was in the air and they were in man-to-man coverage, and explained to his punters the importance of directional kicks. There wasn't one aspect of the game that he wasn't touching with his own experienced mind and hands. He even screamed at his players about the importance of body language and the need to always exude confidence, no matter the score, no matter the circumstance.

"A few guys left the program," said McElroy. "They could take it physically, but they couldn't take it mentally. There was no positive gratification for anything. If you made a good play, well, that was expected, that was what you were supposed to do. But if you did anything bad, you heard about it. Guys struggled with that negativity."

⬤ ⬤ ⬤

Throughout the spring and summer of 2007, when Saban wasn't on the practice field or in his office, he was usually doing one thing: recruiting. At the time the NCAA still allowed coaches to visit campuses during the "spring evaluation period"—six weeks that began on April 15—and no coach in the nation took greater advantage of this than Saban. He had only thirty-five days to put together his first recruiting class the previous February, and he had earned high marks from recruiting experts for reeling in a Top 10 class, but now Saban eyed something bigger and far more ambitious: He wanted his 2008 class to be the foundation of all that he was trying to build in Tuscaloosa. So in the spring of 2007 he spent countless hours on Alabama's private plane, flying throughout the South to check out as many recruits as he could. (The next spring the NCAA would pass a rule prohibiting head coaches from making in-person visits in the spring. The legislation became known as the "Saban rule.")

The junior class in Alabama high schools that spring had a high number of exceptionally talented players, and Saban visited all the elite prospects: safety Mark Barron at St. Paul's High in Mobile, defensive tackle Marcell Dareus at Huffman High, wide receiver Julio Jones at Foley High, and linebacker Courtney Upshaw at Eufaula High. Saban also traveled to Flint, Michigan, to check out running back Mark Ingram, and he flew to Lewisburg, Tennessee, to see Marshall County High linebacker Dont'a Hightower.

On the day Saban and Curt Cignetti, his recruiting coordinator and wide receivers coach, jetted to visit Hightower, the two left Tuscaloosa at 7:30 a.m. The itinerary called for a twelve-hour workday: They first visited Huntsville, Alabama, to look over a few players, then went to Nashville to see more recruits, then lifted off for Lewisburg to watch Hightower, and then they returned to Nashville to see potential recruit Chris Jordan compete in a track meet at Brentwood Academy before returning to Tuscaloosa.

When Saban and Cignetti arrived at Marshall County High, Hightower and his teammates were in the indoor practice facility for the first day of spring practice. As Hightower performed various drills, he noticed that a man on the sideline was following his every move. Confused, Hightower asked a teammate, "Is that one of our new coaches?"

"No."

"Then who is it?"

"That's Alabama coach Nick Saban," the teammate replied. "Um, he's here to see you."

Saban liked what he saw in Hightower, whose only scholarship offers at the time were from Ole Miss and Vanderbilt. Saban coveted big players. That spring he constantly told his assistants that "heavyweights knock out lightweights." And Hightower was big for a linebacker: six foot four, 260 pounds, and capable of running a 40-yard dash in 4.6 seconds. After watching him for a few minutes, Saban turned to Cignetti and asked, "What do you think?"

"We need to offer him," Cignetti replied.

Hightower didn't talk to Saban that afternoon, but later that night the coach called Hightower's home. Though Saban had personally never seen him play in a game, he offered Hightower a scholarship. At the time Hightower wasn't considered a blue-chip player by most recruiting services, but Saban trusted his eyes more than a written report when gauging a player's potential. "What I saw that day in the indoor practice facility at his school was probably the most athletic linebacker in the country," Saban recalled. "I was blown away. I knew right away he could be a perfect fit for what we wanted to do."

Hightower didn't immediately accept Saban's offer, but he couldn't stop thinking about how Saban personally had flown to his small Tennessee town just to watch him practice. *He must really care*, Hightower thought, *and he must really, really want me.* Hightower, who ten years later would have three Super Bowl rings with the New England Patriots, eventually said yes to Saban.

After Saban and Cignetti left Marshall High in Tennessee, they stopped at a 7-Eleven convenience store. Neither had eaten all day and Cignetti purchased a candy bar. "What, do you have a sugar problem or something?" Saban joked. Saban wouldn't eat until the coaches were back in Tuscaloosa at 7:30 that Friday evening. As the pair walked off the plane at the university hangar, Saban looked at Cignetti and smiled like a man who was living his dream. "Just another day in college football," he said.

As the two stepped onto the tarmac and walked toward their cars in the gathering darkness Cignetti didn't know if he'd ever seen anyone look as content as Saban did at that very moment. That was when the realization hit him: *Nick Saban loves the grind.*

🏈   🏈   🏈

The Saban era began in Tuscaloosa on September 1, 2007, at Bryant-Denny Stadium with a 52–6 win over Western Carolina. After games under Coach Shula the Alabama sideline was typically littered with plastic cups and balls of tape that players had torn off their arms and legs. But after this first win under Saban the sideline was spotless—the players knew that only trash cans were the proper receptacle for cups and tape. To Saban, this was just another one of those little BIG things.

Saban's first win at Alabama was followed by victories over Vanderbilt (24–10) and Arkansas (41–38). But over the final ten games of the season, the Tide would go 5-5, including a jarring 21–14 loss in their home finale on November 17 to Louisiana-Monroe, a midpack team in the Sun Belt Conference that Alabama had beaten 41–7 the previous year. Before the game, Alabama had the fastest

Senior Day ceremony in college football—the Tide had only nine on the team, the fewest in the Football Subdivision that season. The last play of the game against Monroe, another incomplete pass by Tide quarterback John Parker Wilson, was emblematic of the entire contest, and the crowd groaned and booed as the ball hit the turf.

Saban fumed in the locker room. He believed that several of the older players had turned against him—and turned against the Process, his philosophy of focusing on the task at hand and what was directly in front in you, not end results. He spotted several cancerous tumors on the team—tumors that were growing. Earlier in the season Saban had suspended five players involved in a textbook scandal. The players missed four games, including the loss to Louisiana-Monroe. He also suspended his best receiver, D. J. Hall, for the first half of that game for violating a team rule. "You either get onboard or get out of here," Saban said in the locker room, according to a player. "I told you this was going to happen. I told you. I told you. Maybe now you guys will start listening to me."

"Nick's program isn't for everybody," said Jim McElwain, the Tide's offensive coordinator from 2008 to 2011. "Nick knows every part of the program and every person who touches the program. To the equipment guys to the janitors to the lawn guys to the players to the coaches, the message is the same—work hard today to be a champion tomorrow. That message never changes. Never. This requires a lot of sacrifice and hard work. But that's the price for success he demands. And if you're not willing to buy in, you won't be around very long, guaranteed."

Alabama lost their last four games of the 2007 regular season before beating Colorado in the Independence Bowl to finish 7-6.

The program was staggering as well off the field. Ten players were arrested in Saban's first year, which inspired rival fans to wear T-shirts emblazoned with the words "Parole Tide." Two assistants then left the program for what they believed were better jobs.

Yet through it all, Saban did one thing every day, no matter his mood, no matter his team's record, no matter how many of his players showed up on the police blotter:

He recruited. And recruited. And recruited.

CHAPTER 4

The Bear Builds

1959 TO 1960

He crisscrossed the Alabama half of the field, his gait like that of a mountain lion. A Chesterfield cigarette dangled from his lips, a string of smoke rising into the warm September air. For several minutes he watched his players warm up before the 1959 season opener in Athens and he liked what he saw. His first recruits—such as quarterback Pat Trammell, guard Billy Neighbors, and defensive back Bill Oliver—were now eligible to play against the Georgia Bulldogs. And the leftover players from the woebegone regime of Ears Whitworth looked different: Their bodies had been hardened by two of Bryant's winter conditioning programs and a pair of his training camps. But most important to the coach, the minds of his players were strengthening as well. Their tolerance for pain—and their willingness to do whatever was required to win, to sacrifice their bodies for the sake of the team—was growing.

Bryant boasted about how he had (metaphorically) kicked his players—just to see which ones would kick back. Now nearly everyone on the field in front of him, he believed, had proven that they would kick back and would even throw a punch or two. Yet Bryant also felt uneasy this early autumn afternoon. A world-class worrier, he had a fear of failure that drove him more than his hunger for victory. He would do anything, he often said, to make sure he didn't "go back to the wagon," a reference to growing up poor in rural Arkansas. If this meant beating the crap out of his players to prepare them for victory, so be it.

Bryant had felt slighted for much of his football life. When he played at Alabama from 1933 to 1935, he bemoaned that he had been "the other end," the one who lined up opposite of future NFL Hall of Famer Don Hutson. When he coached at Kentucky from 1946 to 1953, he joked that he had been "the other coach" at the school, the one who was overshadowed by Wildcats basketball legend Adolph Rupp. But now there was no one at Alabama who could rival Bryant's power or influence or hegemony. This was his team—and his team alone.

Pacing back and forth on the field, Bryant eagle-eyed his players going through their final pregame routines. He understood that many of them came from hardscrabble backgrounds—just as he had. Their families had lived through the shortages and hardships of the World War II years, and the postwar economic boom had failed to reach many parts of the South. "Most of us were country boys," said Charley Pell, the future head coach of Florida who was a member of Bryant's second recruiting class and who passed away in 2001. "If we didn't have that scholarship, it was back to laying blocks or digging ditches or working at the supermarket. Yeah, I was of afraid of doing that."

Bryant, ever the psychologist, preyed on his players' upbringings—and their fears of losing their scholarships, their most glaring vulnerability. He threatened to send anyone home who didn't exert maximum effort in practice, and he implored his players to treat every game with businesslike, clinical focus. He always made sure his boys went through their pregame routines with concentration, precision, and fourth-quarter intensity. "If our opponent was laughing or horsing around on the field before kickoff, we knew we had them," said Bill Oliver. "Football was a serious business to us. It was everything—and I mean everything. Coach Bryant made sure we viewed it that way."

Bryant rarely gave rousing locker room speeches filled with soaring rhetoric or lyrical language. Instead, he would simply tell his players to remember what they had done during practice and to execute the way they had been taught. Now, with kickoff against Georgia moments away on September 19, 1959, Bryant calmly reminded his boys to play with intelligence, poise, and, most of all, fearlessness. Then the tall coach with the wide shoulders led his players out onto the field.

🏈   🏈   🏈

Bryant's team became known as his "quick little boys." They were smaller than most major college players, but that was by design: Bryant viewed speed, quickness, and endurance as the three most important traits in both offensive and defensive players. Unlike some college coaches who played two-platoon football—meaning, the coach gave his first and second stringers almost equal playing time—Bryant kept his starters in the game for as long as they were physically able to play. Bryant schooled his fleet-footed offensive linemen in the art of hitting hard and low, causing the bigger defensive linemen to fall like chopped-down oaks. This opened up space for Alabama's running backs and quarterback. *Sports Illustrated* once noted of the diminutive Crimson Tide team after an Alabama victory, "It was embarrassing, like getting mugged by a kindergarten class."

"We had so many speed drills that we did over and over in practice," said Bill Battle, who played end at Alabama from 1960 to 1962 and later was the school's athletic director from 2013 to 2017. "When I visited Auburn on my recruiting trip they had a dining hall where it was family style, all you could eat. But at Alabama under Coach Bryant you stood in a line and got one serving that included one pint of milk. That was all we got. We really paid attention to keeping our weight down so we could be as quick as possible on the field."

Bryant excelled at coaching defense, his first love. In 1944 he was a defensive assistant at the North Carolina Naval Pre-Flight Training School. When he landed his first head coaching job at Maryland the following year, he implemented his defensive philosophy, emphasizing speed, agility, avoiding blockers, and team pursuit to the ball, which he called the most critical factor in playing defense. He wanted his defenders to play with the characteristics that had defined his life—toughness, resilience, and an edge that bordered on downright nastiness. If one of his defenders didn't display a never-quit, never-surrender mind-set, he wouldn't last long on the field. He commanded his players to never stay blocked and for every defender to chase the ball "like a pack of hounds at full cry." Oklahoma coach Bud Wilkinson, who won three national championships between 1950 and 1956, told rival coaches that he believed that Bryant was greatest defensive coach in NCAA history.

Bryant's defense was predicated on stopping long gains. His goal on first and second down was to hold the offense to five total yards or less; he wanted to force the offense to travel at least five yards on third down to make a first down. When the opponent's quarterback dropped back to pass, Bryant believed his defense should intercept one out of every six attempts. Bryant spent hours in the film room with his defenders reviewing each player's assignment; he wanted every player to know everyone else's responsibilities on any given play. If they did, they could truly trust each other—the very foundation of any successful defense, according to Bryant's philosophy.

Bryant had five objectives for his defense, which he spelled out in a two-page introduction to his defensive playbook: prevent a score, hold every gain to a minimum, force a mistake, get the ball back, and score. Heading into the '59 season, Bryant knew that his defense wasn't yet at a national championship winning level— like a garden, it took time and care to grow any football program. But it was clear that his Bama boys, on both sides of the ball, were vastly improved compared to when he took over the Alabama job eighteen months earlier. He still believed in the promise that he made to his first recruiting class: *Before your four years are over in Tuscaloosa, you will win a national title.*

Bryant's second season at Alabama began with a 17–3 loss to Georgia. His defense couldn't contain Bulldog quarterback Fran Tarkenton, who would guide Georgia to the 1959 SEC title. The next week Bryant returned to Texas to face Houston. Alabama won 3–0, but struggled to move the ball on offense. The same held true the following week in a 7–7 tie with Vanderbilt. Fourteen days later the Alabama and Tennessee offenses sputtered in another 7–7 finale.

Bryant's team was built on defense. During the next four weeks the Tide D surrendered a total of only 21 points in wins over Mississippi State, Tulane, Georgia Tech, and Memphis State. More and more, the Alabama players were becoming a reflection of their coach. After upsetting Georgia Tech on November 14, the Crimson Tide was ranked in the polls for the first time in six years.

Linebacker Lee Roy Jordan, like all of Bryant's players, feared his coach during his playing days at Alabama. One afternoon after meeting Bryant for the first time, Jordan was walking across campus hand-in-hand with his college sweetheart, Biddie Banks, when he spotted Bryant coming toward them. Knowing that his coach didn't approve of his players having girlfriends—Bryant thought they were an unnecessary distraction—Jordan gently nudged his girl into the bushes.

Biddie quickly forgave her boyfriend. A year later the two married with Bryant's blessing. Mary Harmon, Bryant's wife, sewed the wedding veil.

On November 28, 1959, Bryant and his team traveled on buses sixty miles to Birmingham's Legion Field. Their opponent: Auburn. The

Tide hadn't beaten their rival in six years. Bryant viewed this game as the most vital of the season. Not only would a win establish that Alabama was now the king of the state—and help Bryant when recruiting the best players from Alabama's Sand Mountain region to the Wiregrass, from the Black Belt to the Gulf Coast—but it would also raise the national profile of the program.

As soon as the ball was kicked off, Auburn, ranked eleventh in the nation, struggled to gain any yards on Bryant's smallish, quick defense. And on offense, Bryant switched his 140-pound halfback, Scooter Dyess, to split end. Whenever the Tigers played man-to-man coverage on Dyess, Bryant instructed his quarterback to throw the ball in his direction. In the second quarter Dyess caught a thirty-nine-yard pass from Bobby Skelton to score the game's only touchdown in Alabama's 10–0 victory.

Alabama moved up to tenth in the AP poll. The Tide was invited to play in two bowl games—the Bluegrass Bowl in Lexington, Kentucky, and the Liberty Bowl in Philadelphia. Wanting to capture the attention of northern newspapermen, Bryant chose the Liberty Bowl, where the Tide would face Penn State. Bryant desperately wanted his program to be recognized as a national power, not a regional one, and to accomplish this he needed papers in New York, Philadelphia, and Boston to cover and write about his team.

Many in segregated Alabama were upset with the choice; the Nittany Lions would be the first integrated team Alabama had ever played. The chairman of the Tuscaloosa Citizens Council sent a telegram to Frank Rose, the president of the school. "The Tide belongs to all Alabama," the telegram read, "and Alabamians favor continued segregation."

Penn State had five African-American players on its roster. Billy

Neighbors, an Alabama offensive lineman, was going to be facing one of those players, Charlie Janerette. "Now Billy," said Bryant, "a lot of people are going to be watching us and watching how you behave yourself. You play hard, you play clean. You knock him down, you hold out your hand and help him back up."

On a snow-covered field, Penn State won 7–0. Alabama finished the season 7-2-2 and No. 10 in the AP poll. The next day, Bryant and the team rode a train into New York City, where they attended a dinner at Mama Leone's with Mel Allen, the legendary play-by-play announcer of the Yankees. Bryant later met with reporters at a smoky midtown restaurant, where he pressed the flesh and told them about the program he was building from the ground up in Tuscaloosa. With a lit, unfiltered Chesterfield between his fingers, the coach entranced the reporters as he shared story after story about his football life, his Southern charm in full flower. Bryant might have been defeated in his first bowl game as Alabama's head coach, but that didn't mean the trip up East had been a lost cause.

●   ●   ●

A tectonic shift occurred in the Alabama program the following fall when Bryant took his team to Grant Field in Atlanta to face Georgia Tech on November 12, 1960. The Yellow Jackets were 5-3 and they stormed to a 15–0 lead. The 5-1-1 Tide had been so outmanned—and outplayed—that Alabama didn't even get a first down until late in the second quarter.

Alabama trailed 15–0 at halftime. Bryant at first didn't know what to say in the locker room. He typically motivated his players by the element of fear—the same fear of failure he experienced as a kid in Arkansas. But now as Bryant strolled around the locker room he realized that his beat-up and dejected players were bracing for a full-out verbal lashing.

"Two weeks earlier we had played Mississippi State and we were winning 7–0 at halftime and all of us players were thinking we were pretty good," recalled Bill Battle. "Then Coach Bryant comes in and really got on our butts. He scared the heck out of us. So we were expecting him to really let us have it at halftime of the Tech game. They had some stairs that ringed the locker room and every player tried to get to the top of those stairs so Coach Bryant wouldn't have access to us. But then he comes in with a smile on his face and he's whistling."

Indeed, Bryant switched tactics. Once in the locker room he said, "Where are the Cokes? Get some Cokes in here." He grabbed a glass Coke bottle and walked around to each player, patting him on the back, clapping his hands, offering words of encouragement. "Damn, this is great," Bryant told his players, who were drinking Cokes. "Now they'll see what kind of mammas and papas we've got. They'll see what we've got in us."

He kept eyeing his boys, exhorting them, uplifting them. He told his players that they were still going to win the game. "We will win the fourth quarter," Bryant said. "We've been preparing for this moment ever since last season ended. They'll see what kind of team we are when the clock is winding down. Trust me, they won't be able to withstand what we're going to throw at them. We've got them right where we want them. Trust me. We've got them."

Alabama failed to score in the third quarter, but the offense moved the ball. He pulled starting quarterback Bobby Skelton after

Skelton missed a signal from the sideline and called the wrong play—"You'll never play another minute for Alabama as long as you live," Bryant yelled at Skelton on the sideline—and inserted backup Pat Trammell. But then Trammell injured his ankle.

Bryant, who had just upbraided Skelton in front of the team, pulled his starting quarterback close to him. "I'm going to give you one more chance," Bryant said, pushing him back into the game. Inspired, Skelton authored the best fourth quarter of his life, leading the Tide to two scores to cut the lead to 15–13. On the sideline Bryant sidestepped liquor bottles that intoxicated fans heaved from the grandstands.

With only six seconds remaining in the fourth quarter, Alabama lined up for a 24-yard field goal. But the Tide's starting kicker, Tommy Booker, had injured his leg earlier in the game and was hobbling around the sideline on crutches. Bryant turned to Richard "Digger" O'Dell, an end who had never before attempted a field goal in a game. Bryant patted him on the behind and said, "Get on out there, Digger, and kick one." Using a straight-on approach, O'Dell booted a knuckleball that barely flew over the goalpost. Alabama won 16–15.

"We won that game because of Coach Bryant's halftime talk," said Battle. "He was as much a psychologist as a football coach. He was so good at getting people to do what he wanted them to do. When you thought you had it made and you were playing well, he'd kill you. But when you were struggling, he'd uplift you. He was always playing with your mind."

"After the Georgia Tech game we knew that Coach Bryant's words had meaning, that everything he said had meaning," said Lee Roy Jordan. "He always told us that we were going to be the best team in the fourth quarter, and now after the Tech game we knew that we were. His vision for the entire program was taking shape—and we could see that. We were all building something and we could see it grow every single day."

In the jubilant Tide locker room at Georgia Tech, Bryant closely looked at his players. Alabama would finish the 1960 season with an 8-1-2 record and a No. 9 ranking in the AP poll. But here, in the musty visitors' locker room at Grant Field in Atlanta, was the moment when the sea change occurred in the Bear Bryant era at Alabama. This come-from-behind win had injected his program with something more powerful than any words that would ever fly from the coach's lips:

Belief.

CHAPTER 5

The Rising of Saban's Tide

2008

Even in the soft light of Nick Saban's office—where the curtains were usually drawn, as if to conceal secrets—the coach's eyes gleamed when he talked about his favorite subjects: the fundamentals and the X's and O's of football. When recruits came through Saban's thick wooden door, which Saban could close with a remote control, they entered his spacious inner sanctum on the second floor of the Mal Moore Athletic Facility on Bear Bryant Drive. Saban would lead them—and often their families—to a couch. Saban had a large oak desk on the other side of the room, but he preferred to speak to recruits in the more intimate setting he had arranged between his desk and the door: a sofa and a few easy chairs that surrounded a coffee table. Saban would slide into one of the chairs and lay on his singular brand of a well-formulated, focused hard sell: *We will win championships here. I will prepare you for the*

NFL. The best come here. You'll have to earn your way onto the field as well as your right to stay on it. We have a process here. It's an everyday thing. We focus on what is directly in front of us, not end results.

One of the first players to walk into Saban's wood-paneled office—large enough for a few SUVs—was Josh Chapman. As a senior nose tackle at Hoover (Alabama) High in January 2007, Chapman was one of the most coveted players in the South. Scholarship offers from around the country filled Chapman's mailbox. Yet former Alabama coach Mike Shula never extended a full-ride scholarship offer to Chapman, who wanted to go to college in Alabama. In July 2006 Chapman had made a decision that he called ironclad: He committed to Auburn.

Less than forty-eight hours after Saban had landed in Tuscaloosa to take the job at Alabama, he phoned Rush Propst, Hoover's head coach. Saban wanted to know if Chapman might flip his commitment to the Crimson Tide.

"I don't know," Propst replied. "But you can come here and see."

Saban soon met face-to-face with Chapman at Hoover High. Saban told Chapman that he could be a member of a recruiting class that would initiate the turning of the Tide. Chapman was intrigued. Saban just asked for a chance, telling Chapman to come for a visit so that he could make an informed decision about whether Alabama was the school for him. He explained the basics of his 3-4 defense, and how he had developed dozens of defensive linemen in his career who went to play in the NFL. A few days later Chapman and his family made the fifty-minute drive from Hoover to Saban's office.

Once Chapman and his mom, Theresa, were seated on the

couch, Saban began describing how absolutely vital the nose tackle position was in his version of the 3-4 defense, the scheme Saban had honed as Bill Belichick's defensive coordinator with the Cleveland Browns from 1991 through 1994. "Everything we do starts right in the middle of the line," Saban said. "The nose needs to hold the point and demand double teams. That makes the whole thing go."

In his first few months on the job, Saban often came off as distant in public settings, looking bored as he sat at different functions with fans, bouncing his right knee and checking his watch. But here in his office, when he talked football philosophy and techniques, his face lit up, he sat on the edge of his chair, and he spoke with increasing passion, like an excited English professor delving deep into a discussion of Chaucer. When a recruit was in Saban's office, each sell session the coach delivered came off as the most important and urgent of his career. Chapman listened, riveted. He felt Saban's passion and intensity, and he marveled at the depth of Saban's knowledge. "I was like, 'Wow, he really, really knows his stuff and really loves what he's doing,'" Chapman said. "My word is important to me, but playing for Coach Saban was something I couldn't pass up. So I changed my mind."

Chapman played three games during the 7-6 season of 2007 due to a shoulder injury (he was awarded a medical redshirt). But even though Chapman saw only limited action, Saban knew he had scored a recruiting coup—and had sent a message to Alabama's cross-state rival by flipping a prized recruit. Three years later, on October 10, 2011, Chapman would be featured on the cover of *Sports Illustrated* under the headline, "Ram! Jam! 'Bama! The Crimson Tide's Defense Could Be the Best Ever."

The Rising of Saban's Tide

◉   ◉   ◉

Saban didn't rely on game tape alone to evaluate players. He (or a staff member) always talked to a high school player's coaches and grilled them with questions: *What's the player's character like? Can he digest and understand complex concepts? Is he a team leader? Is he a good teammate? What's his family background? Has he gotten in any trouble at school or with the law? How does he practice? Does he listen? Does he show up on time for meetings and appointments? Does he attend all his classes? Is he dependable? Is he active in the community? How does he react to adversity? Can he play through pain? How will he perform when a hundred thousand pairs of eyes are trained on him?* Saban, in short, wanted to know every possible detail about every player.

Even before Saban would enter the home of a prospect or invite a recruit to his office, the Alabama staff usually had delved "seven deep" into the player's life, meaning they had already contacted his friends, family, teachers, coaches—virtually anyone who had an interaction with that player and shaped his development. "We didn't even want to know about a guy's physical ability until we had gone more than a few layers deep into his life to find all the answers about him and see if he had the character to fit at Alabama," said Jim McElwain, the Crimson Tide's offensive coordinator from 2008 to 2011. "We wanted to know if he had the drive to succeed and the character to handle all that we were going to demand of him. It's hard at Alabama. It's not for everybody. You can't be an ego guy at Alabama. Nick won't tolerate it, no matter how much talent you have. But that's why he goes so many layers deep into a player's life before really getting serious about recruiting him."

The Tide staff dug into the background of wide receiver Julio Jones, a six-four, 220-pound wide receiver out of Foley (Alabama) High who was ranked the No. 4 overall prospect in the nation by Rivals.com after his senior year in 2007. Every school in the SEC lusted for Jones, and coach after coach enthusiastically told Jones how much they adored his game and his playmaking ability, and that if he came to their school, they'd turn Jones into a star. But Saban and his assistants had done their research on Jones. They knew he was low-key, shunned publicity, and preferred to blend into the background with players who didn't have his raw talent. But the Alabama coaches also understood that Jones was a natural and he *knew* he was a natural, so there was no point in telling him how magnificent he was. When Jones, who was leaning toward committing to Oklahoma, stepped through that thick, heavy door into Saban's office during his official recruiting visit in December 2007, Saban did one thing—and it was the one thing he did better than any coach in the nation: He exuded conviction, in himself, in the program, and in the Process.

"Well, you know we want you here," Saban told Jones, "but we're going to win with you or without you." No coach had talked to Jones like this before, especially one who had lost four of his last five games. But Jones was sold by Saban's supreme confidence. *There is absolutely no BS to this guy*, he thought. On February 6, 2008—one month after his visit to Tuscaloosa—Jones signed with Alabama. Three years later, he would become the first Crimson Tide receiver to be drafted in the first round of the NFL draft in four decades.

"When you work for Coach Saban, you better make sure you are on top of the guys you are in charge of recruiting," said Sal

Sunseri, the linebackers coach at Alabama from 2009 to 2011 who returned to the staff in 2019. "Persistence is what makes Coach Saban such a good recruiter. If he wants a guy, he'll make that guy feel like no one wants him more than Alabama. That's why you have to be very prepared to respond to Coach Saban when he asks you about a player you are recruiting. It's all about developing relationships with high school coaches, with parents, and with the players. Really, those relationships are the key, and Coach Saban is always making sure that his assistants are keeping up with those relationships."

⬤　⬤　⬤

Prospects and their family members who make official visits to Tuscaloosa typically spend time with Terry Saban, or Miss Terry, as everyone at Alabama, including Saban himself, calls her. Elegant, refined, and an adept conversationalist, Miss Terry is the maternal figure of the entire program. She hosts a large party after the A-Day game each spring at the Sabans' mansion in Tuscaloosa, a few miles north of campus. While Saban works the grill and talks ball with staff and donors, Miss Terry will move from person to person with the skill of a royal, telling humanizing—and often humorous—stories about her husband and making everyone feel comfortable.

Miss Terry also spends time with the players once they arrive on campus, and she makes the parents of recruits feel that their child will be taken care of in Tuscaloosa. "Terry does a fantastic job, I think, of being very supportive, not only in the things we do, or try to do, in terms of recruiting and getting to know and develop relationships with people that are important to feel comfortable when they come and visit our university," Saban said. He added, "She's quick to tell me when we're running it too much up the middle, when we're not passing enough, when we don't blitz enough on defense. I get lots of feedback on all those things. So I would say that she's probably as big a part of the program as anyone in terms of her time, her commitment."

On many road games Miss Terry sat on the team bus next to Mal Moore, the man who had brought the Sabans to Tuscaloosa. The two talked about their lives and families; sometimes she would recite a few lines of Emily Dickinson, one of her favorite poets. At the stadium, she usually engaged in small talk with reporters—embracing her favorite ones—and then watched the action from a private box. After games she moved down to the field and stood near the tunnel that led to the locker room, where she kissed her husband as he made his way to talk to his team. This was their ritual.

Once, when Miss Terry was asked when she last spotted her husband smiling, she quipped, "About twenty-five years ago." Yet in the winter of 2008, Saban would have plenty of reasons to smile.

On February 6, 2008, the fax machine in the Alabama football offices started spitting out scholarship acceptance letters early in the morning. By the end of the day, Saban had signed thirty-two players, including safety Mark Barron, defensive tackle Terrence Cody, defensive tackle Marcell Dareus, linebacker Dont'a Hightower, running back Mark Ingram, offensive lineman Barrett Jones, wide receiver Julio Jones, safety Robert Lester, tight end Brad Smelley, defensive end Damion Square, linebacker Courtney Upshaw, and tight end Michael Williams. The Tide's 2008 recruiting class was universally hailed as the best in the nation. Ten years later, this recruiting class collectively would earn $271 million in the NFL.

Nineteen of the players were from Alabama, and Saban lured the state's top five prospects—according to Rivals.com—to Tuscaloosa, in spite of the fact that the Crimson Tide hadn't beaten rival Auburn in six years. At his press conference that afternoon to announce the signings, Saban was giddy, joking that Miss Terry wanted him to come to their lake house in Georgia to relax for a few days, but he insisted on preparing for spring practice, still two months into the future. "Recruiting is kind of the lifeline for all of us in this profession," Saban said. "When you have good players who can make plays, who are quality people, who are great competitors, things just seem to work out better sometimes."

Saban and his staff devoted time every working day of the year to recruiting, whether it was writing letters, making phone calls, or watching game film. The staff compiled comprehensive reports on every prospective recruit, noting how accurately he fit the prototype the team was looking for at his position. No detail was too extraneous; they'd assess ankle movement, hip flexibility, and knee dexterity. They examined how each recruit communicated to his teammates on the field, how he reacted to getting beaten or manhandled by his opponent, and how he behaved once he'd achieved success on the field. They also probed his behavior at school, analyzing his study habits and his social conduct.

Alabama has a recruiting war room, which sits close to Saban's office. Only key personnel are allowed inside the room, which has a grease board that covers an entire wall and features the players

Alabama is targeting through the upcoming four years. The board includes information ranging from each prospect's grade point average to the names of the school or schools each is leaning toward at the time. The mass of information on the board is constantly updated.

"Recruiting with Coach Saban never stops," said Jim McElwain. "We're evaluating film, writing letters to players, writing letters to coaches. It's nonstop, because it's the lifeblood of the program. Nick doesn't care if a kid has a hundred offers or zero offers; he just wants to know if he can fit in the Alabama program. And if Nick offers a kid, his [recruiting] stars will jump up. But no one at Alabama is concerned about stars or what so-called recruiting experts are saying about players. That's just background noise.

"The evaluation process Coach Saban has is incredibly exhaustive. There are position-specific sets of critical factors that they look for in a high school player. If the player has many of those critical factors, we feel that physically he'll have a chance to succeed at that position at Alabama. It's as much a scientific approach as is possible to what is ultimately a subjective matter. I don't think anyone in the nation can evaluate talent better than Coach Saban."

"A lot of coaches will try to become really close friends with recruits, but that's not Nick. He's matter-of-fact and all business," said Todd Grantham, who was a defensive line coach under Saban at Michigan State in the late '90s. "When coaches do become buddies with the recruit, and then the recruit gets on campus and the coach is no longer his best friend, that's when problems can occur. But Nick just lays it all out there: 'Here's what we have to offer both academically and athletically. I'll launch you to an NFL career. Take it or leave it.'"

"Nick typically only hires coaches who have reputations for

being good recruiters," said Curt Cignetti, Alabama's recruiting coordinator and wide receivers coach from 2007 to 2010. "Every assistant recruits an area, so Nick wants assistants who have relationships with high school coaches in the specific area that he will be in charge of recruiting. Recruiting is information gathering and sales. Once we get film of the player, the position coach will evaluate it. He then passes his evaluation along to Nick. And then if Nick decides to make an offer, he's very good at giving people attention, which is really what people want. He's good at developing and maintaining relationships. He's very, very smart and he has the recruiting down to a science. I think he could have been successful in any business he went into, because he's the rare person who is intellectually gifted and extremely driven. He sets the tempo for everything at Alabama. Everything."

Saban realized that the chemistry of his '07 team—his first at Alabama—had been less than ideal. He told a few in his inner circle that graduation couldn't come soon enough for a few players on that squad, because their poor leadership, poor work habits, and poor decision-making away from the field had poisoned the entire team. Now, in the spring of 2008, after those rotten apples had fallen from the tree, Saban gave daily sermons to his team about the need to exercise better judgment—both on and off the field. He also told his players to spend time with each other away from the football facility and to eliminate small group cliques in favor of big group bonding. The players responded by shooting pool, playing card games, and bowling together in large numbers.

"We now knew what the expectations were going into the 2008 season," said Greg McElroy. "There was more player accountability and more veteran leadership. And Coach Saban eased up a little on us in the winter and spring and summer. We ran out of gas at the end of the 2007 season because of how hard we worked during the off-season. Coach Saban learned from that."

Most of the players from the 2008 recruiting class arrived on May 31. The next afternoon they boarded a team bus at the football facility and rode it to the stadium, where strength coach Scott Cochran told them they would run 110 yards sixteen times. "It was hot and muggy and it felt like it was 120 degrees," said offensive lineman Barrett Jones. "I had never thrown up before, but I threw up about three years' worth of food that day. It was a rude awakening for what the physical expectations were at Alabama."

Coaches also went over a list of rules with the new players. Inside the football facility, shirts always had to be tucked in, earrings weren't allowed, pants had to be pulled up, and hats couldn't be worn. If players wore long hair, it couldn't cover the name on the back of their jersey. For trips to away games, every player had to wear a coat and tie. "The rules were about creating discipline," said Barrett Jones. "Everything about Nick Saban's program comes back to discipline."

Saban knew as much about the mental makeup of his incoming players as any coach in the country. By the time a player walked onto the Alabama practice field for the first time, Dr. Lonnie Rosen had written a detailed psychological profile on him, which was distributed to the staff. A professor of psychology at Michigan State, Rosen had been a mentor figure to Saban since his days in East Lansing in the 1990s, and Saban viewed these profiles as instrumental in developing a player's talent. "The profiles helped us figure out the best way to help the player," said Cignetti. "They showed us what the best way to reach him was and what he responded to and what would turn him off."

That summer Saban brought in instructors from the Pacific Institute, a leadership-development consultancy based in Seattle. At a price tag of $39,000, instructors from the institute met with the players for twelve sessions that lasted between thirty and forty-five minutes. In these classes the players chanted various affirmations, each intended to promote team unity and strengthen their commitment to one another. For example:

"We are a team that's committed to excellence. It's represented in everything we do."

"Our team is a family. We will look out for each other. We love one another. Anything that attempts to tear us apart only makes us stronger."

"Our defense is aggressive. We fly to the ball seeking always to create big plays on every down. We intimidate our opponents."

Before one preseason practice in 2008 Saban also had Dr. Kevin Elko speak to his team. A sports psychologist, Elko first worked with Saban in 2003, when he met with LSU players several times during the Tigers' run to the national title. Elko played a key role in helping to shape and create the Process—"It was something we constantly talked about at LSU: focusing only on what was in front of you," Elko said—and now Saban wanted his trusted friend to deliver a message to Alabama players.

As Elko—who also worked with Green Bay when the Packers won the Super Bowl in 1997 and the University of Miami when the Hurricanes captured the national title in 2001—prepared to speak to the team on the practice field, a few trainers told him to keep his speech short and sweet. Overhearing this, Saban told Elko, "Go as long as you want, man. This is important."

For forty-five minutes, Elko spoke. "You have to have a vision for where you're heading," he said. "Know where you want to go and know what it will take to get there. You also have to eliminate the mental clutter from your life. Get rid of it. It does you no good to be thinking of how you're having trouble with your girlfriend when you're on the practice field. And remember that there is a process to becoming a champion. There's a process to how you play the game and a process to how you prepare. The Process is the price you pay for victory."

In his talks to the team, Elko also discussed eye control and how that factored into the Process. "If you see a little on the field, you see a lot. If you see a lot on the field, you see nothing," he said. "If you're a wide receiver and trying to catch a football, you should just see a little and focus on that ball and nothing else. If you see a lot at that moment the ball is coming and your eyes wander around the field, you won't make the catch. Same with blocking. If you are an offensive lineman, keep your eyes focused on what your assignment is, not what's happening to the guy next to you. Just remember: You see a little on the field, you see a lot. You see a lot on the field, you see nothing."

More than any college coach in America, Saban embraced these unique approaches to team chemistry, mental conditioning, and football playmaking. He frequently repeated phrases that Elko had told him, such as, "Don't worry about accepting failure, worry about the process of preparing," and "Pain instructs." At first, in the summer of 2008, the players were squeamish about these rarely used preparation tactics, but the results were immediate: After beating Clemson 34–10 in the season-opening Chick-fil-A College Kickoff in Atlanta's Georgia Dome—the Tide outrushed the Tigers 239 to 0—every player in the locker room afterward praised the off-season mental conditioning work. "I'm telling you, we're tight," defensive end Brandon Deaderick said. "We're a closer team than last year. We trust each other."

That bonding had cost money to develop, but at Alabama, virtually no expenses were spared if they could benefit the program—a fact that made the job so appealing to Saban when Mal Moore offered him the position in Fort Lauderdale. "Money is absolutely not an issue at Alabama," said Cignetti. "If it can be done legally and within NCAA rules, Nick will do it. He has it all thought out and all of his bases covered. Everyone is on the same page at Alabama. Nick has no battles to fight. Whatever he wants, he gets."

🏈   🏈   🏈

After defeating Clemson in the season opener, Alabama won ten consecutive games in 2008 before facing Auburn in late November at Bryant-Denny Stadium. The Tigers had won six straight against the Crimson Tide—a span that had stretched 2,930 days. But Alabama took control midway through the game on a cool late afternoon in Tuscaloosa behind the powerful running of backs Glen Coffee and Mark Ingram, the offensive line led by tackle Andre Smith, and a stifling defense anchored by defensive tackle Terrence Cody. Late in the fourth quarter, Alabama led 29–0.

With a few minutes remaining, Saban inserted backup quarterback Greg McElroy into the game, without McElroy even throwing a warm-up pass on the sideline. After a few plays, the Tide faced a third-and-six from the Tigers' 34-yard line. The call came to McElroy: "Double Right Y Orbit Jet Left Y Option." The play was designed to go to tight end Brad Smelley for a seven-yard gain—and a first down. But McElroy also had an option: If he saw his wide receiver split out to the right in press coverage with a single high safety in the middle of the field, he could throw the "go" route.

"I look out and see their No. 3 corner is pressed against our best go-route receiver in Marquis Maze," McElroy said. "I take a three-step drop and throw it to Marquis and we score a touchdown. That play was symbolic of what Saban preached. He always said to the quarterbacks, 'We don't care what the score is. The score doesn't matter. You go through your reads and do your job regardless of the score.' Coach Saban was happy with me after the play because I did what I was supposed to do. I think that's when I went from being called 'Hey 12' by Coach Saban to 'Greg.' He started to believe in me. That play was symbolic of the Process, and the final score was symbolic of the changing of the guard in football in Alabama."

Indeed, as Maze ran into the end zone, the crowd exploded, sending a reverberating cheer into the cloudy night sky, as if at that very moment it became clear that there was a new ruler in the state of Alabama. Auburn coach Tommy Tuberville was fired days later—the first of several head coaches in the next decade who would lose their jobs after a blowout loss to Nick Saban, including Phil Fulmer at Tennessee in 2008 and Gene Chizik at Auburn in 2012.

After the game thousands of Alabama fans stood in the dark outside the Tide locker room, waiting to greet their leader. When Saban appeared, they belted another roar, prompting a smile to stretch across Saban's face. A mass of Alabama fans surrounded the Auburn team buses, preventing them from moving down the streets of Tuscaloosa. The fans didn't want the night of celebrating to end; they sensed it was the beginning of something.

In the SEC championship game a week later the top-ranked Tide faced second-ranked Florida and their quarterback Tim Tebow, the reigning Heisman Trophy winner. It was a de facto national semi-final game, and at the start of the fourth quarter, Alabama held a 20–17 lead. Then Tebow took over. He rushed for a team-high 57 yards and threw 3 touchdown passes—each on third-down plays. It was the first fourth-quarter comeback of Tebow's career, and Florida won, 31–20.

And yet, only twenty-three months after he was named head coach, Saban had come within fifteen minutes of reaching the national championship game. Saban would never admit it, but his rebuild project was ahead of schedule. Not even in his most optimistic moments during those first days in Tuscaloosa did Saban ever anticipate that it would be possible for Alabama to be this close to the summit of the sport less than two years into his tenure. Saban's wildest dreams just didn't stretch that far.

Though Alabama ended the 2008 season with back-to-back defeats—the Tide lost 31–17 to Utah in the Sugar Bowl—the program was growing and gaining strength. A hurricane was about to make landfall in college football. A year earlier Alabama had lost four of its final five games; now the Crimson Tide had been a few plays away from vying for its first national championship in nearly two decades. Recruit by recruit, day by day, practice by practice, game by game, Saban was constructing a powerhouse. The Process was beginning to work.

CHAPTER 6

Be Brave

1961

On Saturday mornings before home games Paul Bryant went on a walk with his quarterbacks outside the Moon Winx Motor Court. A few hours before kickoff at Denny Stadium, they'd meet in the lobby of the motel on Highway 11, located less than four miles from campus, and then stroll for about forty-five minutes between the cottages on the property that was shaded by towering trees. In the quiet of the pines, a soft breeze often feathering their faces, the coach and his quarterbacks bonded—the underlying point of the walks.

The coach asked his quarterbacks about their families, their schoolwork, their dreams, their fears, and what made their hearts really tick. They discussed the game plan, the plays the quarterbacks liked, the ones they didn't, and how they should attack the defense they were about to face. At the end of their leisurely walks around the compound where the rooms had the top-of-the-line luxuries such as air-conditioning, television, and telephones, Bryant always told his quarterbacks the same thing, "Be brave."

"All outstanding football teams have two distinct characteristics in common—a great fighting spirit and a great quarterback," Bryant wrote in his book, *Building a Championship Football Team*. "The one [quarterback] everyone is seeking…is a student of the game. He is logical in his thinking, and bold in his action, when necessary to win a football game. He is confident, which in turn gives his team confidence in him and the offense. He is a winner through preparation, and he will give you winners through action and leadership."

In Bryant's offensive system, the quarterback called the majority of the plays. He taught his quarterbacks the principles of his offense, but he also gave them discretion to change course from the game plan if the quarterback saw something on the field that he believed could work. "There are several basic rules by which we expect our quarterbacks to operate," Bryant said, "but I wouldn't give a plug nickel for a quarterback who would not be willing to break every one of these in order to win a game."

Bryant expected his quarterbacks to be physically and mentally tough. The first sign Bryant saw that led him to believe the 1961 season could be special came during a preseason scrimmage. At one point a backup quarterback named Carlton Rankin was tackled and another player's cleat bashed him in the face. Blood poured from Rankin's mouth, falling on his white practice jersey. A doctor escorted him into the dressing room as the blood continued to gush. After a quick examination, the doctor told the backup quarterback that he needed a half-dozen stitches in his upper lip. But Rankin wanted nothing of it.

"You can't do that, Doc!" Rankin said. "I might lose my place! Can't you just put a clamp on it?" When the story of Rankin's reaction was relayed to Bryant, the coach was impressed: This was the kind of never-die, never-retreat, never-surrender attitude that he believed was the stuff of champions.

Bryant's quarterbacks also had to be smart, because as play callers they needed to know the Alabama playbook as thoroughly as the coaches. One quarterback who Bryant later said was as intellectually gifted as any signal caller he ever had was Pat Trammell, the starting quarterback of his 1961 team. The son of a doctor from Scottsboro, Alabama, the six-two, 205-pound Trammell was fiery, in-your-face intense, and profane—so profane that Bryant had to relax the fine system he imposed on his players for swearing. Against Auburn that season, with Alabama leading 34–0 and the ball near midfield, Trammell opted to quick kick on second down.

"What's going on, Pat?" Bryant asked when his quarterback reached the sideline.

"Those—!" Trammell replied, referring to his offensive linemen. "They aren't blocking anybody, so I thought we might as well see if they could play defense."

Bryant relished that his quarterback's internal furnace was always on full blast that autumn. Trammell had been one of the first recruits that Bryant met even before formally accepting the Alabama job. An All-State quarterback at Scottsboro High, Trammell had planned to attend Georgia Tech, but then Bryant told him that if *he* would come to Alabama, then Bryant would follow in his footsteps. Bryant's sincerity and earnestness touched a deep chord inside of Trammell, and he committed to Bryant.

With Trammell running and pitching the ball on the option—and occasionally passing—the Alabama offense burst to life in 1961 and scored twenty-four or more points in seven games. Trammell became Bryant's first star player for the Crimson Tide, a player who Bryant would say for decades was his all-time favorite in Tuscaloosa. (When Trammell died at age twenty-eight of metastatic testicular cancer in 1968, two years after earning his MD from the Medical College of Alabama, Bryant called his passing "the saddest day of my life.")

Through recruiting, Bryant had filled his roster with aggressive, unrelenting players, including linebacker Darwin Holt. During a 10–0 victory over Georgia Tech on November 18 at Legion Field, the Yellow Jackets punted the ball to the Crimson Tide. As the Alabama returner signaled for a fair catch, Holt left his feet and smashed into the face of Georgia Tech's Chick Graning with his left elbow and forearm—an unnecessary block. Graning's face was a bloody mess: He had several fractured facial bones, five missing upper front teeth, a broken nose, and a concussion. The Tech fans in the stands loudly booed, believing it was another example of Alabama playing dirty football. Bryant refused to take Holt out of the game.

Facing reporters after the final whistle, Bryant never apologized for Holt's hit and he later refused to discipline his player. For Bryant, football was blood sport; backing his players who fearlessly attacked the opponent further cemented his reputation for being something of a football outlaw. "I want players who want to go jaw to jaw for sixty minutes," Bryant said. "To go out and be reckless.

You have to fight and bleed. You have to be tough, mentally and physically tough."

To Bryant, football was a game of intimidation and violence as much as it was about strategy and raw talent. Every play, he insisted, could be distilled into eleven one-on-one battles. Whichever team won the majority of those battles would win the play; whichever team won the majority of the plays would win the game.

Against the Yellow Jackets the Alabama defense was as strong-willed as its coach, surrendering only 96 total yards and 6 first downs in the shutout victory. For the season, the Tide was historically dominating, allowing 25 total points—3 touchdowns, 2 field goals, and a point-after attempt—and finished the regular season with five straight shutouts.

Undefeated in the regular season, Alabama faced ninth-ranked Arkansas in the Sugar Bowl. With players who were now as ruthlessly tough as their coach, the Tide defeated Arkansas 10–3 to cap an 11-0 season. The win delivered Bryant, in his fourth year at Alabama, his first national title—and the school's first in twenty years. The core of the team was Bryant's first two recruiting classes from 1958 and 1959.

"Starting with his very first recruiting class, Coach Bryant recruited the right kind of players," said Lee Roy Jordan. "He wanted players with high character who wouldn't back down at the first sign of adversity. We all knew exactly how hard it was going to be to play for him—we'd heard all the stories about his training camps at Texas A&M and how difficult it had been for some of those boys to just survive—but we all were willing to sacrifice because we knew he could lead us to a national championship. He talked about it all the time and prepared us every day to play at a championship level."

Bryant's fame and influence were growing as well. He was paid around $30,000 a year for doing an hourlong television show on Sundays during football season and for making public appearances for his sponsors, Golden Flake potato chips and Coca-Cola. "Coach Bryant came on his television show on Sundays. People would come home from church and watch it in the afternoon," said Bill Battle. "He was so folksy that he really connected to the entire state. Sometimes you couldn't really understand him because he would mumble in that low voice of his, but that didn't matter. It was almost like church continued for the state once his show came on."

Bryant was also a member of the board of directors of the First National Bank of Tuscaloosa and Cotton States Life Insurance. His face was on nearly every Coke bottle in Alabama—as well as on billboards around Birmingham. A chauffeur now usually drove him in his air-conditioned Cadillac. For Bryant, life was good.

In the spring of 1962, a few months after he won his first national title, the town elders in Fordyce, Arkansas, held a dinner in Bryant's honor. Newspapermen from across the nation attended. At the prodding of a friend, Bryant took a few writers and old buddies to his family home in the country. When the group arrived at the small, dilapidated house, Bryant appeared visibly embarrassed by his humble roots. Then Joe Sheehan of the *New York Times* said to the coach, "Why, Bear, I've been hearing for years that you were born in a log cabin."

"Naw Joe," Bryant replied, "That was Abraham Lincoln. I was born in a manger."

Ida and Monroe Bryant raised nine children in a wooden four-room shack in rural Arkansas, on 260 acres of fertile soil between the small towns of Fordyce and Kingsland. They had no electricity or running water and they lived off the land, growing turnip greens and black-eyed peas and watermelons and all sorts of other vegetables in a vast garden. They raised cows and chickens and hogs. On many days little Paul and his mamma would hop on an old wagon that was pulled by two mules named Pete and Joe and ride it on a dirt road seven miles into Fordyce (population: 3,600), where they would sell their milk and butter and eggs, mostly in poor African-American neighborhoods.

One night Bryant's father, Monroe, disappeared into the darkness. A storm had blown through, and Paul's daddy was nowhere to be found. Ida eventually located her husband sitting in a mud puddle on a nearby road. Monroe didn't know how he got in the puddle—he had a reputation among the locals for being lazy—but he soon became sick. Fervent Christians who read the Bible to their children every night, the Bryants didn't believe in doctors and thought it was a sin to be examined by one. Monroe never recovered from that night in the mud puddle—and never saw a doctor. For fifteen years, he was constantly out of breath and rarely was strong enough to help around the farm. He died in 1931 at age forty-six, most likely of pneumonia.

Paul was the eleventh of twelve children—three Bryant babies died as infants—and he was Ida's youngest boy. Born September 11, 1913, little Paul was constantly in his mamma's shadow. "I was a mamma's boy," he once said. "It came naturally because we were together so much." By the time Paul was old enough to work the fields, most of his brothers and sisters had already left home. So the duties of plowing and chopping cotton and drawing water for the cows fell to Paul. At a young age, he learned the value of hard work, that one hour spent out in the fields before sunup was worth two in the afternoon.

Even in the bitter chill of winter, Paul drove the wagon to Fordyce to sell what they raised on the farm, their only income. His mamma would heat up bricks in the indoor fireplace, put them in the wagon, and then pull a tarp over the top to keep warm on the seven-mile ride into town with her youngest boy. Once in Fordyce, Ida Bryant peddled her goods and then she would often head to a hotel restaurant for a hot meal. But Paul, outfitted in overalls, wouldn't join her, because he wasn't sure whether to use a knife or spoon with whatever food was in front of him, which gave him a deep inferiority complex. Instead, he'd pay a dime for a chunk of cheese and soda crackers, sit in a nearby boxcar on the railroad tracks, and dream of one day becoming a fireman. As soon as he would see the clock on top of the courthouse near the 4 p.m. hour, he'd run to meet his mom, and then the two would load the wagon with their supplies and return to their shack in the countryside.

Ida Bryant was a hard, strict woman, and she rarely spared the rod on her youngest boy. During a church revival in nearby Mount Lebanon, Paul spotted a cat, picked it up, and threw it out a church window as the preacher spoke from the pulpit. The cat hit a young girl, causing her to scream. "I am going to whip you for that, son," Ida told Paul. "You did wrong." Later, with Ida using a plum-orchard switch, the beating commenced.

Paul attended elementary school in Kingsland, a few miles from his home. He'd rise at 3:30 a.m. and, in the dark, hitch the mules to the wagon and feed them oats. By the time he reached school in his dusty overalls and was in his seat for the first bell, he'd sometimes be soaked in sweat from the morning's work. One of his teachers repeatedly spoke to the class about the need for good hygiene, hoping that Paul would get the message. He didn't, and the teacher eventually asked Paul to switch seats with a boy in the back of the room, prompting the girls in the class to snicker and laugh. Paul was so ashamed he couldn't lift his eyes from the ground.

Those girls weren't the only ones to make fun of the poor boy who lived out in the countryside. Kids in Fordyce went to school on Saturdays until noon, but because of his chores, Paul and his mother often wouldn't pull up to the schoolhouse doors until just before the final bell rang. Once it did, the more affluent kids from the city would point at Paul and laugh at his smelly clothes and dirty bare feet as they ran out of the doors and passed the old wagon. This was repeated every Saturday, deepening Paul's belief that he was of a lower rank than his peers and intensifying his need for acceptance. The desire for a better life—and an iron-willed determination to achieve that—was formed during these Saturday shaming sessions.

Anger also swirled inside of Paul, who was usually the biggest boy in his class. By thirteen, he was six foot one and 180 pounds. He was lean and muscular, his body hardened by his constant work on the farm. One day he delivered groceries to a man's house in Fordyce. When the man refused to pay, thirteen-year-old Paul raised his fists and the two fought. No one was going to get the best of Paul—not anymore.

Shortly after his first fistfight, Paul walked with a few friends toward the Lyric Theatre in downtown Fordyce. That afternoon a man from a traveling carnival had ridden a wagon into town and was pulling a caged black bear. The man with the bear was outside the theater talking to the owner when Paul and his buddies approached. The man was offering a dollar a minute to anyone willing to wrestle the bear on the Lyric stage. "Why don't you go in there?" one of Paul's friends asked.

Paul then looked at an older girl named Drucilla Smith, a reddish-blond beauty whom he desperately wanted to impress. For a moment Paul weighed his options and then blurted out, "For a dollar a minute, I'd do anything." Paul then insisted that the owner of the bear wave the ten-cent cover charge for his friends; the owner agreed.

The Lyric Theatre was known for showing silent movies, and it had about two hundred seats that sloped to a wooden stage. Once Paul accepted the challenge with the bear, the word-of-mouth news spread throughout Fordyce: The young Bryant boy was daring to do what no one else would. The theater was packed by the time Paul strode onto the stage, and a rumble of expectation rose from the sold-out crowd.

Paul was the first to appear on the stage. He had spent the summer earning fifty cents a day chopping cotton, so the prospect of making a $1 a minute excited Paul. He was ready. Then the man and his bear walked out. Paul's friends would later swear that the bear was scrawny and looked about as ferocious as a puppy dog, but then the man released the bear and it reared up. Suddenly, in Paul's eyes, the bear seemed thirty feet tall.

The crowd howled. Putting his fear aside, Paul charged at the muzzled bear. He grabbed the bear and pinned him to the ground.

For a few seconds, the bear offered little resistance. But then the man told Paul to let the bear up, to give the people the show they had come to see. The owner of the bear wanted blood to be spilled, but Paul wasn't going to let go. The man then walked over and pulled off the muzzle.

Then the bear slipped free. Now angry, Paul pinned him again. The bear got loose again. For the first time, Paul noticed the muzzle was off. He then felt a burning sensation on the back of his right ear. He reached back with his hand, felt his ear, and then inspected his hand. It was covered in blood. The bear had bitten him.

Not wanting to face the bear that was now flashing its teeth, Paul fled the scene, jumping off the stage and landing on the front row of seats. The crowd *ohhhhhh*ed.

Once the show was over, Paul searched for the man with the bear. He was nowhere to be found; he had hurried out of town before Paul could demand his dollar. But on this simmering summer night inside the Lyric Theatre he earned a sobriquet that would follow him into eternity:

Bear.

●　　●　　●

The thirteen-year-old boy lumbered through the autumn afternoon in Fordyce, only weeks after wrestling the bear. His confidence was growing. He no longer dressed in overalls, and he now wore shoes. His mother had moved the family into a small house in town—she earned extra money by taking in boarders—but the Bryants kept the farm. During the weekends Paul still plowed the fields and tended to the cows and hogs and chickens, but during the week he stayed at the house in Fordyce. And now, as he walked down a street on a weekday afternoon after school, the path he would follow for the rest of his life was about to become clear.

Paul had never seen a football before. He had listened to one game on the radio—Alabama versus Washington in the 1926 Rose Bowl—but he wasn't intimately aware of the rules of the game. On his way home from his final eighth-grade class of the day, he sidled past a field where the Fordyce High football team was practicing. The team's head coach, Bob Cowan, spotted Paul in the distance, and was captivated by his wide shoulders and powerful frame. He asked the young man if he'd like to play football.

"Yes sir, I guess I do," Paul replied. "How do you play?"

"Well, you see that fellow catching the ball down there?" the coach asked.

"Yeah," said Paul.

"Well," the coach said, "whenever he catches it, you go down there and try to kill him."

That sounded good to Paul. Lining up with the punt team, Paul tore down the field as soon as the ball was snapped—mimicking the other players. Paul was the fastest kid on the squad, and he was the first to reach the punt returner. He hit the smaller kid so hard that it sent him sprawling to the ground. He had done what the coach had asked: *You go down there and kill him.* The core of his future football beliefs had just been formed.

A few days later he played in his first game. Wanting to wear shoes that resembled the cleats the other players had, Paul visited the town cobbler, took off his black high-tops, and told the cobbler to screw cleats into the soles. For the next few months, his friends and family members could hear Paul coming before they saw him—*clack, clack, clack.*

In his first few games for Fordyce High, he struggled to catch the ball as a receiver, but heaven help anyone who tried to block him. Though only thirteen, he was always one of the biggest—and certainly the meanest—players on the field. He hit opposing players in his lightweight leather helmet like he had something to prove, like he needed them to know that he wasn't some country rube who couldn't afford a pair of shoes anymore. These early games were Paul's release, his way of getting back at anyone and everyone who ever slighted him or laughed at him or looked at him with disgust because he smelled or was layered in dirt. This was the power of football to Paul, and it was a seductive allure—one that would never leave him, the Bear.

The mid-1920s were heady times in America. The economy, which had successfully transitioned from wartime to peacetime, was booming in big cities like New York and Chicago. Model T's rolled off the production line in record numbers. Air, rail, and truck transportation were expanding. Movies with sound were relegating silent black-and-white films to the dustbin of history. People flocked to clubs, where they danced the foxtrot and consumed increasing quantities of alcohol. Radio expanded, as did leisure time. Sports gathered ever-larger audiences. New football teams and a professional league emerged. And Americans adopted athletic heroes. As fans listened over their radios to Babe Ruth hitting home runs, Red Grange breaking tackles, and Jack Dempsey knocking out opponents, these stars captivated the imagination of the country, heroes who seemed to glow in the dark as their exploits were described by announcers over crackling, horn-speaker radios. Indeed, the '20s roared—but not across all of America.

For the most part the prosperity didn't reach Alabama. It was stuck in a minidepression. Joblessness was high. Small businesses succumbed to rising numbers of regionwide companies. Farmers had trouble finding markets for their crops and many had to go town to town in search of work. The state was best known for being the unofficial home of the Ku Klux Klan, which burned crosses at night and pushed candidates into state office during the day. Hopes for a better future were low.

It was against this backdrop that Wallace Wade led his team onto the football field at Alabama for preseason practice in August 1925. Hired in 1923, Wade had never lost a game in his previous two years as an assistant at Vanderbilt. He was as demanding as any coach in America. Wade offered his players two options: Give your entire effort on the field or sit on the sideline. And he was feared. In the middle of one practice he was summoned off the field to take a long-distance phone call. The conversation went on and on and, after he hung up, Wade went home. But the assistant coaches and players, not wanting to upset Wade, stayed on the practice field for several more hours, even into nightfall. They were waiting for Wade to yell his customary phrase—"All right, that'll do"—to signal that practice was over. A coach eventually called Wade at his home and asked if they could stop practice. "Yes, well, let them go in. It's dark now," Wade said.

Wade's coaching philosophy could be considered the genesis of the doctrines of Bryant and Saban. "What I try to do is get the very best out of every boy who becomes a member of the Crimson Tide team," Wade told the *Birmingham News*. "I try to impress upon boys that I am fair and square with them; I never try to appeal to their sentiment. I never ask a boy to try to win a game for my sake, but on the other hand put him on his mettle to do his level best and failing, he feels the discomfort of not having done his duty, measuring up to the best that is in him. A coach gets and fails to get results on account of his ability to handle boys; he must inspire them with confidence and enthusiasm."

Wade's 1925 team, led by running back Johnny Mack Brown, finished the season 9-0 and outscored its opponents 277 to 7. After their final game against Georgia, the team traveled around the state for celebratory banquets; in Birmingham more than nine hundred fans attended a team party. Everyone thought Alabama's season had come to its end. At the time there was only one postseason bowl game—the Rose Bowl—and no Southern team had ever been invited to play in Pasadena, California, on New Year's Day. The Rose Bowl committee asked Dartmouth, then Yale, then Colgate to play, but the three Eastern powers declined because of a recent report by the American Association of University Professors that stated, "Football promoted drinking, dishonesty, and poor academics." When the idea of inviting Alabama to play in the Rose Bowl was broached by the committee, one member said, "I've never heard of Alabama as a football team and can't take the chance of mixing a lemon and a Rose." Nonetheless, in early December, Jack Benefield of the Rose Bowl formally invited Alabama to make the 2,013-mile train trip to Southern California.

Wade called a team meeting and asked the players to vote whether to accept the invitation. Before the ballots were cast, Wade spoke. "Fellows, this is what a trip to the Rose Bowl means," he said. "There will be three weeks of tough, hard practice. I want you all to realize that to the full and think about it. But here's something else to remember: Southern collegiate football is not recognized as being anywhere near what it is in the East, West, and Midwest. So here's your chance to be a part of history." Minutes later, the vote was a landslide: Alabama would play in the Rose Bowl against Washington, a West Coast powerhouse that compiled a 10-0-1 record in '25, including a 108–0 thrashing of Willamette on September 26.

Alabama president George Denny understood the magnitude of the cross-country trip and the game itself. Not only were most Alabamians living in the grip of poverty, but the state was also alienated from the rest of the nation culturally and, Denny believed, it had been branded with the stigma of inferiority. And even though Alabama, like other states in the South, had dealt with the legacy of military defeat for sixty years, Southerners still proudly believed that one Confederate soldier was worth a half-dozen Yankees on the battlefield. Now it was Alabama's chance to prove, on a different kind of field, that they still knew how to fight.

Before the team departed for Pasadena on December 19, Denny spoke to students and players. "Our team will strive to represent worthily our great commonwealth and our great section," he said. "We recognize the difficulties and the handicaps of a long trip to that distant region in which we shall be strangers, both to the climate and the people. We recognize that we shall meet the champions of the Pacific Coast, one of the greatest teams in the country, one of the most powerful America has produced. Such is the colossal task to which our boys have set their hands. Win or lose, this trip means more widespread and sustained publicity for Alabama than any recent event in the history of the state."

Though a round-trip train ticket to Pasadena cost $250, several Pullman cars of fans joined the team on a special train for the journey. As the steam engine pulled the train along the long iron lines across America, the players looked out the windows at a world they'd never seen before. When the train stopped, the players got off, stretched, and tossed footballs. After brief practices, they would climb back on the iron horse, take their seats, and—with its wheels grinding and steam engine hissing—continue their westward charge.

Between stops, Wallace meticulously laid out a game plan and handed his players scouting reports on every Huskie. A reporter, Zipp Newman, who was traveling with the team noted, "There isn't a player on the train who can't tell you the name, weight, disposition, and few other little things about every eligible player on the Washington team." Wade also emphasized that this game was a challenge to Southern character. He stocked the train with fifty-five-gallon barrels of Alabama spring water, so his players wouldn't get sick from drinking that "foreign" water in California, as if the state was some third world country.

Finally, after six days on the rails, the train carrying the Alabama team and its fans eased into the depot at Pasadena on Christmas Eve. The press soon mobbed the players. In that golden era of journalistic hyperbole, reporters framed the game as the second coming of the Civil War—even though the state of Washington had not participated in America's deadliest conflict. The press simply referred to the Huskies as the "Yankees from Washington."

At the time, twelve-year-old Paul Bryant had never listened to a radio broadcast of a college football game before, but this was one he couldn't miss. On New Year's Day in 1926 he sat riveted in front of the radio in his home in Fordyce, awaiting the kickoff of the Rose Bowl. Like millions in the South, Paul leaned toward the radio speaker and strained to hear every bit of the action and the rise and fall of the crowd noise. The word pictures the announcers painted transfixed young Paul: the images of the hard hits, dashing runs, arching throws, and crowd-pleasing touchdowns unfolded vividly in his mind. He couldn't get enough of the action.

After falling behind 12–0 at halftime, Wade growled in the locker room, "And they told me Southern boys could fight." The Crimson Tide stormed back in the second half. When Johnny Mack Brown caught a 63-yard touchdown pass from Grant Gillis, Alabama seized a 14–12 lead in the third quarter. The teams then traded touchdowns. With a few minutes remaining and Washington trailing 20–19, the Huskies drove deep into Alabama territory. But Johnny Mack Brown intercepted a pass thrown by George "Wildcat" Wilson. The play ended the game. Alabama captured its first national title.

Young Paul became mesmerized with Alabama football. "I never imagined anything could be that exciting," Bryant recalled years later. "I still didn't have much of an idea of what football was, but after listening to that game, I had it in my mind that what I wanted to do with my life was go to Alabama and play in the Rose Bowl like Johnny Mack Brown."

Once he started playing high school football, Paul learned that the sport could be his escape from Fordyce and his pathway to a better life. He wasn't the most talented player on his team, but through his force of will—and his joy of violence—he was named an All-State player in 1930 after his senior season. More important, he had found something he loved—his true love. Everything about the game fired his imagination, from the X's and O's to the camaraderie of the locker room to traveling on chartered trains across the state to play rival towns to letting opposing players know just how tough the boys from Fordyce were. By the time his high school career was over, Bear hoped his future would be tied to football.

🏈   🏈   🏈

One summer during high school, Paul and a friend hitchhiked to Ohio to spend time with Paul's sister Ouida, who lived in the town of Parma, seven miles outside Cleveland. Paul got a job at a factory that made spokes for automobile wheels. When he wasn't working, he often rode the train to Dunn Field in Cleveland to watch the Indians play baseball.

One Friday morning at the factory an irate young man approached Paul, believing Paul had taken this man's girlfriend on a date. Paul didn't deny the accusation. The young man then said he'd be waiting outside the factory for him when Paul's shift was over.

Paul was scared, but he wasn't going to back down. He had a plan. *No matter what*, he told himself, *I'm going to swing first.* Advance, never retreat was his fighting philosophy on this day— and would soon become part of his football philosophy as well. Once his shift was over, Paul exited the factory to find a circle of spectators awaiting him. In the middle was the angry man. Paul approached. When the young man opened his mouth to utter a few words, Paul swung and connected with the man's face, badly bloodying his opponent's mouth and ending the fight with one mighty swing. Paul's aggression had carried the day.

That aggression powered him on the football field, too. In the spring of 1931, an assistant coach from Alabama named Hank Crisp visited Coach Cowan at Fordyce High. Crisp wanted a set of twins—Click and Jud Jordan—to play for Alabama. But the twins were set on attending Arkansas. *Do you have any other blue-chip players?* Crisp asked Cowen. The Fordyce coach mentioned Paul Bryant, explaining that he was a fighter and was so tough that his nickname was Bear. Crisp asked to meet Bear.

Minutes later, player and coach were shaking hands. The coach asked Paul if he'd like to play at Alabama. Bear excitedly nodded. His dream was becoming real.

CHAPTER 7

"This Is the Beginning"

2009

He usually met with his starting quarterback once a week in his office, one-on-one, checking on him, wanting to make sure his life was going well. Nick Saban could be hard on his quarterback on the field—if he threw an interception, Saban would be waiting for him on the sideline with a what-the-hell-was-that expression on his face, and then he'd often rip into him using the bluest of language. But after the initial outburst, Saban would calmly explain what he saw on that play and how, for instance, the defense tricked his quarterback into unleashing an ill-advised pass. In the quiet of his office, Saban continued to coach his quarterback, asking him about plays he liked in the game plan, but these sessions were more about connecting with his quarterback on a more personal level, creating a bond. For his team to play at its peak, Saban's quarterback needed to be an extension of himself on the field, and he needed to trust him like a parent trusts his child—his good child.

At this stage in his coaching career Saban asked his quarterback to manage games, not win them on the strength of his passing arm. To Saban, it was far more important that his quarterback avoid taking risks, such as trying to feather passes between two defenders to his receiver. Saban considered it a positive play if his quarterback, failing to see an open receiver, threw the ball away. Punting was rarely a negative outcome to Saban, because he preferred to win games with field position, an unbending defense, and a powerful running game—the same rudimentary formula that Bear Bryant employed early in his tenure at Alabama. It took an intelligent, team-first quarterback to accept this role, and Saban lucked into Greg McElroy, a 4.0 student and a Rhodes Scholar finalist who was on the Tide roster when Saban arrived in Tuscaloosa.

Four decades earlier, Saban had played quarterback on his father's Pop Warner team and in high school. During many long-ago evenings in their West Virginia home, father and son would watch eight-millimeter film of Nick's high school games in their living room, the father critiquing and instructing as the son listened intently. These one-on-one tutorials in front of the flickering black-and-white images helped transform young Nick into one of the top high school players in the state. In the late 1960s he was nowhere near the most athletic, the strongest, or the quickest high school quarterback in West Virginia, but Saban's football IQ was higher than any other QB in the state.

Saban had always wanted a son of a coach to lead his team. "Sons of coaches don't get rattled," said Phil Savage, who was on the staff of the Cleveland Browns with Saban in the 1990s. "They have a depth of knowledge that other players don't have just because they've been around the game their entire life. It's almost like having an extra coach on the field."

Now, in his third year as Alabama's coach, Saban's quarterback was McElroy, whose father worked in the front office of the Dallas Cowboys and had taught his boy the game in Texas. "I basically grew up in a locker room," McElroy said. But Saban didn't just want to talk about life and X's and O's in his meetings with McElroy; he also mined his cerebral quarterback for information on other players. "Coach Saban really wanted to know how the young guys on our team were doing all the time," said McElroy. "He'd ask me, 'How is Marcell Dareus coming along with his stuff? How is Marquis Maze doing with his position switch?' He was really using me to fact-gather, which I was fine with because I think guys on the team trusted me."

McElroy added, "Coach Saban relishes the role of being a father figure to players, but I didn't need that. I had a dad who was involved in building me up and giving me confidence. So my relationship with Coach Saban was very professional and not all that deep, but I tried to help him out by letting him know what was going on with some of the guys who may have needed him more than me."

Saban was demanding of McElroy when he was the backup to John Parker Wilson in 2008. Routinely during practice, Saban would yell at the top of his lungs at McElroy, "What are you doing? What the HELL are you doing?" Once practice ended, Saban would walk off the field with his young quarterback, explaining in a conversational voice precisely his expectations.

"This Is the Beginning"

"Coach Saban does everything for a purpose and players very much like him, even when he's yelling at you," McElroy said. "Every conversation we ever had was in some shape or form about football. It never got personal and was always business. If I had a rough practice, he'd come up to me and ask, 'How can I help you?' He'll do everything in his power to help you improve and maximize your potential."

Saban never said it, but those close to him believed he saw a bit of himself in McElroy—an overachiever's overachiever who succeeded more with his mind than his arm.

⬤ ⬤ ⬤

He didn't want to tell anyone, not until he had to reveal his secret. Eddie Lacy was a four-star running back from Dutchtown High in Geismar, Louisiana, and in February 2009 he knew where he was going to go to college, but he was reluctant to share the news with his friends, fearing they wouldn't understand why he would leave his home state to play football for LSU's most bitter SEC rival.

Nick Saban knew that recruiting in Louisiana would be crucial to the long-term success of his program. Saban had yet to land a marquee player from this talent-rich state, and he turned on his full persuasive powers when he visited Lacy and his family in their home, telling them that he was only in the early stage of his empire building in Tuscaloosa. He told Eddie that he could be the first of many Louisiana kids to gain glory at Alabama, and Saban said he would prepare him for the NFL. As Saban detailed his vision for the Tide program over the next four years, explaining how national championships would be won as long as the players didn't grow complacent and focused each day on what they could control, Lacey was spellbound, enamored by the prospects. On National Signing Day at a press conference at his school, Lacy stunned his friends and classmates: He would play for Nick Saban.

"I couldn't stop thinking about what Coach Saban has done at Alabama," Lacy said. "In just two years they are like the best team. It's incredible and it's only going to get better." Left unsaid was that the state of Louisiana was now open for business for Saban, and in the years to come the Bayou-to-Bama pipeline would produce stars such as safety Landon Collins, defensive end Tim Williams, tackle Cam Robinson, tight end Irv Smith Jr, and linebacker Dylan Moses.

In February 2009 Lacy was part of a group of recruits who were widely regarded to be the best in the nation for the second consecutive year. "We had [Alabama] ranked No. 1 in 2008 and '09," said Allen Wallace, publisher of *SuperPrep* magazine. "Right now Nick Saban is probably the smartest coach out there. With his grasp of X's and O's, motivational skills, program discipline...he combines all the most important aspects of what kids are looking for."

●　　　●　　　●

The 2009 team went 12-0 in the regular season and faced top-ranked and defending national champion Florida in the SEC championship game. "The entire offseason was all about beating Florida," said McElroy. "All I wanted to do was beat Tim Tebow. The Gators roster had ten times the recognition that we did. We were the blue-collar team back then. Going through the week before the game we had our best practices in my five years at Alabama. There was no doubt in my mind we were going to kill them."

In Alabama's first two offensive drives, McElroy was five of seven for 62 yards as the Tide built a 9–0 lead over the Gators, who were favored by five points. Alabama never trailed and won 32–13. It was a program-altering flogging that left Gator quarterback Tim Tebow on the sideline in tears and sent Florida coach Urban Meyer to the hospital with chest pains. McElroy lingered on the field so long during the postgame celebration that the rose he had been handed—Alabama would face Texas in the Rose Bowl for the national championship—wilted before he went to the locker room.

"We mentally broke through in that game against Florida," said offensive lineman Barrett Jones. "Something happened among the players that day. We started believing and reaching our potential. The Process was underway and taking hold. Coach Saban's system was working, and we knew it. Something powerful was taking place. We felt like we were going to be a force on the national stage for a long time."

A month later the Tide flew west to play in the Rose Bowl— the site of Alabama's first national championship in 1926, the first game that Bear Bryant ever heard on the radio. The Crimson Tide players entered the game against the Longhorns flush with confidence, still relishing their dismantling of Florida in what was viewed as a ground-shifting victory in the SEC. Two days before the Bowl Championship Series national title game, tight end Colin Peek said Alabama had "left about twenty-one points on the field" against the Gators and nose tackle Terrence Cody revealed that he was looking forward to getting a few carries on offense as a fullback "if we go up by two or three touchdowns" against Texas.

Trying to keep his team focused, Saban spent the week before kickoff reminding his players about the 1980 gold-medal winning USA hockey team and how, after they upset the Soviet Union, the Americans still had to beat Finland to win gold. To emphasize this point, on the night before the BCS title game Saban took his players to a nearby theater to watch the film *Miracle* about that very "Miracle on Ice" team.

In the days before the game, the practice sessions were among the most intense of the season. Saban knew what this meant: His players were ready. "The way Alabama practices is a huge part of its success," said Curt Cignetti, the wide receivers coach and recruiting coordinator at Alabama from 2007 to 2010. "No one stands around. There's a lot of putting guys in game situations. It's all business. People are constantly on the move. I worked for Johnny Majors for four years [at Pittsburgh] and he came to watch us at Alabama practice. Afterward he grabbed me and said, 'That was the most impressive practice I've ever seen.' And the amazing thing was, that was just a Thursday practice, a dress rehearsal with just shoulder pads and helmets. But it was high tempo and highly organized. The goal is always to make practices harder than the games...And our practices before we played Texas were intense. We were ready to go."

◉   ◉   ◉

The national title game started under a cloud of smoke. With haze still lingering from the pregame fireworks, Marcell Dareus delivered the hit of the night. Saban had prophesied to Dareus during his recruitment in 2008 that he would "win a championship" before he left Tuscaloosa, and now Dareus was intent on fulfilling that vision. On the Longhorns' first possession, quarterback Colt McCoy—a four-year starter who had won more games than any other quarterback in college football history—took a snap and ran to his left on an option play. Before he could pitch the ball, Dareus barreled through the offensive line and rammed into McCoy, slamming him to the ground. The pad-popping collision echoed through the stadium. The Texas medical staff ran onto the field as McCoy lay on the grass, holding his right arm, squirming in pain. McCoy suffered a severely pinched nerve in his right shoulder, and he was immediately taken to the locker room. As he disappeared into the bowels of the Rose Bowl, so too did the Longhorns' hopes of winning the national title. McCoy wouldn't return (and he didn't fully recover from the injury for two years).

The Tide won 37–21, capturing its first national title in seventeen years. As the final seconds on the clock ticked down, a few Tide players dumped a bucket of red Gatorade on Saban. The coach frowned as his white shirt turned pink. Even though he was about to become the first coach since the AP poll began in 1936 to win a national championship at two different schools—he led LSU to the 2003 national title—Saban looked unhappy after the game, as if he was already worried about the trials of trying to repeat, which reinforced his national reputation for being a curmudgeon. As Saban climbed onto a makeshift stage near the roses painted on the 50-yard line and then held the Crystal Ball Championship trophy over his head, his wife knew that he wasn't actually drinking in the moment and savoring its sweetness. "I guarantee you," she said of her husband of thirty-eight years, "he's already thinking about next week."

In the postgame locker room there emerged the sense, at least among the players, that more national titles were on the way. "We have something special going on here," McElroy said. "Hopefully this is something we can build on, and hopefully we're back in this position a year from now. But this is a big start, and a big moment for Alabama."

Outside the locker room Mal Moore beamed. He spoke glowingly about Saban, how he resuscitated the program in only three years, and how he would soon lobby university president Robert Witt to commission a statue of the coach he had doggedly pursued on a secret mission to South Florida and convinced to come to Tuscaloosa. Four Alabama legends were memorialized outside of Bryant-Denny Stadium—Bear Bryant, Gene Stallings, Frank Thomas, and Wallace Wade. Now Moore wanted to add a fifth. It might have seemed premature, but it underscored how deeply and completely Moore—and the entire Alabama fan base—had fallen for Saban.

Yet as Saban stood in a near empty locker room, with the clock nearing 10 p.m. Pacific time, he was already focusing on all that had to be done in the coming days—and it left him in a brooding mood. In his postgame speech to his players he had told them that they should have played better in the second half and that they had let Texas back in the game. Instead of celebrating, he was still coaching and searching for perfection, while also worrying about the missed recruiting time the extra weeks of practice before the national championship game had cost him. "The adage that 'success breeds success' is not necessarily true," he said. "The challenge to our returning players will be: Is this the beginning, or the end? Do you want to build on this and have *more* success, or are you guys going to be satisfied and take the easy way out and not make the commitment necessary?"

No, Saban was not content. He wanted more. As he walked out of the stadium into the warm California night, he gave the thumbs-up to the hundreds of Alabama fans waiting by the team buses, but Saban could only muster a half smile as cameras flashed in his face. There were duties that needed to be completed, plans that had to be made, recruits who needed to be called, written to, and visited. The next morning at 9 a.m. at the team's hotel in Orange County, Saban phoned all of his assistants and told them to gather at 10 a.m. in a specific hotel conference room. In the meeting Saban initiated a critique of the game—"We shouldn't have let them come back in the second half," he said to his coaches—and then told his assistants it was "time to move on." "It was amazing," recalled Cignetti. "There was a real sense of urgency in his voice as he spoke to us."

On January 16 Saban and the players were inside Bryant-Denny Stadium to celebrate the national title. The temperature hovered around freezing and drizzle fell. Still, more than thirty-eight thousand fans filled the west side of the stadium to see the players and to hear Saban speak.

Saban rose from his seat on the stage at the 50-yard line. He looked up at the vast crowd before him and thanked a few people, including Mal Moore and Robert Witt, the two figures at Alabama who had given Saban every resource he had asked for since arriving in Tuscaloosa three years earlier. Then, wearing a gray jacket and crimson sweater, he leaned closer into the microphone.

"I want everyone here to know," he said, stretching his hand forward like a preacher in front of his congregation to signal he was about say something very important. "This is not the end. This is the beginning!" The crowd thundered and rose, believing every word their coach had said.

Saban returned to his seat on the stage, and a few hours later he was back in his office, back to building his ascending program. Indeed, the engine that powered the entire operation at Alabama could be summed up in two words: hard work. That was the ethic Saban learned as a boy from his father in West Virginia.

⬤   ⬤   ⬤

In the foothills of the Allegheny Mountains, the two-lane road snakes north–south the entire length of West Virginia, twisting and turning through the heart of coal-mining country. Stretching 249 miles, Route 19 was a road that Nick Saban traveled frequently in his youth—either in his parents' car or by hitchhiking with locals, a common practice for the teenage Saban, especially when he needed a ride to see his girl. Like Saban, her family roots burrowed deep into the West Virginia coal, and she would be by his side when he stood at his most critical crossroad.

In September 1973 Saban, a graduate assistant coach at Kent State in bordering Ohio, drove south on Route 19 to tiny Helling's Run, a dot on the map southwest of Fairmont, and parked his car. He was home again. At age twenty-one, recently married, and with his future spread before him like a buffet of choices, Saban was about to make the biggest decision of his life. And now he had no idea what he should do, because he was as heartsick as he'd ever been.

"This Is the Beginning"

The only buildings at this intersection on Route 19 were Saban's Service Station, a Dairy Queen his family owned, and the three-bedroom house behind the station where the Sabans lived. Two miles south on Route 19 was the one-street town of Worthington; a few miles north was the hamlet of Monongah (population: 1,500), not far from the mine with the same name in which 362 miners were killed in 1907. The neighboring Helling's Run was just a nook, tucked into the rugged, undulating terrain, but it was where locals from neighboring small towns often gathered to share news, fill up on gas, and talk sports with Nick Saban Sr., the founding father of Pop Warner football in the area.

In 1962, when Nick was ten, his dad formed the Idamay Black Diamonds, a Pop Warner team for kids in four nearby small towns. Big Nick, as the locals called him, acquired a few dozen pairs of black-and-orange hand-me-down uniforms from a team that had long since disbanded, and he recruited two college-aged boys to serve as coaches. Big Nick, who was of Croatian descent, had hoped to be a commissioner of sort for the team, but on the first day of practice the college kids didn't appear. So even though he had never before coached football, Big Nick became the head coach. He bought every book about coaching football he could find. But in his first season of leading the Idamay Black Diamonds, which was named for the coal mining towns in the area, his team won only one game. He needed a couple talented kids or at least one special player. And he didn't have to look far to find him. He tapped his son.

Nick Lou Saban Jr. was born on Halloween in 1951. When Big Nick's wife, Mary Saban, was pregnant with their second child, he told his daughter, Diana, who was almost two at the time, that she soon would have a brother. Big Nick was joking; they had no idea what gender the baby would be. But from that day forward Diana called Nick Jr. "Brother"—as did just about everyone else as he grew up in coal country.

As soon as he could walk, Brother had a ball of some kind in his hands. He and his sister liked to shoot baskets at the basketball hoop in their yard. Their mother, who worked at the family's Dairy Queen, often joined them. And when Big Nick could break away— he ran the service station from 7 a.m. to midnight and sometimes made extra money working in the coal mines—he'd become the fourth player in games of two-on-two.

Little Nick began working at the gas station when he was eleven, only weeks after his dad had started coaching the Pop Warner team. Father and son would throw a football to each other in front of the pumps until a car pulled in. One of them would then grab the nozzle and pump the gas while the other would check the engine oil and clean the windshield. Brother did everything at the station: He checked tire pressure, washed cars, collected money, made change, did grease jobs, changed oil and air filters, and re-placed oil. One time his father asked him to clean out a floor drain at the station. He was a perfectionist even then: By the time he finished hours later, the drain was as shiny clean as the counters at the Dairy Queen across the street.

"The biggest thing I learned and started to learn at eleven years old was how important it was to do things correctly," Saban said. "There was a standard of excellence, a perfection. If we washed a car—and I hated the navy blue and black cars, because when you wipe them off, the streaks were hard to get out—and if there were any streaks when [my father] came, you had to do it over."

"This Is the Beginning"

The quest for perfection followed Brother onto the football field, where at age eleven he became the starting quarterback for the Idamay Black Diamonds. Though the team practiced on a field that was littered with rocks—each player had to pick up ten rocks at the end of practice and remove them from the field—that didn't stop Big Nick from holding marathon practice sessions. He always announced the starting time for practice but never the ending time, in keeping with one of his favorite mottos, "Practice Makes Players." On countless occasions when darkness descended and players wanted to go home or watch a local high school football game, Big Nick wouldn't call practice to a halt. Instead, he'd start his car, flip on its headlights, and run his boys through additional drills illuminated by the car's high beams.

But Big Nick cared deeply about his boys. With what little extra income he had, Big Nick purchased a used bus that he drove to pick up his players for practice and drop them off afterward. After painting the bus orange to match the team's color, his wife plastered positive sayings, inspiring quotations and affirmations on the inside of the bus—"When the going gets tough, the tough get going"—for the boys to read as Big Nick drove forty miles daily along the narrow, winding roads chiseled into the West Virginia mountains, traveling up and down the hills and hollows to the four different towns where his players lived. He considered them his own blood. In return, not wanting to disappoint the man who had given them so much, they played their hearts out for Big Nick. Little Nick carefully studied it all.

To build the fittest team in the league, Big Nick ordered his players to run up a hill in the back of the end zone after practices. A tree stood atop the incline. To make sure his players reached the top, Big Nick told them to bring back a leaf or a twig to prove that they had completed the task. After every game, win or lose, the team ran at practice. And even if his team won, Big Nick was never satisfied. One season the Idamay Black Diamonds beat an inferior team, but the Diamonds' defense allowed that squad to score. At the next practice Big Nick had his players form a circle and run in place for nearly an hour. If he believed that a player's knees weren't pumping high enough, Big Nick ordered them to run the dreaded hill.

He was as tough on his son as any player. If Nick Jr. threw a touchdown pass, Big Nick always had a critique: His throwing technique wasn't fundamentally sound or the ball didn't travel in a tight enough spiral or he didn't look off the safety before unleashing the pass. Big Nick was a natural-born perfectionist, and his attention to detail was rare among Pop Warner coaches. He wasn't as concerned with results as much as he was with his players performing at their maximum potential, which was something he reminded his players of nearly every practice. Little Nick soaked it all in. Many of the phrases his father used—"Invest your time, don't spend it"—he still uses today.

Saban's father also didn't tolerate insubordination or disrespectful behavior—from his team or his boy. One day after the Black Diamonds had lost a game, Nick Jr. was working at the gas station when an elderly homeless man approached. The man had been to the station many times before and had been given free coffee and a snack, but now Nick Jr. was in no mood to offer a handout. He was still disgusted by the recent defeat and he had just struggled to repair a flat tire. Frustrated, Nick teased the elderly vagabond. His father heard the comments and slipped off his belt. He quietly approached his son and then smacked him in the butt. He told his boy, "I don't ever want to hear you talk to someone older than you like that ever again." The son apologized, learning his lesson.

On another occasion Big Nick saw that his son was being short with customers and wasn't being as courteous as he'd taught his boy to be. Little Nick had just broken up with his girlfriend and was failing to say "Thank you" to the paying customers. His father confronted him.

"Your mom told me you broke up with your girlfriend. You're a little upset about that?" he asked.

"Yeah, I'm a little upset about that," Nick Jr. replied.

"Let me just tell you this," Big Nick said. "When you let one bad thing that happens to you affect other things, sometimes you create more negative consequences than you like. You're about ready to cause a couple more. You don't have a girlfriend right now. Pretty soon, you're not going to have a job, because I'm going to fire you. And if I fire you, I'm going to whip your ass." The son learned another lesson.

The father had great expectations for his boy, which included going to college. When young Nick was in the eighth grade, he earned a D in music. He was so shy that he wouldn't stand in front of the class to sing. After seeing his son's report card, Big Nick ordered his son to turn in his basketball uniform—he wouldn't be allowed to play until his grades improved—and then the two drove to a nearby coal mine. The father told his son to stand on the shaft elevator, Big Nick pushed a button, and they descended 550 feet deep into the earth. Standing in the cold darkness of the mine, Big Nick said, "Is this what you want? You want to work down here for the rest of your life?" Nicholas Lou Saban Jr. has not been in a coal mine since.

●   ●   ●

On the football field Brother had no equal in his Pop Warner League. Led by Nick Jr.—an elusive, athletic quarterback who called his own plays and wore jersey No. 12 in honor of former Alabama quarterback Joe Namath—the Idamay Black Diamonds strung together extended winning streaks. After each win, the owner of a local store would allow the boys on the team to play free pinball for a week. In one victory, the Diamonds toppled a Pop Warner squad that featured a young quarterback named Joe Montana. Though Big Nick's team didn't possess the most talent, they had traits that proved to be more powerful: desire, toughness, and unrelenting hustle. "He took these country kids that didn't have an opportunity to play, taught them how to be successful, how to compete," Saban said. "That certainly is something that stuck with me as a person and as a player... It made me better. The work ethic he taught, the standard of excellence, the integrity that you do things with, the attitude that you carry with you and the character that you carry with you, what you do every day. Those kinds of values affected me."

The Idamay Black Diamonds even had cheerleaders. Terry Constable, dressed in her cheerleading skirt that fell halfway down her shin, always flashed a smile at young Nick, the seventh-grade quarterback. She desperately tried to catch his eyes—one time, when Nick walked by, she did a dramatic twirl in her skirt—but he didn't notice. That would change when Nick was in eighth grade and Terry was in seventh.

"This Is the Beginning"

They attended a 4-H science camp in Marion County over the summer. Nick had no desire to go to the camp—he wanted to be playing sports from sunup to sundown—but his parents forced him. His attitude and interest changed, however, when he started talking to another camper, the dimpled-cheeked brunette with a heart-melting smile. A member of the junior Audubon Society, Terry suggested they go bird watching at 5 a.m. Nick said yes, but after agreeing to the early-morning meet-up he realized he had a softball game at 8.

Fearing he would miss his game, Nick stood up Terry on what was to be their first date. He would, however, soon be forgiven.

◉   ◉   ◉

After learning the game from his father, Saban became the starting quarterback at Monongah High early in his sophomore season. Late that fall Monongah traveled to Masontown for a critical game: The winner would advance to the state playoffs, the loser's season would be over. As the team bus ferried the Monongah players thirty-five miles to Masontown Valley High, a river of cars followed, as nearly every resident of the town motored behind. To reach the football field at Masontown Valley from the locker room, the players had to walk across a cemetery. Adding to the sense of gloom, the lighting of the field was poor. Nick Jr. felt that he had the weight of his entire town upon him.

With Big Nick and the Saban family watching from the stands, the fifteen-year-old quarterback called the team's offensive plays, but none worked. At halftime Monongah trailed 18–0. As he ambled across the cemetery to the locker room, he remembered what his dad had taught him: *No matter what the circumstances, never stop fighting.*

The second half was a different game. Behind the running and passing of Saban, Monongah cut the lead to 18–12. With 1:27 left in the game, Masontown Valley punted the ball. Saban quickly guided his team down the field. Facing a fourth-and-twelve on the 25-yard line with only seconds remaining, Monongah coach Earl Kenner called a time-out. Saban ran to the sideline, relieved that Kenner would tell him what play to call on what would be the final snap of the game.

"Coach, what do you want to run here?" Saban asked.

"I tell you what," Kenner replied. "You have a three-time All-State split end and the left halfback is the fastest guy in the state. I don't care what play you call, just make sure one of those two guys gets the ball."

Saban, surging with confidence, ran back onto the field. In the huddle he said, "26 crossfire pass." Monongah lined up and Saban took the snap. He pump-faked a pass to his left halfback, then rifled the ball to his split end in the corner of the end zone. It landed in his arms for a touchdown and Monongah won, 19–18. Afterward Kenner approached his young quarterback and said, "It really doesn't make any difference what play you call sometimes. It's what players you have doing it." Those words would one day become the first commandment in Saban's coaching bible.

🏈   🏈   🏈

Saban guided the Monongah Lions to the small-school state football championship in his senior year, 1968, beating rival Fairmont

High School for the title. During that game Terry had cheered for Fairmont, where she was a majorette, but her loyalties were split. Earlier that autumn Terry and Nick had renewed their earlier grade school friendship after they bumped into each other at a football game. Saban was so taken with this stylish, classy, cute-as-a-button brunette that he would often hitchhike ten miles from his house in Helling's Run to her home in Fairmont on weekends to spend time with her. Their first date was over Thanksgiving weekend, when Saban took her to the Lee Movie Theatre to see *Gone with the Wind*. Then, on many weekend nights, they'd go to dances at the Pleasant Valley Fire Department. Though the physical distance between them would grow when Saban left for college—Terry was a year behind him in school—it wouldn't sideline their relationship.

Before graduating from Monongah—where Saban was also a two-time All-State player in baseball, a one-time All-State player in basketball, and sports editor of the yearbook—Saban had planned to attend the Naval Academy. He had been awarded an appointment to Annapolis by West Virginia senator Robert Byrd and passed all the required tests. But he later withdrew his application. The Vietnam War was raging and Saban knew he'd likely serve multiple tours on the other side of the globe during the five-year military commitment required of graduates. When he told his father he was no longer interested in Annapolis, Big Nick replied, "I want you to leave the state of West Virginia. You need to see what it's like someplace else. And if you choose to come back, then come back."

Four small universities offered Saban a football scholarship: Marshall, Ohio University, Miami of Ohio, and Kent State. Saban picked Kent State in Kent, Ohio, because it was only a 186-mile drive from Helling's Run and his Terry. He spent his freshman year learning the college game and switching from quarterback to cornerback—and missing his girl dearly. The two wrote letters every day and talked on the phone frequently, cementing what they both already knew in their hearts: They were going to spend the rest of their lives together, even though at the time, Saban said, "she didn't know what a first down was."

In May 1970 the Kent State campus was the scene of anti–Vietnam War rallies. The ROTC building was burned to the ground, and on May 3 hundreds of Ohio National Guard soldiers arrived to quell a protest and guard against further disruption during a scheduled rally at noon the following day, a Monday. That afternoon, after Saban had attended his 11 a.m. English class, he met friend and teammate Phil Witherspoon, and the two went to lunch in the cafeteria. After eating, Saban was leaving the cafeteria when a frantic student approached, yelling that shots had been fired at the protestors. Saban and his friend quickly made their way to the quad area—the rally site—but were prevented by the guardsmen from getting too close. Through a cloud of smoke, Saban saw several people lying on the ground, covered in blood. He later found out that four students had been killed, including Allison Krause, who was in his English class.

The shootings at Kent State weren't Saban's first encounter with death. Tragedy in his corner of the country was a part of life. Tales of disasters in the mines were woven into the fabric of West Virginia culture. In 1907 the collapse of the nearby Monongah Mine killed 362 miners, the worst mining disaster in American history. On November 19, 1968, at the Consol No. 9 mine just outside of Farmington, his grandfather Conroy barely escaped being en-tombed when the mine was sealed to prevent oxygen from feeding a fire within; seventy-eight men lost their lives. Saban's experience with disaster—and how to lead others in times of tragedy—would one day mean everything in Tuscaloosa.

◍   ◍   ◍

The following season, 1971, Don James was hired by Kent State. Detailed, organized, and systematic in how he approached every-thing, James had as large an influence on Saban as any coach other than his father. Even as a player, Saban was constantly in James's shadow, absorbing how he watched film, how he talked to players, how he dealt with his assistants, how he interacted with the media, how he handled problems. James built his defense around middle linebacker Jack Lambert—who would become a Hall of Fame player with the Pittsburgh Steelers—and Saban. In 1972 Saban and Lambert helped the Golden Flashes win five of their last six games and clinch a berth in the Tangerine Bowl, which was the high point of the program's history. "I think everybody felt like something really good had to happen at Kent State," James later said of that '72 season. "The school needed positive publicity, and the community wrapped its arms around the sport."

After graduating with a degree in business, Saban was playing baseball one day at Kent State when James walked up to him. At the time Saban considered opening a car dealership; he had been looking into entering a General Motors program for owning a dealership. But now James asked Saban if he would stay at Kent State and work as a graduate assistant on the football team. Saban was thrilled. He and Terry had gotten married during the winter break of his junior year—their honeymoon consisted of an overnight at a Holiday Inn in Wheeling, West Virginia, and a dinner at Bob's Big Boy, where they enjoyed strawberry pie—and now Saban was waiting for his wife to finish her degree at Kent State, where they lived in married housing. This coaching job would allow him to earn a little money while Terry completed her studies. Plus, it would give him more time to figure out how he could work his way into the car business.

Saban excitedly called his father to share the news. Neither of Saban's parents had attended college, and now here was their boy, a college graduate who was going to receive a paycheck to coach. Saban's parents, particularly his dad, couldn't have been prouder. Nick Sr.'s son was on his way in the world. Dreams were being fulfilled.

It would be the last time father and son would ever speak.

On September 22, 1973, the Kent State football team traveled to Louisville to play the Cardinals. With Saban on the sideline as a graduate assistant, the Golden Eagles beat Louisville 35–7. Overjoyed, Saban wanted to share the news of the victory with his father. Before he boarded the team bus, he called home to tell Big Nick that now he genuinely believed he had discovered his passion, his calling: coaching football. It was as if he'd solved the biggest mystery of his life, and he couldn't wait to tell his dad that, like him, he was going to be a coach. But when he phoned his house and the gas station, no one could find his father.

"This Is the Beginning"

After riding the bus 340 miles back to the Kent State campus, Saban received a call. The news was devastating: Big Nick, at age forty-six, had died of a massive heart attack—the same age Bear Bryant's father had passed away. In shock, Saban and his wife drove down Route 19 toward Helling's Run. Now Saban, at age twenty-one, faced the biggest decision of his life: Should he quit his job at Kent State and return home to run the service station? Or should he continue to coach?

As Nick Sr. neared his midforties, he had grown slightly over-weight. A family doctor suggested that he start running and stop coaching. Big Nick agreed to jog, but not to walk away from the sidelines. "I can't," he said to the doctor when told he should quit coaching. "I have to do that."

On the last day of his life in 1973, Nick and Mary Saban were driving home from a track when Nick asked to be dropped off. Big Nick had already run some laps at the track, but he felt like he hadn't completed his workout. So he told his wife to drive on without him and he'd just jog the rest of the way home. Within a few hundred yards of his house, the man who was rarely satisfied, the man who had passed the gene of hard work down to his son, collapsed to the ground. He later died at a local hospital.

It seemed as if every kid and every parent of every kid who had played for Big Nick attended his funeral. Mourners came from a four-town area to pay their final respects to Nick Saban Sr. He was buried on a hillside; his tombstone featuring two black diamonds and the engraved epitaph that defined his life: "No man stands as tall as when he stoops to help a child."

After the funeral Saban stood on the family porch with his mother when he announced he had made his decision: He said he wanted to leave Kent State and return to Helling's Run to handle the day-to-day duties at Saban's Service Station. He would now take charge. The son explained that he had thoroughly considered all options and determined he needed to help his family, to assume the role of the provider, the man of the family. That was what sons did in West Virginia coal country when their fathers passed away. It was the way of things.

But his mother reacted sharply to her son's proclamation: Never would she allow that. Her boy needed to make his own mark in the world, not pick up the shattered pieces of what Big Nick had left behind. Her forceful words were firm and final: Nick and Terry Saban would return to Kent State and pursue their own dreams, whatever they be, and go wherever their passions would take them.

And so the young couple did, leaving behind the heartbreak in Helling's Run and returning to Ohio. In 1974 Don James promoted Saban to be a part-time coach, while also promising to help Terry find a teaching job. Saban stayed at Kent State until 1977, when he accepted a position to coach outside linebackers at Syracuse University, the first of what would eventually be thirteen moves in his coaching career.

🏈   🏈   🏈

At Alabama, Saban abides by a strict routine. On a typical day he'll awake at 6 a.m., flip on the Weather Channel and, sitting close to his wife, drink two cups of coffee and eat two Little Debbie oatmeal crème pies for breakfast. He'll devote the mornings at the office to football matters—he'll ask the team nutritionist, for instance, why a player has a certain percentage of body fat and, if high, he'll then want to know what can be done to lower it—and at noon he'll have the same lunch every day: a salad of iceberg lettuce and cherry tomatoes topped with turkey slices and fat-free honey Dijon dressing served in a plastic container. In the off-season Saban organizes a pickup basketball game a few times a week at the university's Coleman Coliseum. He's the league's commissioner—"I pick the teams, so I have the best players," he said, "I also pick the guys who guard me"—and he's the league's referee. Not surprisingly, he's never fouled out of a game.

The middle of his days are filled with meetings with coaches and players, and then the afternoons are spent on more football-related issues, such as watching film of an upcoming opponent or breaking down his own team's practice film. And at some point every day he'll focus on recruiting—sometimes thirty minutes, sometimes an hour, sometimes several hours. Saban never stops recruiting; it's a 365-day-a-year endeavor. "More than any coach in America, Nick understands that the jockey doesn't carry the horse, it's the horse that carries the jockey," said Saban's longtime friend Phil Savage. "He knows he needs talent to win and that's why he'll never get out-recruited by anyone." Saban typically tries to be out of the office by ten.

When Saban goes on vacation in midsummer each year, he travels to his lake house in North Georgia. Located on the shoreline of Lake Burton on the North Carolina border close to where the movie *Deliverance* was filmed, the house isn't adorned with pictures of football or mementos of his life along the sideline. Saban loves nothing more than simply jumping in the water with his wife and family. It has a calming effect on him. Saban has joked that he only has three outfits that he wears at the lake—three swimsuits to go with hundreds of T-shirts. Saban also spends hours on the water in his pontoon and speedboat, pulling friends and family on inner tubes and listening to the Eagles—his favorite band—as he sits at the helm. "He could spend all day and all night on his boat with the Eagles blaring out of the speakers," said a family friend. "I think that might be one of the few times he can really enjoy some down time and be content with simply relaxing."

But football is never far from Saban's thoughts, not even when he's at his lake house. His father was a high-strung workaholic who devoted his life to the game, and Saban is just like his old man. The son recognizes that life is short—Nick Sr.'s death, at age forty-six, tragically taught him that—but it simply isn't in the genetic makeup of the Saban men to savor sweet moments and spend hours reflecting on past experiences. Life, to Saban, is to be lived, not reviewed.

Even when he's at Lake Burton, Saban stays in contact with his assistants, and his mind rarely strays from contemplating how he's going to accomplish the upcoming tasks that await him in Tuscaloosa. And during those few, fleeting days of vacation at the lake before the start of the 2010 season, the coach didn't allow himself to revel in the memory of winning the national championship months earlier. It just wasn't his nature. He may have recently become the only coach in college football history to lead two different schools to the national title, but even now he only worried about one thing:

What it would take to repeat.

CHAPTER 8

The Founding Football Document

1962 TO 1966

The metal tower rose high into the Alabama sky, thirty-three spiraling steps that led to a small platform. This perch was where the coach lorded over practice, the Alabama Zeus atop Mount Tuscaloosa. To see him, players and assistant coaches and trainers and water boys on the field had to raise their heads and squint into the sun. Everyone feared the same thing: Having your name called down in that thick Southern accent from high above in the bullhorn, the voice thundering down from a metallic mountaintop. Even worse, when he unhooked the chain at the top of the tower to climb down the stairs, the sound of its rattle and clank, clank would cause everyone on the field to come to attention. That was when Old Testament–level fear invaded the hearts and minds of the players and managers and coaches and water boys—it meant the Bear was coming, and he might be coming for you.

By returning the Tide to football glory and leading the school to its first national title in two decades, Bryant had become a near deity in Alabama, where now more than ever on the single-lane roads that threaded across the state there were banners with the cursive A flying on porches and Crimson Tide flags rising out of the backs of pickup trucks. "In Alabama," former Georgia coach Wally Butts once said, "an atheist is someone who doesn't believe in Bear Bryant." But believe they did: In a state that ranked near the bottom nationally in most meaningful statistics—education, income, infant mortality—Bryant had given his faithful a reason to be proud of their roots. The masses in Alabama worshipped their coach: The Bear had become their religion.

No coach or player had ever ventured up those thirty-three swirling stairs other than Bryant. Governor George Wallace once watched practice with Bryant from the tower, and so did the university president Dr. Frank Rose. But players and coaches knew: The tower was Bryant's domain, and his alone. To them the thought of scaling the tower was as frightening as flying too close to the sun.

Then one afternoon in August 1961, an eighteen-year-old from Beaver Falls, Pennsylvania, walked onto the practice field with assistant coach Howard Schnellenberger. The fresh-faced teenager had landed on a plane at the Birmingham airport the previous evening, outfitted in a checkered sports coat and a silvered blue-straw hat. A toothpick dangled from his mouth. Now, in the middle of a practice on a summer day, the young man stood on the sideline as the Tide players performed drills on the practice field. Freshman center Gaylon McCollough, spotting the nattily dressed Northerner, who was still wearing his straw hat, asked a graduate assistant coach, "Who is that cat?"

"That's going to be your new freshman quarterback," the coach said.

"Are you kidding me?" replied McCollough. "He won't last two days here."

Just then, the chain dropped and rattled. Practice stopped, everyone looked skyward to the tower. Bryant grabbed his bullhorn and yelled, "Joe, come on up here!"

The young player from Beaver Falls strolled to the base of the tower and, to the astonishment of the players and coaches and water boys, began climbing the stairs. Every set of eyes was locked onto this Pennsylvania kid who looked like he belonged in a Manhattan nightclub, not on an Alabama football field.

He reached the platform. For forty minutes, Bryant explained in his rumbling, mumbling voice how much he adored this young football player and how he could help lead Alabama to more conference titles and more national championships. He told the player he would look after him, be a strong father figure to him, and turn him into the best quarterback in the country. Joe Willie Namath later said he only understood one word that Bryant uttered:

"Stud."

·   ·   ·

In Joe Namath, whom Bryant regarded as the greatest quarterback he would ever coach, Bryant had what he had always been looking for: A QB with the mind of a coach, the arm and quick release of an elite NFL starter, and the legs of a running back. After hearing glowing reports about Namath from two assistant coaches who had watched high school film of Namath in Beaver Falls with Namath's coach, Frank Bruno—Bruno set up a projector in his kitchen, shut the blinds, and narrated the black-and-white images of Namath that flashed on the kitchen wall—Bryant was intrigued. Namath was the kind of player who could revolutionize the Alabama offense, transforming it from a plodding, powerful unit that relied on long, sustained drives to one that could move the ball with quickness and speed—on the ground and through the air.

At the end of his senior year in Beaver Falls, Namath was one of the most sought-after high school players in the country. That June he signed a letter of intent to play for Maryland—in return for playing football, the letter stated, Namath would receive free room, free board, free tuition, free books, and $15 a month for laundry as long as he carried a C average in his classes. But Namath had yet to score 750 on his SAT, the number he needed to gain admission to the school. In the spring he had scored in the low 730s. Maryland coaches figured Namath would pass the test in August. Namath had all summer to study, but instead spent most of his free time in a pool hall at a bar in Beaver Falls drinking Seven and Sevens, which cost thirty-five cents a pop. Namath failed to reach 750 on the test.

With only weeks before the start of the college's fall semester, a Maryland football coach who wanted to help Namath—and wanted him at a faraway school so the coach would never have to face him— called the staff at Alabama, telling them that Namath was available. Bryant immediately sent Schnellenberger, his offensive coordinator, to Beaver Falls and told him to bring back the quarterback.

But Namath wasn't sure where Alabama even was—and he certainly didn't know if he wanted to play for their demanding and dictatorial coach. He had heard the stories of the Junction training camp in Texas and the hellacious preseason camps in Tuscaloosa. "Alabama?" Namath said. "That's Bear Bryant, isn't it?"

For about a week Schnellenberger stayed in Beaver Falls, trying to convince Namath and his mother, Rose, that Tuscaloosa was the perfect place for him to play football and acquire an education. Schnellenberger quickly realized that Rose was calling the shots, and so he worked her hard, telling her that Bear Bryant would take care of his son, instill discipline in him, and help him win a national title—maybe even a few. Finally, after dinner one night, Rose marched upstairs and packed a suitcase for her son. She returned and told Schnellenberger, "Take him."

Days later, Namath joined Bryant on the tower. The coach had landed his star quarterback.

●　　●　　●

Before the start of the 1961 season, Bryant handed his freshmen players, including Namath, a document he called "Winning Theory at Alabama." The outline included:

1. Beat your opponent physically
   A. Better physical condition
   B. Be aggressive and "out-mean" them
   C. Consistency—110 percent on every play
2. Genuine all-out desire for team victory
   A. Goal—to win them all
   B. Personal sacrifice instead of personal glorification
   C. What one can contribute, not what you can receive
   D. When you win there is enough glory for everyone

3. Winning Edge
   A. Second and third effort (Run beyond initial contact)
   B. No penalties, broken signals, fumbles or interceptions
   C. Sudden change
   D. Something extra when behind and in 4th quarter
   E. Know and play zone and field position
4. Defense
   A. No long runs
   B. No passes for touchdowns
   C. Force mistakes
   D. Score on defense
5. Offense
   A. Never give up the ball without a kick
   B. Discipline
   C. Intelligent recklessness
   D. It takes 11 to move the ball

Nearly forty-five years later, this outline would aptly describe the coaching philosophy of another Alabama coach. Indeed, "Winning Theory" could be considered the founding document of Crimson Tide football.

🏈　　🏈　　🏈

Namath played on the freshmen team in 1961. During one Monday night scrimmage between the freshmen and varsity, Namath ran an option play to the left. As he was about to pitch the ball, a defender hit him, causing Namath to fumble. Bryant noticed that Namath hadn't tried to recover the ball. Irate, the coach ran to his freshman quarterback, who had been pinned to the ground by a defender and couldn't move to go after the loose ball. "It's not your job to pitch the ball and lay down there on the ground not do anything," Bryant yelled. "You don't just lay there."

Namath pushed himself up and began walking to the huddle. But Bryant wasn't done. He forcefully grabbed Namath's face mask and told his player, "Namath, when I'm talking to you, boy, you say, 'Yes sir!'" Shaken, Namath replied, "Yes sir." For the rest of his time in Tuscaloosa, Namath never failed to answer all questions from his coach with those same two words: *Yes sir*.

Namath led the freshman team to wins over Mississippi State and Tulane before it tied Auburn 7–7 in their season finale, ending the three-game season 2-0-1. Namath ran more than he passed, but Bryant knew that he would soon unleash Namath's full spectrum of talents. Bryant was risk averse as a coach—he preferred to win with a suffocating defense and a run-first, ball-control offense—and he viewed passing the ball as the riskiest play in football. Yet he'd also never had a quarterback like Namath, who had wowed the coaches and teammates with his arm in practices and scrimmages throughout the fall of 1961 and the spring of 1962.

Gaylon McCollough, Namath's center, lived across the hall from Namath in the players' dormitory. In the off-season they shot pool together at the Shamrock Inn and played in pickup basketball games. On the court Namath was typically the quickest player and could dunk a basketball behind his head. "Joe could run like a gazelle and could jump out of the gym," said McCollough. "And on the football field, I'd never see a stronger and more accurate arm. He was unlike any athlete I'd ever come across."

But early in his career in Tuscaloosa, Namath wasn't entirely happy. He spent spring break of '62 with friends on the beach at Panama City, Florida. The quarterback had been contemplating leaving Alabama—he didn't like how African-Americans were treated in the South and at one point called his mom and told her he was quitting school—but his experience that spring break helped change his mind. The weather and the women and the azure waters of the Gulf Coast stood in stark contrast to the bitter cold of working-class Beaver Falls. Then in mid-May, Namath's right arm—the quick release, the tight spirals, the beautiful, high-arc rainbows that landed in the hands of receivers thirty yards down the field—stole the show at the annual Red-White scrimmage at Denny Stadium. He completed 12 of 17 passes for 156 yards in front of 10,500 fans, one of the largest crowds ever to witness the Crimson Tide spring game.

Even Bryant was impressed with his bold and brash young quarterback—"that Yankee," some sportswriters in Alabama already were calling Namath—but the coach still told reporters in the preseason that his 1962 team was destined for mediocrity a year after Alabama had won the national title. A number of key players had graduated—tackle Billy Neighbors was now in Boston playing in the American Football League, and quarterback Pat Trammell, Bryant's all-time favorite player, was in medical school—and his offensive and defensive lines were small and young. Bryant predicted that Alabama would finish 5-5 or, if the team caught a few breaks, 6-4.

On September 22 the Tide opened against Georgia at Legion Field in Birmingham. In front of a national television audience—and fifty-four thousand Crimson-clad fans in the stands—Namath trotted onto the field for his first possession as Alabama's starting quarterback. After a few plays, the Tide had the ball on its own 48-yard line. Namath faked a handoff to the fullback, then dropped back to pass. Wide receiver Richard Williamson sprinted down the right side of the field. Namath cocked his arm and flicked the ball into the Southern sky, almost making the throw look effortless. The crowd rose to its feet as the ball spiraled through the warm afternoon air. Williams looked over his left shoulder, extended his hands and, without breaking stride, caught the ball for the fifty-two-yard touchdown pass. The fans roared: This wasn't "three yards and a cloud of dust," this was the new brand of Alabama football under Bryant. This was football of the future. In his varsity debut, Namath threw for three touchdowns against the Bulldogs, tying a school record, as Alabama won 35–0.

Undefeated and ranked No. 1 in the country, the Tide traveled to Atlanta on November 17 to face Georgia Tech, a team still seething over Darwin Holt's cheap hit during the previous season. Alabama was riding a twenty-six-game unbeaten streak. On the Tide's first snap from scrimmage, Namath lined up in the shotgun formation on Alabama's 23-yard line and threw a pass. A professional scout in the press box nearly fell out of his chair. "Who is he trying to kid?" the scout yelled. "Bear's teams don't pass on the first play from scrimmage. They don't pass from the 23-yard line, and they haven't run from a shotgun once this year." Later in the game Namath dropped back to throw from Alabama's own end zone—an act no one in the press box could ever remember a Bryant-coached team doing.

Namath tossed three interceptions and Alabama lost, 7–6. Bryant, believing he had made several poor coaching decisions late in the game, was the last person to enter the locker room. Bryant asked his players to take a knee and he led them in prayer. "Lord, let these young men forgive me," he said. "If I'd stayed at home, we'd have won the game."

Bryant then rose to his feet. "I just want to tell you guys how proud I am of you," he said. "You never quit, you weren't beaten. Time just ran out on you. If you pick up where you left off today, in the fourth quarter, when we play Auburn we'll be OK. Feel sorry for yourself and you'll get beat again." Fourteen days later, on December 1, 1962, at Legion Field, Alabama beat Auburn 38–0. Namath ran for a seventeen-yard score and threw two touchdown passes.

At season's end—Alabama finished 10-1 and ranked No. 5 in the nation—Namath had single-season school passing records for yardage (1,192) and touchdowns (13). The New Age Bear Bryant offense was just beginning to take flight.

Bear Bryant had three rules of coaching:

1. "Surround yourself with people who can't live without football."
2. "Recognize winners. They come in all forms."
3. "Have a plan for everything."

Bryant's plan for the 1963 season was unlike any he had envisioned to this stage of his coaching career. He understood he needed to change his offensive playbook to take full advantage of Namath's skills. So he hired quarterback coach Ken Meyer, who had been at Florida State, to open up his offense even more and draw up plays that featured a drop-back passing game with two wide receivers.

The first touchdown of the '63 season was a forty-seven-yard strike from Namath to Charlie Stephens in Alabama's 32–7 win over Georgia in Athens. Bryant trusted his junior quarterback so much that, midway through the season, he let Namath call all the plays except one with no advice from the sideline. Against Georgia Tech—a team that had beaten Alabama 7–6 the previous year in a game in which Namath had attempted 31 passes—Namath threw only 4 passes and completed just 1. But the quarterback realized that the running game was working, so there was no need to drop back and risk interceptions. The Tide won 27–11. Bryant later called this performance Namath's "finest hour," because it was the quarterback's intellect—not his arm—that won the game.

But then on December 7, while Alabama (9-2) was preparing to play at Miami University in a late regular season game that had been postponed because of the assassination of President John F. Kennedy, Namath and a few of his buddies went out on Saturday night in Tuscaloosa. They attended a frat party, flirted with girls on Sorority Row, and had some drinks at Captain Cooke's, a favorite bar among many of the Alabama players. The stories of what happened next vary—one tale has it that Namath was drunk and directing traffic downtown—but one thing was clear to Bryant: His star quarterback had been drinking, and that was a violation of the no-alcohol policy he instituted before every season.

Bryant confronted his quarterback two days later in his dorm room, asking him if he drank on Saturday night. "A few sips," Namath said. "Not even a full glass."

Bryant returned to his office, spoke to his assistants about the matter, and then asked to be alone. The Bryant Training Rules were both the core of his program and the foundation of everything he had built. These rules laid out his standard for excellence. If a player broke one of the rules, it amounted to a sin, one that Bryant would find difficult to forgive. But Namath was different from any athlete he'd ever had. Not only was he Bryant's best player, but he also was Bryant's mind on the field, his football alter ego. For a long time, Bryant sat by himself in his office like a judge in his chambers, pondering how justice could be served and his rules upheld.

Bryant ate lunch every day with his quarterbacks, asking them about their personal lives and their families. He talked about his own childhood and his own struggles, dispensing life lessons he'd learned over the years. He wanted his quarterbacks to view him like a second father, to trust him, to work hard for him, and to always do the right thing because of him. But now Bryant felt as if he'd somehow failed Namath and that he hadn't connected with him the way he needed.

Every one of his assistants told Bryant not to suspend Namath. Finally, he called the quarterback into his office. Bryant explained that he could let him play, but if he did, he'd have to resign because he would no longer be able to uphold his training rules.

"Sir," Namath said, "I don't want you to do that."

Bryant then suspended his star sophomore quarterback for the Miami game and the subsequent Sugar Bowl against Ole Miss. Namath would have a chance to re-earn the trust of his teammates the following spring and then—if he kept his nose clean and was both a model citizen and student—he could perhaps once again be a member of the Alabama Crimson Tide. But nothing was guaranteed. Both coach and player left the meeting heartbroken.

A few hours later, with her husband still at the office, Mary Harmon invited Namath to the Bryants' home for dinner. She embraced Namath and said, "Joe, what happened? You couldn't do anything bad. You're just too good a boy to do anything bad." At the dinner table, she continued to comfort Namath, telling him everything would be fine, everything would work out. These were the maternal outpourings that Namath needed to hear, words that kept Namath from leaving Tuscaloosa and never coming back. That night Mary Harmon did even more:

She helped Alabama win a national championship.

◉　　◉　　◉

It was completed in the spring of 1963, a $1 million athletic dormitory that featured a lounge with a color television, wall-to-wall carpeting, and a dining hall where the players could order steak. Up to that year, no building in Alabama had been named after a living person, but the politicians in the state legislature in Montgomery voted unanimously in 1965 to grace this plush living space for the Crimson Tide football players with but one name: "Paul W. Bryant Hall."

The brick colonial dorm, which had massive Greek columns and looked like an antebellum mansion, was air-conditioned and housed one hundred football players. It featured a library, two study rooms, a rec room, a large fireplace, four luxury guest rooms for visiting parents, and two full-time dieticians in the dining room to make sure all the players' nutritional needs were met. Bryant wanted his boys—many of whom came from poor families—to feel like they had ascended to royal life now that they were playing for Alabama. Some called the dorm "the Bear Bryant Hilton."

For a few months, Joe Namath had to move out of Bryant Hall. But before the end of spring practice in 1964, Namath had exhibited enough good behavior that his sentence was commuted: He was allowed back into the dorm—and onto the roster. In front of 14,500 fans at Denny Stadium for the annual spring scrimmage, Namath led the Red team to a 17–6 win over the White team. Namath had played with an injured arm and a bruised foot, but Bryant expected—demanded—that anyone wearing the Alabama uniform play through pain. "Namath was terrific," Bryant said, "particularly when you consider that he's all banged up and shouldn't even have been playing." Bryant didn't say it, but his complimenting Namath's toughness and character in the media was his way of expressing how proud he was of his quarterback for sticking with him when he could have transferred.

In the season opener against Georgia, Namath's gifts were on full display: He completed 16 of 21 passes and ran for three touchdowns in the 31–3 victory. Namath looked like a future Heisman Trophy winner, but then in the fourth game of the season at home against North Carolina State, Namath took off on a scramble to his right. Not seeing any of his receivers open, he tucked the ball in his arm and started running. But then, with no defender close to him, he fell to the ground after hitting a clump of turf that had been torn up from the Denny Stadium grass field. Namath grabbed his knee. A trainer ran onto the field. Then Bryant came. After a few minutes, Bryant walked back to the sideline in the quiet stadium, his face expressionless. Namath hobbled off the field—no player of Bryant's was going to get a free ride on a stretcher if he was able to stand—and in the locker room his knee was wrapped in ice. After the 21–0 victory, a team doctor called the injury a "twisted right knee" and said Namath should be able to play the following week. The injury would later be diagnosed as torn ligaments and cartilage.

A week later against Tennessee, Bryant put Namath in the game in the fourth quarter. With Namath gimping in the backfield, Alabama won 19–8. The next game was against Florida. To again show the fans and the team how much Namath had matured, Bryant named his quarterback a co-captain. He was clearly still hurting—"He moves like a human now," said Bryant, "he did move like a cat"—but he started against the ninth-ranked Gators. Namath reinjured the knee on a run in the first quarter and left the game, but third-ranked Alabama survived, 17–14.

The Tide was 9-0 on November 14 when the team traveled to Atlanta to face Georgia Tech. The two teams had been playing each other since 1902, but because of the increasing animosity between the two schools—the hit by Darwin Holt two years earlier was still a hot topic—this was slated to be the final contest in the long-running series. At the team meeting on Friday night at the Biltmore Hotel, Bryant told his players, "Tech hits hard, but they don't hit hard all the time. They play tough, but they don't play tough all the time because they don't live tough like we do."

Bryant expected to be pelted with whiskey bottles when he walked onto the field at Grant Stadium, so he donned a football helmet for pregame warm-ups. Bryant was the first member of the Alabama team to walk out of the tunnel, and for several minutes he strolled around the field as fans screamed profanities. He lingered in front of the Georgia Tech student section, as more insults were hurled like sharpened spears at the coach. Bryant didn't flinch; he acted like he was checking the condition of the grass, but he really wanted the fans to know he wasn't afraid—and his team wasn't afraid, either. He then walked to the Alabama sideline, took off the helmet, and put on a brown felt hat—the houndstooth hadn't yet become his signature.

Namath entered the game late in the second quarter, the score 0–0. In the span of less than eighty seconds, he threw a forty-eight-yard strike to end David Ray, which set up a short touchdown run by fullback Steve Bowman. After a successful onside kick, Namath hit Ray for another score. Bryant then pulled his quarterback from the game. Alabama won 24–7. In the dressing room after the victory, every player and coach had filed out except Bryant and Namath. Alone together, the two spoke for several minutes. "I want to look you in the eye," Namath said. "I want to look right in the eye and tell you, 'You were right.' And I want to thank you." Bryant was never more proud of his quarterback.

Against Auburn on Thanksgiving Day at Legion Field in Birmingham, Namath threw a late touchdown pass to Ray Perkins to seal a 21–14 victory. The major wire services at the time awarded their national championships prior to the start of the bowl season, and the AP and UPI declared the Tide to be the 1964 national champions. Alabama would lose to Texas in the Orange Bowl 21–17, but the school claimed the '64 title. The next day Namath signed a professional contract with the AFL—an act that would change the landscape of professional football.

Bear Bryant loved routine. Most mornings he'd rise before five, shower, and drive through the predawn darkness to his office. At his desk he'd catch up on his mail and write letters. Once finished, he'd often slide back behind the wheel of his Cadillac, cross the Black Warrior River to Northport, and take a seat in his corner booth at the City Cafe. Smoking a Chesterfield, he'd order his breakfast and read the newspaper to catch up on events around the world. He liked to review the performance of different stocks—Wall Street stirred his passions almost as much as football—and check out what the media was writing about his team. In 1965, the year after Namath graduated, the news reports about the Tide were once again effusive.

With quarterbacks Steve Sloan and Ken Stabler leading the way, Alabama finished the regular season with an 8-1-1 record and ranked fourth in the AP poll. On the evening of January 1, 1966, the Tide faced third-ranked Nebraska in the Orange Bowl. Earlier that day top-ranked Michigan State had lost in the Rose Bowl, and second-ranked Arkansas had been defeated in the Cotton Bowl, setting the stage for the winner of the Orange Bowl to be crowned national champions by the AP.

Nebraska outweighed Alabama by an average of twenty-five pounds per player. For most of the season the passing game had been an afterthought for the Crimson Tide, but on this New Year's night Bryant had Sloan and Stabler throw the ball all over the field. Alabama's first play from scrimmage was a trick play—the tackle eligible. The play took advantage of a little-known rule that allowed, with a slight shift in the formation, the weak-side tackle to become an eligible receiver. Bryant was so excited about the trick play that several times he came down from his tower to work one-on-one with tackle Jerry Duncan, showing him how to fake a block on the play, blast off the line of scrimmage, run his pass route, and catch the ball.

Against Nebraska in the Orange Bowl, Duncan reported to an official before the first play of the game that he was an eligible receiver and then he squatted in a three-point stance just off the line of scrimmage. The 180-pound Duncan was helmet to helmet with the Cornhuskers' Walt Barnes, a 245-pound defensive tackle. The ball was snapped, Duncan faked a block on Barnes just as Bryant had taught him, and then ran down the field. The Nebraska defense, confused, didn't cover Duncan and he caught a pass from Sloan for thirty-five yards. That set the tone of the game.

Nebraska's roster featured black players, and before kickoff Bryant told his all-white team that they were to display sportsmanship on every play. He instructed his players to help Cornhusker players get up off the turf and on their feet after every whistle—no matter the color of their skin—and told them he wouldn't tolerate any dirty play. Howell Raines of the *New York Times* later wrote:

> The Alabama players' insistence on helping fallen opponents to their feet bordered on the comic. But the intention was not to humiliate or patronize their rivals. It was, as everyone in Alabama knew, to show the national sports audience that the state's football team was more civilized than its governor. Alabama played with a kind of desperate politeness...If Bryant had refused to confront [Governor] Wallace, his team had at least shown that Alabamians were capable of sane conduct in a racially charged atmosphere.

The Founding Football Document

The Tide beat Nebraska, 39–28. It was Bryant's third national title in five years. It was also the last time an all-white team of his would reach the summit of the sport.

🏈　🏈　🏈

It arrived in the mailboxes of Alabama fans the second week of August in 1966, the *Sports Illustrated* magazine that featured Bear Bryant on the cover. Except something was different about the Alabama coach: He was wearing a black-and-white checkered fedora hat known as a houndstooth.

The stories vary on who gave Bryant the first houndstooth—they range from New York Jets coach Weeb Ewbank to Oakland A's owner Charlie Finley to New York Yankees announcer Mel Allen to a Birmingham tailor named Butch Baldone—but the hat became a fixture on Bryant's head beginning with the '66 season. More than a half century later, houndstooth is still the most popular game-day apparel pattern in Tuscaloosa.

The Tide steamrolled through the '66 season, capping a perfect 11-0 record with a 34–7 victory over Nebraska in the Sugar Bowl. Alabama was the only undefeated team in America, but finished third in the final polls behind Notre Dame and Michigan State, which had tied late in the season. Though denied the national championship, it was clear what team Vince Lombardi, the head coach of the Green Bay Packers, thought was college football's best in 1966. After the Packers won the Super Bowl in January, a reporter asked Lombardi what it felt like to have the world's greatest squad. "I don't know," he replied, "we haven't played Alabama yet."

Bryant never said it, but many claimed that the Tide was deprived of the national title because of Alabama governor George Wallace, who preached a policy of segregation, and the fact that Alabama had yet to integrate its football team, both of which caused voters to punish the Tide in the polls. Alabama had also refused to schedule home games with Big 10 or West Coast schools—teams that had black players.

Bryant, aware of the growing anti-Alabama sentiment, had tried to sway opinion in 1965, when during a nationally televised game against Auburn he had an African-American supporter of the team stand close to him on the sideline. Bryant hoped the ABC cameras would capture the two side by side. "Normally when I'm on the field I don't want anybody around me," Bryant said. "But I knew that TV camera would be on me."

Bryant was acutely aware of what was happening in the world around him. After the final polls were released in 1966 and the Tide had been denied the national championship, he knew he needed to do something. He eventually did what he did best:

He came up with a plan.

CHAPTER 9

The Genesis of the Process

2010 TO 2012

Walking into his office in August 2010, Nick Saban passed a small black case on a coffee table that featured a ring. Even in the dull fluorescent light, the diamonds on the national title ring sparkled like sun rays dancing atop rippling water. The scene was eye-catching and almost hypnotizing, which was precisely why Saban kept his ring on the coffee table by the door to his office. "I like to keep it there for the recruits to look at," Saban said, cracking a devilish smile. "Some of them kind of think it's a pretty cool thing to have."

Saban moved across the room, slid behind his massive desk, and took a seat in a high-backed leather swivel chair. Even though he was only seven months removed from the night he and his Crimson Tide earned that diamond-crusted ring with a victory over Texas in the BCS national championship game, Saban was concerned, on edge, anxiety ridden, like a man who feared losing his job. He thought all the adoration and praise both the fans and the media were heaping on his team—the Tide was preseason No. 1 in the polls—was unwarranted. He was especially uneasy about his defense. He had to replace nine starters from the 2009 unit that had finished second in the nation in total and scoring defense. But it was something else about his 2010 squad that caused even greater consternation—and it *really* kept him up at night: He didn't like the collective demeanor of his team. "I always worry," Saban said, leaning forward in his chair, his eyes bright with intensity. "We've got so far to go to get where we want to be. I mean it's not even funny."

In the world of Saban's Process, what happens during winter conditioning is as important as what transpires on Saturday afternoons in the fall. Named "the Fourth Quarter Program," Saban's off-season conditioning program is led by strength coach Scott Cochran, a super-charged, in-your-face, goal-driven coach who is known in Tuscaloosa for his screams of "Yeah, yeahh, yeahhhhh!" that are played on the big screen in Bryant-Denny before the start of every fourth quarter. His voice normally hoarse at the end of every day, the blond-headed, blue-eyed Cochran is the epitome of an Army drill sergeant who constantly challenges the Alabama players—at the top of his lungs—to do that extra rep in the weight room or run that extra wind sprint at the end of a conditioning session. To keep revving the internal engines of his charges, Cochran—hired by Saban from the NBA's New Orleans Hornets in 2007—challenges his players with inspirational sayings drawn from a computer file of some two thousand pages. Kirby Smart, the defensive coordinator in 2010, called Cochran the second

. most important person in the Alabama program, because Cochran spends more one-on-one time with—and exerts more influence on—the players than any other coach.

The Fourth Quarter Program is as grueling as any winter workout regimen in the nation. Though the lifting and running routines are similar at other top schools, it is the endless quest for perfection that sets Alabama apart from the others. Under Cochran's watchful eyes, the players must perform every lift and every drill with textbook precision; if they don't, Cochran immediately is on them like a shark on fresh chum, telling them to do it again and again and again until every exercise is completed correctly. It is also Cochran's responsibility to indoctrinate all incoming freshmen into the culture of the Process and the pursuit of perfection that it requires day after day—a pursuit that is as taxing mentally as it is physically for eighteen-, nineteen-, and twenty-year-olds. Yet despite his screaming and the exhausting workouts, the players— veterans and freshmen alike—universally admire Cochran. He repeatedly asks about their families and possesses an avuncular demeanor; he often plays the role of the good cop to Saban's bad cop.

The goal of Alabama's winter conditioning program is to win the final fifteen minutes of every game come the fall, which Alabama did in 2009, outscoring opponents 121–32 in the fourth quarter. But Saban was concerned by the reports he received from Cochran in the winter of 2010. Players weren't as sharp or as dedicated as they had been the previous year. Their focus and intensity had fallen. Goals weren't being achieved. So even though Saban had a returning quarterback who hadn't lost a game as a starter since the eighth grade (Greg McElroy), a reigning Heisman Trophy winner (running back Mark Ingram), the most dangerous wide receiver in the SEC (Julio Jones), and perhaps the top linebacker in the country (Dont'a Hightower), Saban felt his team was too content, too willing to live in the past and bask in all they accomplished the previous season. As talented as his roster was, Saban told those close to him that he instinctively believed his team was vulnerable—his coaching experience had taught him that.

● ● ●

Before arriving at Alabama, Saban had been a coaching nomad, wandering the nation with Terry at his side. After spending three years as an assistant at Kent State from 1973 to 1976, he began steadily climbing the professional ladder. In '77 he was the linebackers coach at Syracuse. The next year he became the defensive backs coach at West Virginia, where he spent two seasons. In 1980 Nick and Terry moved to Columbus, Ohio, where Saban was an assistant at Ohio State under Earl Bruce. In 1982 he joined the staff at the Naval Academy, where he once considered becoming a midshipman. From 1983 to 1987 he was an assistant at Michigan State, first as the defensive backs coach and, later, as the defensive coordinator.

At one point in these early coaching years Terry told her husband that she wanted to buy a piano. She had found a cheap one that they could afford, but Saban objected: If she wanted a piano, she needed to buy one that was up to the family's standard of excellence. They wound up paying $68 a month for a few years, but Terry got the elegant piano she had dreamed for years of having.

"Because Nick is so relentlessly single-minded about football, it would be tough for him to do his job the way he wants to do it without Terry," said Phil Savage. "She does the bills, takes care of the cars, and makes sure their personal house is in order. Nick just doesn't have time for that. They have a true partnership. She makes it so he doesn't have a lot of distractions. Her role in his career has just been enormously important."

Life changed for the Sabans in 1988. Saban landed his first NFL job that year with the Houston Oilers. While coaching defensive backs for the Oilers, the Sabans adopted a son, Nicholas, and later adopted a daughter, Kristen. In 1990, Saban was hired by the University of Toledo for his first head-coaching job. He guided the Rockets to a 9-2 record in that initial season and suddenly appeared to be on the fast track to becoming a head coach at a big-time, Top 20 school. But then Saban took the almost unprecedented step of leaving Toledo after one season to become an assistant— a defensive coordinator—for the Cleveland Browns in 1991 under new coach Bill Belichick.

Saban had met Belichick nine years earlier when they were assistant coaches at Navy. The two were obsessed with the fundamentals and philosophies of football and immediately clicked, forming a close personal relationship and developing an easy, back-and-forth rapport that was rare for either of them. The day that Saban told his Toledo players he was heading to Cleveland, he cried for the first time since his father passed away, eighteen years earlier. "The opportunity to be a coordinator with an NFL franchise, especially one with the tradition of the Cleveland Browns, puts you in a position where the next step might well be consideration for a head coaching job in the NFL," Saban said on the day he announced he was leaving Toledo.

When Saban arrived in Cleveland as a thirty-nine-year-old assistant—it already was his ninth coaching job since leaving Kent State—the Browns were preparing for the upcoming 1991 NFL draft. But unlike other coaches who used scouts who had their own ideas and matrices of judging and measuring football skills, Belichick wanted to develop the team's own system for evaluating talent. So before the coaches looked at individual college players, the staff defined what they wanted in a player at each position. Debates ensued, ideas were exchanged, notes were taken, and before the draft the Browns had identified the ideal height, weight, size, and speed for every position. At center, for example, the team determined that the desired size was six foot three, 280 pounds, with a 5.19-second 40 time. A player was then evaluated based on those ideal measurables. Other important factors at every position were also weighed, such as athletic ability, strength, playing speed, and character. But when a player was assessed, he was always compared to the Browns' created prototype. And Saban learned never to look simply at players; rather, he examined players in the context of the definitions of what the team wanted at each position.

"It took a number of months to build that system, and we enlisted the help of Gil Brandt [a longtime scout for the Dallas Cowboys], but by the end we had a weight-height-speed template that really is the basis of what Saban and Belichick are still using today in evaluating players," said Phil Savage, who was a quality control assistant with the Browns from 1991 to 1993 and became the team's general manager in 2005. "Our quarterback needed to be six-three or taller and weigh 218 pounds. If he met those requirements, he was considered 'clean.' If he didn't, we'd designate him on the chart with a red flag. But this system was particularly important on the defensive side of the ball. We wanted tall corners, big safeties, and big, strong linemen. If you look at Alabama today it's a height-weight-speed program. There are some outliers like Javier Arenas [who was a five-foot-nine cornerback for Saban from 2007 to 2009] and Nick has certainly made some modifications, but what he's doing today really started in Cleveland."

In his first season with the Browns, Saban revamped a defense that was last in the NFL a year earlier in points allowed and transformed it into the No. 1 unit in 1994. Saban and Belichick grew exceptionally close. The two would spend hours together in the football offices talking the finer points of defense. Back and forth, they would trade ideas about the 3-4 defense they both ardently believed in, and discuss blitz concepts, presnap adjustments, and different coverages based on down and distance and field position. They debated—often in expletive-filled language common in Cleveland football offices—how best to scout, motivate players, and prepare for an opponent. It was the football equivalent of Socrates and Plato waging great debates over the art of playing defense. Unlike most coaches, the two didn't use a chalkboard; they could perceptively visualize complex schemes and communicate them with astonishing mutual clarity and recognition—masters of the string theory of football.

"I've never been around two coaches with higher football intellects than Nick and Bill, but the two really had different personalities," said Savage. "Bill is much quieter. He's steady, almost monotone, and he can be very sarcastic and his criticism can be biting. Nick wears his emotions on his sleeve, particularly behind the scenes. He's much more animated in the hallways and in the meeting rooms. He won't tell you that you're doing a good job, because he doesn't have time for that. But he will make it very clear to you if you're not doing a good job…Watching Bill and Nick work together on game day was as impressive as anything I've ever seen in football."

In Cleveland Nick and Terry hosted a Kentucky Derby party every year for friends and colleagues. While Terry moved effortlessly from guest to guest, Saban preferred to talk shop with other Browns staff members. The job was always on his mind. "When you work for Nick you always feel like it's fourth-and-one on the goal line and the Super Bowl is on the line," said Savage. "He's the pacesetter. Players at Alabama will swear to you that they've never seen him close his eyes in meetings and that they've never seen him yawn. He's got a lot of firepower in that engine. You feel like if you don't get something done, then you're letting him down. It's intense with him. Meetings, practices—everything is intense. That's one reason why Alabama plays so well in big games, because it's almost easier and more relaxing out there on the field in the game than it is with him at practice and in the building."

When Saban left Cleveland in 1994 to become the head coach at Michigan State, he carried the Browns grading system with him—and has used a variation of it since. So has Belichick, who has won six Super Bowls with the New England Patriots using that same core grading system. The two coaches have remained close since they parted ways more than two decades ago, frequently speaking over the phone and tossing a range of football thoughts at each other. The four years Saban spent at Belichick's side did two key things: They sharpened Saban's ability to scout talent, and they refined the style of defense he would play during the remainder of his coaching career.

The Genesis of the Process

● ● ●

Before he took over at Michigan State, Saban was awarded an $8,000 bonus when the Browns reached the 1994 playoffs. Cleveland lost in the divisional round to the Pittsburgh Steelers, 29–9. On Christmas Day Saban gave his father-in-law a Cleveland Browns jacket. When Paul Constable put his hand in the pocket, he felt something inside and discovered that Saban had used the bonus money to pay off the mortgage on their home. Terry's father, who had been a coal miner in West Virginia, couldn't hide the tears that welled in his eyes.

Once at Michigan State, Saban installed a new strength and conditioning program, which nearly caused a player revolt due to its intensity. But as the linemen began to shed fat and other players became more sculpted, the collective attitude of the team started to change. Saban asked the Downtown Coaches Club, a Michigan State booster club, to buy five desktop computers that would be housed in a computer lab for the players. Saban emphasized to the boosters the importance of supporting academics among players and the correlation of that to recruiting. The request was approved.

Though the Spartans lacked talent in Saban's first season— Michigan State had gone 5-6 in '94, and most local reporters believed that another five-win season would be considered a successful year for Saban—the Spartans reached the Independence Bowl, where the team lost to LSU, 45–26, and finished the year 6-5-1. Fans in East Lansing, witnessing the improved play on the field, were smitten with Saban. At the final regular season game, at home against Penn State, a fan held up a sign that read: "Saban Is God."

Before the start of his second season in East Lansing, Saban interviewed Todd Grantham for the defensive line coaching position. Grantham had spent the previous six years at Virginia Tech. Five minutes into the interview Grantham demonstrated to Saban the stance he liked his defensive linemen to line up in. Saban vehemently disagreed with Grantham's philosophy, arguing that he was completely wrong. "He got in my face a little bit," Grantham said. "He can be a pretty intimidating guy when he wants to be. I thought I had no chance at getting the job. But then we moved on, and an hour and a half later he offered me the position."

As soon as Grantham arrived in East Lansing, he was stunned by how Saban had essentially created an NFL type of operation on the college campus. The most important space in the football office was the staff meeting room, which served as the recruiting command center. On a floor-to-ceiling dry-erase board, Saban ranked the recruits he was targeting. The rankings were based on the grading system Saban learned in Cleveland. "The measurables" were listed next to every name on the recruiting board: the player's height, weight, and speed. "The rankings allowed us to see on the board who we felt was going to be All-American, who was a freshman starter, who was a starter by year two, who was a developmental player, who was going to be a situational player, and who was going to be a role player," Grantham said. "I'd never seen anything like it before. He was ahead of his time in college football. If a guy fell off the board for some reason, then you just moved on to the next guy in the rankings."

Grantham was hired in January 1996—the college football off-season—and Saban assigned each of his assistants special projects that had to be completed before the start of spring practice. One project, for instance, was for an assistant to find out who the best team in the Big 10 was at converting third downs, and then figure out why that team was so successful in those critical situations. "Nick is always looking for an edge," said Grantham. "He has a detailed agenda for every day in the office, even if it is the off-season. He creates a business atmosphere and so when you're working, man, you're *really* working."

Saban also kept his eye on the pro game while in East Lansing. In 1998 he was intrigued with what the San Francisco 49ers were doing with linebacker Charles Haley that season. The 49ers had created a new position for Haley—called the "Elephant"— that allowed the weak-side defensive end to move around the formation and rush the passer from either side of the line in a two-point stance. After speaking to the San Francisco coaches, Saban installed an Elephant package into his defense and moved linebacker Julian Peterson into that role. Playing the Elephant in 1999, Peterson was named an All-American.

🏈   🏈   🏈

In his fourth season at Michigan State, Saban and the Spartans were 4-4 when they traveled to Columbus, Ohio, on November 7, 1998, to play undefeated Ohio State, the nation's No. 1 ranked team. During practice that week Saban opted to try something new: He told his players not to worry about winning the game. Rather, they should treat each play as if it were the game itself, and focus on what needed to be done during that play to be successful. And as soon as the whistle blew after each play, it was to be wiped from memory; all that mattered was the next play and zeroing in on what actions needed to be completed in order to "win" that play. Saban found during the week that his players appeared more confident and were as crisp in practice as they'd been all season. A twenty-four-point underdog, Michigan State then went into Columbus and upset the Buckeyes 28–24. As Saban jogged off the field that afternoon, he knew that a significant new element of the Process had been born.

●   ●   ●

After building Michigan State into a team that cracked into the Top 10 in 1999—the Spartans finished that season 10-2—officials from LSU contacted Saban's agent, Jimmy Sexton, to see if he'd be interested in moving to Baton Rouge. In December 1999 Saban met with LSU chancellor Mark Emmert at Sexton's house in Memphis. Saban walked into the meeting carrying a yellow legal pad that was filled with questions. For several hours, it was Saban who conducted the interview, asking Emmert about the school's facilities, recruiting, and academic support for the program. Emmert was so impressed that he offered Saban a $1.5 million annual contract and a guarantee that if he won the national championship, he'd become the highest-paid college coach in America by one dollar.

Why did Saban leave East Lansing? Saban had earlier done research and discovered that both NFL and college football rosters were populated with players from Louisiana and other Southern states. There was simply more raw football talent in the Deep South than in the north. And Saban never forgot what his high school coach had once told him: *It really doesn't make any difference what play you call sometimes. It's what players you have doing it.* Saban needed access to blue-chip players if he was ever going to contend for a national title.

LSU officials sent a plane to East Lansing to pick up any of Saban's assistants who wanted to join him in Baton Rouge. The plane returned with no passengers. To those who don't care for Saban, this anecdote has been referenced repeatedly over the years as evidence that he's a hard driving, no-fun boss who is impossible to please. But in reality, the main reason the Michigan State assistants didn't board the LSU plane was because they felt loyalty to fellow assistant Bobby Williams, who was elevated to replace Saban in East Lansing.

So is Saban liked by his assistants? "The thing about Nick is that he clearly spells out for you what he expects and what your duties are," said Jim McElwain, offensive coordinator for Saban at Alabama from 2008 to 2011. "He can be tough, but he's all about one thing: winning. That's it. He has a clear plan and a clear organizational calendar. There's no wondering with Nick; everything is clearly defined. He doesn't have any set office hours. You get in as early as needed and you stay as late as needed. During the season you're usually in at 7 a.m., but it's not like Nick and his assistants put in any longer hours than other staffs in the country. He's not overbearing as long as you're doing your job. He leaves the assistants alone for the most part. Like all good managers, if he believes that the area you're in charge of is in good shape, he'll let you do your job without much interference. I personally found it very easy to work with him, and so did the other assistants on the staff during my time with Nick."

"When you interview with Coach Saban, he'll tell you over the course of several hours exactly the job he's hiring you to do," said Sal Sunseri, the linebacker coach at Alabama from 2009 to 2011 who returned to the school in January 2019. "He tells you very clearly what he wants, what he expects, and what he wants you to develop. As he's telling you all of this, he's asking, 'Are you OK with this? Are you OK with that?' I was, and that's why I worked for him. The staff was very professional and very, very focused. You have to be when you're working for Coach Saban; otherwise you won't be working for him very long."

"It's normal working hours of seven to ten with Nick," said Curt Cignetti, Alabama's recruiting coordinator and receivers coach from 2007 to 2010. "The difference is you're working all the time. There is no socializing, no BS sessions. You're always doing purposeful work and you're making your time count. It's relentless, which is one of Nick's favorite words."

Added another assistant who coached under Saban, "Everything is good until you do something that upsets Coach Saban. He doesn't get over things easily. I won't say he holds grudges, but you need pretty thick skin to be on his staff. He'll yell at someone on staff just for the sake of yelling, I think, like it's set on his calendar. So yes, he can be difficult."

Four years after being hired, with the Process fully ingrained in the culture of the Tiger program, LSU advanced to the BCS title game against Oklahoma in the Sugar Bowl. The 12-1 Tigers looked radically different from the team Saban had inherited in 2000. Saban's first task then was to improve the strength of his players. On the LSU game tapes that he had reviewed shortly after accepting the job, Saban saw that the Tigers wore down in the fourth quarter, which translated into several last-minute losses the year before. When Saban got to Baton Rouge, only two players could bench 400 pounds and only two could squat 500 pounds. By the time the Tigers vied for the national title, the Tigers had thirty players who benched 400 and twenty-five who did 500-pound squats. When hired by LSU, Saban said he would base his program on four principles: effort, toughness, discipline, and commitment. Those principles turned the Tigers into a power. "No one around here was used to the kind of discipline that Coach Saban brought in," said defensive tackle Chad Lavalais, who also remarked about the intensity of the off-season workouts and the emphasis on good grades.

Before the national title game Kristen Saban, age thirteen, gave her father three pennies to carry for good luck. She normally handed him just one before his earlier games, but with so much on the line against Oklahoma on January 4, 2004, she felt he needed three. Those pennies jangled in Saban's pocket as he boarded a bus outside the New Orleans Marriott at ten minutes past five that afternoon, three hours away from the kickoff of the biggest game of his life.

LSU had allowed only 10.8 points a game during the regular season, the best in the nation. Oklahoma led the country with an average of 45 points a game, but the Sooners had only 22 possessions that lasted more than ten plays. As Saban and his staff watched film of Oklahoma's Heisman-winning quarterback, Jason White, they noticed that he took chances and threw the ball down the field rather than check down and make easy, more certain passes. LSU had blitzed on nearly 80 percent of their defensive snaps in the regular season, but Saban was going to throw a curveball at the Sooners: The Tigers would start the game with five defensive backs and they would rarely blitz. Saban wanted to test White's patience and see if he could bait him into making mistakes down the field, which would be covered in his new scheme by an extra defensive back.

The plan worked: White looked confused in the first half, and Oklahoma gained only 44 total yards. Trailing 21–14 late in the fourth quarter, the Sooners' last chance to tie or win the game ended with six consecutive incomplete passes by White. Saban had done it: The Tigers won their first national title in forty-five years. Moments after the final whistle sounded, Saban found his wife on the field and the two kissed. "Nick is very serious about the theory that football epitomizes the American dream," Terry Saban said. "His feeling is that if you work hard, stay disciplined, and refuse to cut corners, the playing field is a place where a person of any shape, size, or background can succeed."

A day after winning the BCS national title the New York Giants asked LSU for permission to talk to Saban. He would eventually be offered the Giants job, but he turned it down. "I like college football and I like being here," he said. But then he also added, "There's always the chance of that being different someday."

That someday would come one year later, when Miami Dolphins owner Wayne Huizenga flew into Baton Rogue on his private jet and convinced the Sabans to move to South Florida. It wasn't easy. Saban and Terry agonized about the $5-million-a-year contract offer for four days. At one point Saban boarded Huizenga's plane in Baton Rouge, then stepped off and drove away in his car, needing more time to consider his decision. Saban had earlier turned down overtures from at least five NFL teams in the past, as he and Terry opted to stay in the college game where Saban believed he could personally touch more lives. But the lure of the NFL was simply too strong, especially because Huizenga committed to handing Saban complete control of the franchise. Saban wanted to test his football philosophy at the highest level. When Saban and his LSU team landed in Orlando on December 25, 2004, for the upcoming Capital One Bowl, he announced that he was taking the job with the Dolphins.

"I've always been driven by challenges," Saban said after accepting the Miami contract offer. "I don't care if it was Little League baseball. What it was, it was always the next challenge that makes driven people want to take advantage of the next opportunity."

How driven was Saban at Miami? In July 2006 he turned down an invitation to dine with President George W. Bush at Joe's Stone Crab in Miami Beach. Why? Because it fell on the second day of training camp and Saban had work to do.

◉   ◉   ◉

A year after LSU won the national championship in 2003, the Tigers lost their third game of the '04 season to Auburn and then again fell two weeks later to Georgia, 45–16. LSU finished the season with three losses. Recalling that past disappointment and sensing another letdown season was fast approaching, Saban summoned all of his persuasive powers during preseason camp to ensure the 2010 Tide team didn't suffer the same fate as the '04 Tigers. He warned his players that complacency after winning a national title was the most dangerous disease for a team trying to seize back-to-back crystal trophies. The warnings were frequent. He issued them in the locker room, on the practice field, and on television (Saban usually looks into the cameras at his press conferences when he's sending a message to his team, not at the reporter who asked the question).

During some preseason practices Saban, wearing his customary straw hat, unleashed profanity-laced tirades at players who he believed were giving less than full effort, yelling that losses were certain to come if attitudes and approaches didn't change. Saban's temper was legendary on campus—student workers on the team were careful not to misstep out of fear of being on the business end of an expletive-filled rant—and among the beat reporters. ("You haven't covered Alabama football if you haven't gotten yelled at by Nick Saban," said one veteran reporter of the Tide beat.) Now, in the days before the season opener, Saban raised his voice time and again to commandeer the attention of every one of his players.

"[It] can't be about trying to prove something, because you've kind of already done that," Saban said in August. "It needs to be about, 'Are you driven to be the best player you can be?'...I think I learned a lot of this from the first time around at LSU because I wasn't aware of how that success would affect the next team. I really wasn't."

Saban's premonition was confirmed. His Crimson Tide team didn't compete the way Saban had wanted. Top-ranked Alabama opened the season with five consecutive victories—including a 31–6 thrashing of Florida on October 2—but then lost two of its next four games. South Carolina defeated the Tide, 35–21, on October 9 and then LSU knocked off Alabama, 24–21, on November 6. After that game Saban pointed to the main reason his squad wasn't going to repeat as national champions: a failure to follow the Process. "This whole year, everyone around us has been very concerned about the results in comparison to what was accomplished a year ago, and that has not been the best thing for the development of this team," Saban said. "They have become too result oriented, and we never have developed to become as good a team as we can be."

The Tide finished their 10-3 season with a 49–7 win over Michigan State in the Capital One Bowl—a victory that many players would later say put the program back on track.

🏈   🏈   🏈

On the afternoon of April 27, 2011, after spring practice had wrapped up, Saban sat alone in his second-floor office in the Mal Moore Athletic Facility, unaware of the increasingly threatening weather reports. Saban was preparing for a videoconference scheduled for 6 p.m. with former Crimson Tide coach Gene Stallings. He needed to change clothes, so at 4:20 p.m. he got in his black Mercedes and drove to his ivy-covered, French-chateau-style home across the Black Warrior River a few miles from campus.

As he neared his house, jagged bolts of lightning repeatedly ripped the blackening sky and booms of thunder rumbled through thickening clouds. The storm-warning sirens were blaring in Tuscaloosa, but Saban, like so many in the city, had become desensitized to their piercing sound. They had gone off a few times every week over the previous month or so, and except for the tornado twelve days earlier that had caused minimal damage, each time they had been false alarms. But then, as he drove closer to his house, his cell phone bleated; his son, Nicholas, was calling to say that the winds were picking up at his house in town. Saban detected a tone of fear in his son's voice. He told Nicholas to shelter in his bathtub. Saban pulled into his driveway and walked into his house. At 5:13—the precise moment a half-mile-wide tornado touched down on the southwest outskirts of Tuscaloosa several miles from Saban's home, a twister that would take sixty-four lives over an eighty-mile path—he was changing clothes.

Unaware of the approaching tornado and the magnitude of what was transpiring, Saban left his house after ten minutes, around 5:25. He steered his car back to his office for the videoconference with Stallings. After it was over, he phoned Nicholas, checking to see that everyone was safe. His house was intact, his son replied, but a few blocks away several homes and structures had been destroyed.

Saban drove to Nicholas's house. Darkness was beginning to fall, but when Saban looked out the window, he could faintly detect that something terrible had just happened to his town. "You could see it a little," he said. "But more than anything, you could feel it. That's when I was starting to realize it was bad, but at that point the police didn't even know. Communication was down." Even though he still wasn't aware of the full scope of the tragedy, Saban's life—and the lives of everyone in Tuscaloosa—had just radically changed.

Saban reached his son's house. Eventually Saban—along with his son, four of his son's friends, and his son's dogs—went back to the family home, which was safely seven miles beyond the tornado's path and where electric power never went out. Saban opened the garage doors; immediately his three dogs bolted and raced toward something that demanded their attention in the dark distance.

The Genesis of the Process

Saban's daughter, Kristen, and several of her sorority sisters were in the living room, where they had gathered soon after the first reports of threatening weather. In the same room, later that night, they would learn from a post on Facebook that Ashley Harrison, one of their Phi Mu sorority sisters and the girlfriend of Tide long-snapper Carson Tinker, was missing. Tinker and Harrison had been huddling in a closet at Tinker's house when the tornado hit. Ashley's friends at Saban's house spent the entire night texting Ashley, calling other friends, and scouring Facebook trying to learn Ashley's whereabouts. At 5:30 a.m. they were joined by Saban, who took a seat in a reclining chair. When they told him that Ashley was unaccounted for, his heart dropped.

At daybreak Saban drove to the football offices to meet with Thad Turnipseed, the director of the athletic facilities. They filled the back of a pickup truck with bottles of water and sports drinks that had been left over from the spring game and then drove into the heart of the devastation. As the morning sun rose over Tuscaloosa, Saban saw for the first time the devastation that the tornado's swath had carved into the heart of T-Town, leaving little but destruction and death in its whirling wake. Up and down the streets and throughout many neighborhoods of Tuscaloosa, Saban handed out water, but mostly he just listened and hugged, allowing victims to vent or cry in his arms. He met with business owners who picked through what was left of their livelihoods and with homeowners who sorted through what remained of their homes, gathering what few possessions they could find. Some moved about in a what-in-heavens-will-I-do silence, others openly sobbed, uncontrollably. A local man with only one leg explained to Saban that he had worked for three years to purchase a specially designed truck that allowed him to drive. Now, the man said, the truck had been cartwheeled away by the storm. Saban heard sad tales like this all day, nonstop, and all he could do was grab those in pain, pull them close, and tell them that he would do everything in his power to help.

This was a side of Saban that only Terry and their children knew: compassionate, emotional, and capable of great empathy. As the most revered figure in the state, Saban wielded a great power—the power to soothe, to make people believe that a new day of promise was on the horizon, that together they would rebuild Tuscaloosa, brick by brick, life by life. For hours on the Day After, Saban comforted and consoled, spoke about the town being one team together, and embraced more people in a six-hour stretch than he ever had in his fifty-nine years. This was a critical moment for Saban: His friends say that this was when his roots became firmly planted in Tuscaloosa—and why they believed he would never leave Alabama for another job. Now Saban was no longer just a coach of a college football team; he was, for the first time in his career, a true community leader.

The next afternoon Saban spoke to his team in a meeting room at the football facility. He knew his players were hurting. Some of the young men sitting in front of him had pulled the injured and the bleeding from the rubble, and Saban was concerned that many of his players might suffer posttraumatic shock. So he arranged to set up a treatment center for the players where they could meet with psychologists to help them understand what they had just experienced. The university had canceled classes for the semester; Saban told his players they were welcome to go home the following day. "It might be for the best for some of you to leave, especially if you don't have power [in your homes]," he said. "That's up to you and it's a personal decision."

After the meeting Saban—who met with a counselor himself "to give me direction," he said—traveled to Tuscaloosa's main hospital, Druid City Hospital, to visit Carson Tinker, whose girl-friend, Ashley, had been one of six students killed by the tornado. Lying in his hospital bed, Tinker could only remember being in the closet with Ashley and wrapping his arms around her in the seconds before the tornado virtually atomized his house, causing Ashley to be thrown seventy-five yards across the street into an open field, where she died of a broken neck. Saban tried his best to comfort his long-snapper. Standing at Tinker's bedside, he didn't have any magic words for him—they simply didn't exist—but he emphasized that he wasn't alone.

"You have to have gratitude for being alive," the coach said softly, grabbing Tinker's hand. "We are here for you, all of us, everyone on the team and the entire university."

Tears rolled down from Tinker's cheeks as his coach em-braced him.

🏈   🏈   🏈

Nine months after the tornado—nine months after the event that had deepened Saban's roots in Tuscaloosa—Alabama faced LSU in the Superdome for the BCS national championship on January 9, 2012. With kickoff only a few minutes away, Saban told his players to listen up. He spoke about the need for everyone to do their job, to focus on their responsibility each play, and to finish strong. He ended his pregame speech by yelling, "We fight, we fight, we fight!" The players ran onto the Superdome field, confident that their forty-three days of preparation would give them the edge, that their film study would pay off.

With five minutes remaining in the fourth quarter and Alabama up 15–0, quarterback AJ McCarron handed the ball to Trent Richardson, who darted around the left edge, cut down the sideline, and galloped into the end zone, icing the game and national championship for Alabama. "It was probably the sweetest touchdown we've ever scored," said Barrett Jones after the game, looking at the scoreboard. The final score: Alabama 21, LSU 0.

Thirty minutes later, after the on-field celebration had ended, Saban and his players walked into the locker room. As soon as everyone was inside the small, cramped space, the door was shut. Saban told his players to gather around close. As they took a knee, Saban raised his right hand. The locker room fell absolutely silent. Then the Crimson Tide coach said in an emphatic voice, "We buried the pain tonight!"

Two days after capturing his second national title in three years, Saban spoke to his players in a meeting room in the Mal Moore Athletic Facility on a bright and cold winter afternoon in Tuscaloosa. Saban, a type-A perfectionist, had hardly rested. It was time to go back to work—even though not even sixty hours had passed since he held aloft the Waterford Crystal trophy. "Nick will never take time to smell the roses, because he always has something more to do," said Phil Savage. "I know people at Alabama would wish he would enjoy it more, but that's just not him. He's always looking at that next task and that next hurdle and what it will take to get over it. That's simply who he is."

Now in the football building, Saban told his team that their time to celebrate was over. "You are *not* the national champions," Saban sternly told his players who would be returning for the 2012 season. "We have a lot of good players coming back, but you haven't done anything yet. We're going to have to work our tails off to do something special."

The last time Alabama had won the national title, in 2009, Saban's squad struggled the following season, losing three games and finishing tenth in the final BCS standings. Reflecting on that disappointing team, Saban—who constantly reviews and analyzes his past performances, scouting himself as vigorously as an upcoming opponent—believed it became complacent during winter and spring workouts. The Process is synonymous with preparation and mastering detail, and how Saban's squads prepare usually will foretell how they will perform. Saban now understood that the failings of 2010 were rooted in poor off-season workouts. So to keep his players sharp and focused for 2012, he continually reminded them during winter and spring of the letdown the program had suffered in 2010.

"Fighting complacency after you've had success might be the hardest thing for a coaching staff to do," Saban said in his office a few days before the spring game in April 2012. "It's a daily thing you have to guard against. But I like the effort I've seen and so far that hasn't been an issue. I like this mental makeup and toughness I've seen. I like this team."

Alabama won its first nine games of the 2012 season by an average of nearly thirty points. But in mid-November Texas A&M and their freshman quarterback, Johnny Manziel, came to Tuscaloosa and defeated Alabama, 29–24. Operating out of a shotgun spread offense, Manziel confounded Alabama's defense as he zigged and zagged on runs or flung the ball to open receivers. He completed 10 of his first 11 passes and rushed for 74 yards in the first quarter alone as the Aggies sprinted to a 20–0 lead. Playing hurry-up, sandlot-style football, Manziel awed the sold-out crowd at Bryant-Denny. Alabama defenders, who were often out of breath, struggled to keep up with him and the quick pace of play. The secondary didn't have enough time to communicate and make their adjustments before the ball was snapped—something Saban and his staff discussed at length after Alabama's only loss of the 2012 season.

At a meeting after the game Saban and defensive coordinator Kirby Smart emphasized that they had to get faster on defense. Alabama played a base 3-4 defense, which was designed to stop the run with a massive nose tackle, but the Tide now was forced to play most of their snaps out of their base defense because they were facing so many spread offenses that featured four wide receivers. "We knew after that Johnny Manziel game we had to change some things on defense," said one former Alabama coach. "We had to figure out how to get used to the faster tempo, which Coach Saban called 'fastball.' "

In a few months, once the season was over, Saban would begin working on how to solve the problems that Manziel had created for his defense.

The Genesis of the Process

In spite of the loss to Texas A&M, Alabama advanced to the 2012 SEC championship game, where the Tide faced Georgia in early December. On the day before kickoff Saban met with the media at the Georgia Dome. A reporter asked Saban, *Do you enjoy your successes more now than you did when you were a younger coach?* Saban's answer was surprisingly reflective and revealing, because it encapsulated the core of his coaching philosophy and explained the fundamentals of how he constructed his empire in Tuscaloosa—in 144 words. "There's no continuum in success," he said. "It's an ongoing process. You have to look at the next play, the next game, the next season, the next recruiting class. If you're going to continue to be successful, you're going to continue to have success, that process is ongoing.

"When I came to Alabama, they put it on all the books and everything, 'The Process Begins.' Well, it's still beginning every day, every game. Regardless of what you've accomplished in the past, this is the most important game we're going to play this entire year for our team. As a coach, you want to do the best job you can to have your team have the best chance to be successful relative to the hard work they've done. I'm always looking forward to the next challenge. When I can't do that, I probably shouldn't do this anymore."

A day later the Tide beat Georgia, 32–28. Alabama would face Notre Dame in the Orange Bowl on January 7, 2013, in the BCS National Championship Game.

On January 2 the Crimson Tide left the gray chill of Alabama and landed in the warm sunshine that bathed the Miami airport. After Saban walked off the plane, he approached a group of waiting reporters. In the span of four minutes, he was asked twice about his departure from the Miami Dolphins back in January of 2007, when he left for Alabama two weeks after defiantly saying, "I guess I have to say it. I am not going to be the next head coach at Alabama."

Ever since leaving the Dolphins for Tuscaloosa, Saban had been a popular punching bag in the local South Florida media. *Miami Herald* columnist Dan LeBatard called Saban "a loser" and "a gasbag" and "a weasel." Now, six years later, Saban faced the local reporters for the first time as Alabama's head coach. "We all learn things about ourselves as we go. Some things we all would like to do differently," he said. "I just think we all make mistakes and would like to do things differently. You know, you don't get the opportunity to get it back."

The team piled into four tour buses. Led by a police escort, they drove into the pulsing heart of South Beach and pulled in front of the swanky Fontainebleau Hotel, now the team's headquarters. The next morning Saban met with his players in an expansive hotel ballroom. Standing in the front of the room, Saban told them it was now time to turn up the intensity, to work harder than they had in Tuscaloosa, to be sharp in practice, to pay attention to every detail. It was Coach-Speak 101, but the players knew from past experience that upcoming practices would be critical.

A few hours later, on the well-manicured soccer fields at Barry University in Miami Shores, eight miles south of Sun Life Stadium, Saban liked what he saw: The pace of Alabama's first practice in Florida was quick, the pads were popping loudly, and his team's edge had suddenly returned after the sloppy practices in Tuscaloosa. After the two-hour practice was over, Saban was virtually certain his team would be ready to play in four days.

● ● ●

At this time in January 2013, Saban was 3-0 in BCS title games. Since arriving at Tuscaloosa, counting season openers and bowl games, when Saban has had at least a month to prepare for an opponent, he had a 12-1 record (the lone loss coming to Utah in the 2009 Sugar Bowl). In every championship game, Saban's defense had smothered the opposition's offense. In the 2003 BCS title game Oklahoma quarterback Jason White, who had won the Heisman weeks earlier, completed only 13 of 37 passes for 102 yards and was sacked five times; the Tigers won 21–14. In the '09 BCS championship Alabama picked off four Texas passes in the Tide's 37–21 win. And in '11 Alabama sacked LSU quarterback Jordan Jefferson four times, held the Tigers to only 92 total yards, and went on to win in a 21–0 rout.

So why had Saban's defenses been so dominating when he had extended time to prepare for a BCS title game? Several SEC coaches who knew Saban well pointed to three factors. First, Saban, a film study addict, excelled at pinpointing an offense's tendencies in every down-and-distance situation and then devising a game plan based on his film study to counter what he expected the offense would do. Second, because Saban's scheme was more complex than most college defenses (and many NFL defenses), he recruited only defensive players with high football IQs, which enabled them to digest more information over the course of a month or so of preparation than typical college players. And third, it was difficult for opposing offenses to game-plan for the Alabama's defense because Saban featured more blitz packages than any coach in the nation—and since Saban assiduously scouts himself and his own tendencies, the opposing offense hadn't been able to predict what blitz or coverage Saban's D would employ based on down, distance, and field position.

"The extended time to prepare for [a national title] game is a huge advantage for Saban," said an SEC assistant coach. "Alabama plays an NFL type of scheme. They say, 'Not only will we beat you with our athletes, but we're also going to out-scheme you.' Saban has more blitz packages than any coach in the country. And it's a very complicated scheme, with more shifting based on the presnap motion of the offense than any team in the country. If one guy on the Alabama defense doesn't get lined up correctly, you can burn them for a long play. But...[the players] will study like crazy and...they'll know what's coming a good deal of the time."

In the days leading up to the Notre Dame game Saban was convinced Alabama would need to do two things to slow the Irish offense. It had to tightly cover Notre Dame's talented tight end, Tyler Eifert, but not with a linebacker or safety; instead, Saban would assign his best cover corner, Dee Milliner, to shadow Eifert from snap to whistle. And also, Saban would attempt to confuse Notre Dame's freshman quarterback, Everett Golson, with an exotic blitz package and endless presnap alignment switches. The one thing Saban fears the most is a quarterback who can run and improvise—the best way to beat a perfectionist like Saban, as Texas A&M proved, is to bring a backyard, draw-it-up-in-the-dirt style of play that is difficult to simulate in practice and therefore hard to prepare for—and so Saban would do everything in his power to pressure the young quarterback into making poor reads and poor decisions.

⬤ ⬤ ⬤

He walked onto the Sun Life Stadium field in Miami Gardens at 7:37 p.m. EST on January 7, 2013, flanked by three police officers, a liquid glimmer of intensity in his brown eyes. He immediately gathered a cluster of his players around him in the south end zone fifty-four minutes before kickoff, clapping his hands, yelling that now was Alabama's time to seize the moment, the night, the national title. Players always take their emotional cue from the head coach, and now Saban looked as confident as ever.

He briskly moved to midfield, where he paced with his arms folded, like a philosopher deep in thought. He closely watched his players, who were outfitted in white jerseys, white pants, and crimson-colored helmets, as they went through their now well-ingrained warm-up routine. For three, four, five minutes, he strode back and forth across the BCS national championship logo painted onto the grass field. At five foot eight, 180-pounds, the sixty-one-year-old Saban didn't cut an intimidating physical presence, but his players kept glancing at him, as if to make sure he was there, watching, assessing, analyzing.

He shook hands with Notre Dame coach Brian Kelly. Saban is not big on small talk. Even with his assistant coaches, it's rare for him to stray from the business at hand. "In all my time with Nick,

I think we only had one conversation that wasn't about football," said Jim McElwain, Saban's offensive coordinator for four years before becoming head coach at Colorado State in 2012. "He's the most focused, driven person I've ever met." And when Saban is with friends at a restaurant, he will dig deep on social subjects, but won't indulge in idle chatter. "Put it this way: The topics of discussions aren't usually about insignificant things," said a family friend. "He likes to get to the point and move on." So Saban certainly wasn't going to chitchat with the opposing coach at midfield before a national championship game.

After a few seconds, Saban moved away from Kelly and then, from the back pocket of his khaki-colored pants, he pulled out a piece of paper that was similar in size to the folded lineup card a baseball manager usually tucks into his uniform pocket. On this paper were Saban's "field notes," as he calls them, that he had prepared in his suite at the Fontainebleau Hotel, reminders of what he had learned in the more than a thousand hours of his film study of Notre Dame games during the previous thirty-five days. Saban let his eyes fall over his words one more time and read through all that he hoped to accomplish in the coming three hours. Minutes later, he scribbled a few more notes and returned the paper to his back pocket.

He spoke briefly with quarterback AJ McCarron before heading across the field. He couldn't stand still; his eyes darted back and forth from sideline to sideline, looking, looking, looking. Bear Bryant used to lean against the goalpost and watch his team passively in pregame warm-ups, as if his job of preparing his players was done. But Saban acted like there was still work to be done, even in these final, frenetic minutes before kickoff.

The Genesis of the Process

Greg McElroy, Mark Ingram, Trent Richardson, Mark Barron, and Julio Jones—all key figures on the 2009 title team—sat side by side in the north end zone stands. As McElroy watched his former team warm up, he marveled at all the talent on the Alabama side of the field. "That's a totally different team than what we had in 2009," McElroy said. "We had a bunch of really solid players and a few stars, but now Alabama has stars across the board. Their lines are huge. Our 2009 team wouldn't have stood a chance if we had to play that team."

Notre Dame won the coin toss, but deferred to the second half. Irish kicker Kyle Brindza swung his foot into the ball and Alabama's Christian Jones gathered it a yard deep in the end zone and took it to the 18-yard line. On first down McCarron handed the ball to Eddie Lacy, who gained one yard. On second and nine, McCarron rifled a deep out to the right sideline to Kevin Norwood for twenty-nine yards. Lacy and running back T. J. Yeldon then rushed on three consecutive plays to the left behind tackle Cyrus Kouandjio, guard Chance Warmack, and center Barrett Jones, the last a barreling twenty-yard touchdown gallop by Lacy. Notre Dame hadn't allowed a touchdown drive of more than 75 yards all season, but in just two minutes and fifty-seven seconds, and with startling ease, the Tide wracked up 82 yards.

After Notre Dame went three and out—with cornerback Milliner attached to the hip of Eifert, two attempted throws to the tight end fell incomplete—the Tide took possession on its own 39-yard line. Again pounding the left side of the line with running plays, Alabama methodically moved down the field. Lacy rushed for three

177

yards on the first play, then eight, then five, then five again, then twenty. It was all so simple, just Football 101—beat the hell out of the man in front of you. This was precisely how Saban and his staff had drawn up the beginning of this game during their five weeks of preparation; the ebb and flow was exactly as they expected it to be. The ten-play second drive was capped when McCarron hit a wide-open Michael Williams, a senior tight end, over the middle for a three-yard touchdown. Less than ten minutes into what had been one of the most hyped games in college football history, the Tide led, 14–0. What's more, the discrepancy of the talent on the field was as striking as the difference between gold and rust.

By halftime, as chants of *S-E-C! S-E-C! S-E-C! S-E-C!* thundered throughout Sun Life Stadium, Alabama was up, 28–0. It was the largest halftime lead of the BCS championship era. ESPN sideline reporter Heather Cox asked Irish coach Brian Kelly, before he headed to the locker room, "Where do the fixes need to come in the second half?"

"Uh," said Kelly, "maybe Alabama doesn't come back in the second half? It's all Alabama."

Late in the fourth quarter, two Tide players grabbed a jug of Gatorade and dumped it over Saban. Alabama won 42–14. As a makeshift stage was pulled onto the Sun Life Stadium field, the players swarmed Saban, tightly hugging their coach. Saban wasn't an easy coach to play for, but he connected with his most dedicated players in a way that was unusual in college football.

Because Saban is a perfectionist—and because he is constantly in the faces of his players explaining what they're doing wrong and how to right the wrongs—he forces his players to make a decision: Either listen and react or languish on the bench (or, in some cases, quit). And when they do pay attention and take his advice, a stunning transformation frequently occurs: The players perform at a level they never fathomed could be reached. On all of Saban's national-title-winning teams, that realization had spread, virus-like, affecting nearly every player on the roster. Suddenly Saban is no longer viewed as a screaming tyrant; rather, he's some sort of coaching whisperer who knows precisely what it will take for each player to flourish and enable his team to win on Saturdays. "It's hard to explain," said Barrett Jones, "but we all love and respect the heck out of Coach Saban."

Once the stage was in place, Saban climbed the few stairs and made his way toward the podium but he suddenly stopped and gazed back into the crowd. He was searching for someone, his eyes dancing around the throng of Alabama fans. Then he saw the object of his search and stepped back down onto the field, where he embraced Terry Saban. It was a sweet, loving moment, one that replicated their victory hugs in the Superdome a year earlier and at the Rose Bowl following the 2009 title game.

In the locker room, Saban triumphantly declared to his players, "You dominated!" About an hour later the coach took his seat in the front row of a team bus. Then the engines revved, the wheels began to roll, and the headlights shot through the cool South Florida night. Saban and his team were on their way to yet another victory party, but this one was also a celebration of an emerging college football dynasty.

No one said it on the bus—no one close to him would *ever* dare say it to Saban—but the chase of the Bear was now officially on.

The scorecard read: Bryant, six national championships; Saban, four.

CHAPTER 10

A Secret Plan

1967 TO 1970

They flew south to Miami in late December 1969, the Bear and Mary Harmon, searching for sunshine and, possibly, a new life. The previous three seasons each had ended in bowl game losses, and now Bryant was only days removed from finishing 6-5—the most defeats he'd ever suffered in a single season of his coaching career. Some hard-to-please fans in Alabama were calling for Bryant to resign, arguing the game had passed him by, evidenced by his 11-6-1 record in SEC play between 1967 and 1969 and his failure to finish higher than No. 8 in the AP poll over that stretch. Bryant later said the program slipped because he had been "big dogging it" and spending too much time vacationing in California's Palm Desert in the off-season instead of focusing on football and recruiting.

Upon arriving in Miami, Bryant and his wife took up residence at the Palm Bay Club, located on the western shore of Biscayne

A Secret Plan

Bay, sixty-five miles south of Palm Beach. Earl Smalley and Harper Sibley, part owners of the Miami Dolphins, showed the Bryants around the area, wining and dining them, believing they were getting to know their next head coach and his wife. They took Bear and Mary Harmon to the Jockey Club, an opulent high-rise with condos that had panoramic views of the Intracoastal Waterway, and explained that this could be their new home, the locus of a new life in South Florida. The Bryants were impressed. It felt like a continent away from Tuscaloosa and a world away from where Bryant had grown up in Arkansas.

Days earlier in a Birmingham hotel room Bryant had shaken the hand of Joe Robbie, the managing partner of the Dolphins, agreeing in principle to coach the NFL team in 1970. Robbie had offered Bryant a sweetheart deal: a five-year contract that paid Bryant a total of $1.7 million and included stock options, living quarters, cars, and a $10,000 annual stipend for Mary Harmon to fly to and from Tuscaloosa during the season. It was an almost too-good-to-be-true offer, though some details still needed to be worked out with Bryant's lawyer, Winston McCall.

"The one thing Coach Bryant loved as much as winning football games was money," said Gaylon McCollough, a former Alabama player who became one of Bryant's closest friends. "He worried about it a lot—probably more than he should have."

Now in Miami with his wife, Bryant continued to consider the move to South Florida. Joe Namath, who had just finished his fifth season with the New York Jets, was in town and Bryant asked him to come to his Palm Bay Club condo. Bryant opened up to his former quarterback, spilling his secret about the handshake deal with Robbie. Bryant asked Namath how much talent the Dolphins had on its roster—a team that was then only three years away from authoring the first and only perfect season in NFL history. "Shoot, Coach," Namath said. "You could win here left-handed."

Bryant also asked his former assistant Howard Schnellenberger, now the receivers coach for the Los Angeles Rams, the same questions. Schnellenberger gave him a similar answer: The Dolphins were a young team loaded with potential. Convinced he could win—and win big—in Miami, Bryant called Robbie and told him he would definitely take the job. But first, Bryant explained to Robbie, he needed to speak with the Board of Trustees at Alabama.

The Bryants flew back to Tuscaloosa. Bryant called David Mathews, the president of the university. "Look, they've got this new team in Miami, the Dolphins," Bryant said. "You wouldn't believe the amount of money that they have offered me and you know I've got to think about Mary Harmon and our future and I just don't see how I could say no."

"Well, you've done so much for the university, how could I object?" Mathews replied. "Although this is not, you know, what we like."

Bryant met with the Board of Trustees. Although he had ten years remaining on his contract, he told the members it was time for somebody else to coach Alabama and that the move would be best for the school. He asked to be let go. Bryant later remarked that he believed the Alabama brass would quickly open the door for his exit, happy to see him leave, because his program had struggled each of the previous three seasons.

Bryant was wrong. The board said they would release him from his contract on one condition: He needed to find a replacement that was his coaching equal. Bryant called John McKay, the head coach at University of Southern California, who he thought might be interested in coming to Tuscaloosa to get away from the hustle of Los Angeles. But McKay said he needed time to think about it; Bryant replied that he didn't have time. He needed a yes-or-no answer. McKay didn't commit.

That night Bryant struggled to sleep, tormented about what he should do. At 6 a.m. the next morning he phoned Mathews, the university president. "Is it too early for you to have a cup of coffee?" Bryant asked.

"I've been up an hour myself," Mathews replied.

The two men spoke in Mathews's office. Bryant broke the news to him. "I can't get anybody as good as me," he said with a smile to Mathews.

Later that day Bryant flew to Mobile, Alabama, where the Senior Bowl was being held. At the airport he bumped into Joe Robbie. The coach shook Robbie's hand, looked him in the eyes, and said, "I'm sorry and I apologize, but I'm not interested in a new deal. I just can't do it. There's no way I can leave Alabama." A week later Robbie hired Don Shula to coach the Dolphins.

Once back in Tuscaloosa, Bryant called a coaches meeting. It was time to rebuild the Tide. Smoking a cigarette, a tone of urgency in his voice and fire in his eyes, he told his staff that the days of haphazard recruiting efforts were over. He emphasized that fans were calling for his head because Alabama no longer had the players necessary to win national championships. Now it was time, Bryant proclaimed, for every assistant coach to treat recruiting like it was their personal oxygen—if they didn't convince the best players in America to come to Tuscaloosa, the air surrounding Alabama football would soon vanish.

"I can get a job," Bryant said. "I'm not sure about the rest of y'all. If I was you, I'd get out there and get us some players." The message was heard. Within hours, the Alabama coaches were big-game hunting, stalking elite recruits.

"Coach Bryant decided to get back into the recruiting business in a big way," said Scott Hunter, who played quarterback at Alabama from 1966 to 1970. "The program slipped in the late '60s. We had good players then, but just not enough of them. But then Bryant really got after his assistants to get him the best players, and he himself started making more calls and making more visits. He started using former players in the NFL to make calls for him to recruits. He'd give NFL players a telephone credit card number and tell them to call a recruit he was after. He used every trick he could."

Four months after reaffirming his commitment to Alabama, in April 1970, Bryant flew to Southern California to see close friend and USC coach McKay. The two met at the Western Airlines Horizon Room at the Los Angeles International Airport. Bryant was in town for the Bob Hope Desert Classic golf tournament, but he had far more important business to take care of.

After ordering drinks, Bryant proposed to McKay: Would USC like to play Alabama at Legion Field in the season opener of the 1970 season? McKay was intrigued. "Paul, how about this?" he asked. "We'll play you in Birmingham, and we'll give you $100,000 more than you give us if you'll agree to play us in Los Angeles to open next year."

Bryant agreed to the idea. The two men then shook hands. The first integrated football team from the West Coast would arrive in five months to play in Alabama.

🏈   🏈   🏈

After the 1970 spring game, Bryant held a team meeting. The coach began by delivering his standard post–spring practice speech, spelling out his expectations for the players when they returned in the fall: They needed to get stronger and faster and needed to stay away from temptations and trouble. But then the players noticed something different—the words coming out of Bryant's mouth gained horsepower, quickening with every syllable, and his voice was rising.

Bryant finally arrived at the heart of what he needed to say. Eyeing his players, he told them that he was going to start aggressively recruiting the best high school players in the country—and yes, this included black players. "If any of you don't like it," Bryant said, "then you can get the hell out of here." Not a single player rose from his seat. The issue of whether Bryant would populate his roster with black players was resolved then, there, and forever.

"Four years ago we had the finest football team that I have ever seen," Bryant told reporters before the start of the 1970 season. "In three short years we worked our way down to where the ordinary people are. I believe in three years we can be back on top, and I'm hoping it doesn't take three. This has to be the first sound basic building year."

🏈   🏈   🏈

The Crimson Tide had already played an integrated team at Legion Field. The previous season the Tennessee Volunteers had traveled to Birmingham and beat Alabama, 41–14, in the stadium that proclaimed itself the "Football Capital of the South." Two of Tennessee's best players, receiver Lester McLain and linebacker Jackie Walker, were black. But no integrated team with the tradition or star power of USC had ever crossed over the state line to take on the Tide.

Two days before kickoff against the Trojans, Bryant sat in his office and pondered the approaching freight train of a football team that was coming to Legion Field. The Tide's once vaunted defense had struggled the previous two seasons—things were so bad in 1969 that Bryant turned an offensive lineman and a second-string fullback into linebackers in the season's fourth game—and Bryant understood that his team was a big underdog against the Trojans, ranked third in most preseason polls.

"It might be a little early [for us to compete with USC]," Bryant told a reporter before the game. "Probably a year too early. But darn, if you get down and want to get back up you've got to play some great teams and win. Still, I wish it was next year."

That same day Bryant spoke to reporters from Los Angeles, inviting them into his inner sanctum. The West Coast writers were struck by the grandeur of Bryant's office, with its mahogany paneling and his massive desk. Wearing a dress shirt and tie, Bryant explained how much he admired the Trojan's Clarence Davis, a black tailback who was born and raised in Birmingham. A player with Davis's talent, Bryant emphasized, would not be leaving the state in the future. Adeptly, Bryant was using the reporters to convey a clear message to Crimson Tide fans and beyond: The widespread integration of his football team was coming. Bryant was trying to paint Davis as a symbol to explain why the Tide had fallen behind traditional powers in recent years.

Forty-eight hours later, the buses carrying the USC team drove though a lower-income neighborhood on their way to Legion Field. The Trojan players saw young black boys and girls rush toward the buses, waving and cheering. Later, in front of 72,175, the USC players jogged through the stadium tunnel into a hot and humid night. A few of the African-American players—USC's starting quarterback, tailback, and fullback were all black—were astonished by what they saw and heard: Scores of black Crimson Tide fans rising to their feet and cheering for them.

From the opening kickoff, the Trojans dominated the action. USC rushed for 485 yards—compared to Alabama's 32—and doubled up the Tide for a 42–21 victory. The star for the Trojans was sophomore fullback Sam Cunningham, who carried the ball for 135 yards and 2 touchdowns on only 12 rushing attempts. But Cunningham wasn't the only USC player who would plow through the Crimson Tide defense. Clarence Davis, the Birmingham-born back who would go on to play for the Oakland Raiders, continually ran over the Alabama defensive linemen and into the secondary. On the sideline, Bryant once again bemoaned that Davis wasn't playing for Alabama.

"USC was bigger, stronger, and faster than us," said Scott Hunter, Alabama's starting quarterback in the game. "Not recruiting skilled black players put us at a disadvantage, there is no doubt about that. And there were so many of those players in our area."

After the final whistle blew, Bryant and McKay met at midfield. In spite of the defeat, Bryant had a smile on his face. "John," Bryant said, "I can't thank you enough." Bryant then met Cunningham outside the USC locker room, congratulating the fullback on his fine effort and wishing him a safe trip back to California. Through it all, Bryant did not act like a coach who just lost a football game by twenty-one points.

The Crimson Tide fans at this moment understood what Bryant already did: Integration was the future of football. Now more than ever, Alabama supporters realized that the Tide squad needed to be integrated in order to compete with the likes of USC and other heavyweight teams whose rosters featured black players. As Jerry Claiborne, a Bryant assistant, later said of the USC game, "Cunningham did more for integration in Alabama in sixty minutes than Martin Luther King Jr." This was an exaggeration, but those close to Bryant said that this was why the coach was so pleased after the game: The lopsided loss created the atmosphere he needed in the state to start signing big-time African-American prospects.

"The point of the game will not be the score, the Bear, the Trojans; the point of the game will be Reason, Democracy, Hope," wrote Jim Murray of the *Los Angeles Times*. "The real winner will be the South."

Bryant already had one black player on his team. Freshman wide receiver Wilbur Jackson, the first African-American to be offered a scholarship by Bryant, watched the USC game from the Legion Field stands with the other Alabama freshmen. Bryant had first noticed Jackson on game film that he watched with assistant coach Pat Dye, telling Dye to recruit him. When Jackson came to Tuscaloosa on his recruiting visit, he spent time with other recruits in Bryant's home. At one point in the evening Bryant pulled

Jackson aside and said, "If you come here and if there are ever any problems, you come see me and I will take care of it." That pitch sold Jackson, who committed to Alabama and would never have any problems at the school due to the color of his skin.

As far back as 1967, five African-American players had attempted to make the Tide team as walk-ons. That February a black freshman named Dock Rone, who had played guard in high school in Montgomery, ambled into Bryant's office and asked if he could try out for the team. Bryant said he was welcome as long as he passed a physical, adding, "I admire your courage, young man." In April four other black walk-on players joined Rone in tryouts, becoming the first black Alabama players to wear practice jerseys. Bryant told his white players not to make a big deal out of the occasion, and no incidents of racial animosity were ever reported. None of the walk-ons made the final roster, but three—Rone, Andrew Pernell, and Jerome Tucker—played in the spring game.

"The players on the team were never concerned about race," said Scott Hunter. "We welcomed anyone who could help the team. We were there to win football games, not have social arguments over things. And if someone could help us win, that player's skin color didn't matter to anyone on that team. We didn't have time to worry about anything but one thing: winning."

🏈 🏈 🏈

Even though the USC game had accomplished what Bryant had hoped and crystallized the issue of integration on his football team, he was still upset with his players. Bryant told them that the upcoming practices were going to be as physically demanding and draining as the Junction practices he'd held in Texas. He told his players that he was determined to find out who was worthy of the Alabama uniform and who wasn't. The players knew what was coming.

More than a few considered quitting. Jim Simmons, the starting tight end, drove home to Yazoo City, Mississippi. Simmons told his parents he wanted to transfer to Troy State. His father then reminded his son that the car he was driving was registered in his name, and it was to be driven to one place and one place only: Tuscaloosa. At 2 a.m., Simmons was back in his Chevy and heading east. At 5 a.m. he was sitting on the steps outside the building of Bryant's office. Minutes later, Bryant pulled up in his Caddy and strolled right past Simmons, not even acknowledging him. The coach eventually called for him and, once inside his office, unleashed an expletive-filled diatribe on commitment and what it took to win. Still, Bryant let Simmons back on the team.

In spite of the hard practices, Alabama finished the 1970 season with a 6-5-1 record. That winter Bryant met John McKay in Houston to talk about off-season plans and their teams. Over cocktails at a restaurant, the pair eventually discussed a few West Coast recruits that Bryant was interested in, but then McKay mentioned a black linebacker from Mobile, Alabama, named John Mitchell, who was finishing up junior college at Eastern Arizona. "Well, hell, Paul, the best one out there isn't even on your list," said McKay, who believed Bryant wouldn't recruit Mitchell because he was black. "He's from Mobile, Alabama, and I want him."

Intrigued by this prospect he had never heard of, Bryant excused himself and phoned his office in Tuscaloosa, asking for information about Mitchell. McKay was right: Mitchell was a special player.

At Eastern Arizona he played on both offensive and defensive lines and, while in junior college, he'd gained thirty-five pounds of muscle and was now a sturdy six-three, 230 pounds. Bryant then called one of his assistants and told him to drive to Mitchell's house in Mobile, where Mitchell was home on vacation.

Bryant liked that Mitchell was mature and would be entering his junior season in the fall. He thought the linebacker could handle the pressure of breaking the color barrier on the Crimson Tide team. Bryant eventually spoke to Mitchell over the phone while his recruiter sat with the player and his parents in their living room. "John, you'll be the first black we ever started [at Alabama]," Bryant said, "and that should mean something to you."

Bryant then asked to speak to Mitchell's mother. "Mrs. Mitchell, John and I have talked this thing out, the problems that might arise," Bryant said. "But you trust me."

Mitchell's parents wanted their son to come back to the state of Alabama to play football. Late that summer, eight years after Governor George Wallace—an Alabama graduate—had stood in a schoolhouse doorway in an attempt to prevent black students Vivian Malone and James Hood from enrolling at Alabama, Mitchell strolled across the campus of the state's flagship university and greeted Bryant in his office. It wasn't always easy for Mitchell; he felt more than a few stares when he and his white teammates went out together to restaurants and stores in town, but for the most part students and fans viewed him as an Alabama football player, not a *black* Alabama football player. There were never any conflicts or protests surrounding his presence on the team. Three years later, a third of the starters at Alabama would be black.

Playing in the first game of the 1971 season—against USC at the LA Coliseum on September 10, 1971—Mitchell made the tackle on the opening kickoff against the Trojans. Bryant's plan had come to fruition: His team was integrated. After the game Mitchell's mother was standing near Bryant when a sportswriter approached. She overheard him ask the coach how many black players he had on his football team. "None," Bryant replied. "I don't have any white ones, either. All I have are football players."

Just then, the mother knew her son had made the right decision. And just then, the renaissance of Bear Bryant's career—and the Alabama program—began.

CHAPTER 11

The Play That Changed Nick Saban

2013 TO 2014

Defending national champions rarely undergo philosophical changes to their style of play. But in the spring of 2013 Nick Saban faced a crisis. On the grainy film of his memory, the haunting images of Johnny Manziel and the fast-paced Texas A&M offense constantly flickered, a horror show featuring the Aggies torching his defense the previous autumn in the Aggies' 29–24 win at Bryant-Denny Stadium. Led by Manziel, A&M routinely moved the ball up and down the field on the Alabama defense, gaining 418 total yards and catapulting "Johnny Football" to the Heisman Trophy. Saban knew he needed to change his defense and adapt to the proliferation of hurry-up, no-huddle, spread offenses in the SEC. The transformation began in spring practice.

Saban, an organizer's organizer, plans every second of every practice. But now he agreed with his assistants to have one period of unscripted live football—something he had never before done. The first-team offense went against the first-team defense in a no-huddle, fast-paced duel. The defense had no idea what plays were coming, and that was the point: Saban and his defensive coaches wanted his defenders to learn how to react to the hurry-up offense in real time. The Alabama defenders, especially in the secondary, had repeatedly been burned by the no-huddle A&M offense, mostly because they were slow in making their presnap calls and adjustments, causing them to be out of position at the snap of the ball. Now the Tide defense spent the spring learning how to perform against this new breed of offense that was sweeping across the college football landscape.

Once preseason practices began in August, Saban continued these unscripted, no-huddle sessions in his practice regimen that featured the ones against the ones. At the end of every Tuesday practice, this period of fast-paced football forced the defenders to think and instantaneously react on the fly. Realizing that Johnny Manziel and company had provided a blueprint for teams on the upcoming schedule, the coach purposefully put his players in time-compressed, rapid-fire, predict-read-react situations. The Tide needed to be ready, because the secret was out. "The way to beat Alabama," one opposing SEC offensive coordinator said that fall, "is to go tempo, tempo, tempo. Don't let that big ol' defense of theirs slug you in the mouth. Go fast and you'll confuse them and wear them out. A high-speed spread offense is the ultimate equalizer when you don't have Alabama's talent. And trust me, no one does."

The Play That Changed Nick Saban

Nick Saban paced up and down the sideline of Jordan-Hare Stadium in Auburn on November 30, 2013, his eyebrows furrowed, a foreboding look on his face. With the clock ticking down and forty seconds remaining in the fourth quarter of the Iron Bowl, top-ranked and undefeated Alabama led fourth-ranked Auburn, 28–21. The Tigers had the ball first-and-ten on the Tide's 39-yard line. At this moment, Saban had no idea that what was about to transpire would change the course of his program.

Lined up in the shotgun, Auburn quarterback Nick Marshall took the snap. He faked an inside handoff, tucked the ball, and ran with it to the wide side of the formation—a classic run-pass option play (RPO). The Tiger offensive linemen blocked as if it was a running play; in college football, it is against the rules for O-linemen to release from their blocks more than three yards beyond the line of scrimmage on a pass play. As Marshall continued to execute the RPO play and run toward them, more than one Auburn offensive lineman moved beyond the imaginary line three yards downfield. Alabama cornerback Cyrus Jones, seeing the Tiger blockers charging beyond that mark, stopped covering wide receiver Sammie Coates, who was nine yards beyond the line of scrimmage, and ran toward Marshall to tackle him.

Just before Jones put his shoulder into the quarterback, Marshall shot-putted the ball to the wide-open Coates, who then ran untouched into the end zone for the tying score. Saban fumed furiously on the sideline, telling referees that the pass to Coates was illegal because Auburn had ineligible receivers blocking beyond three yards of the line of scrimmage. The referees ignored Saban, who after a few minutes of red-faced screaming returned his attention to the game.

At first Saban appeared content to play for overtime, but then, with seven seconds remaining on the game clock and Alabama on their own 38-yard line, quarterback AJ McCarron pushed the ball into the gut of running back T. J. Yeldon, who burst through a gaping hole in the line and ran twenty-three yards before stepping out of bounds. Sixty percent of the homes in the Birmingham market were tuned to the game broadcast by CBS—as were more than 10 million across the country—and no one could miss the chyron on the screen that read: END OF REGULATION.

But Saban again rushed at the officials, and asked them to review the play. They did. "After review," referee Matt Austin announced to the Iron Bowl crowd, "the runner's foot touched out of bounds at the 39-yard line with one second on the clock."

Saban sent his backup kicker, Adam Griffith, onto the field for a 57-yard attempt, believing he had a stronger leg than starter Cade Foster, who had already missed two fieldgoals in the game. "Let's freeze the kicker," Auburn coach Gus Malzahn said into his headset. The Tigers took a time-out. Auburn defensive coordinator Ellis Johnson, who was sitting in the press box, told coach Rodney Garner, who oversaw the field goal block unit, "We need to put one of our return guys deep." Malzahn agreed and told Chris Davis, who led the SEC in punt return average, to stand with the back of his cleats on the end line.

The ball was snapped and Griffith gave it a boot. The kick sailed toward the goalposts and faded slightly to the right. The try came up short and the ball fell into Davis's arms. He ran three steps forward and then made a slight cut to the right. The move signaled to the rest of the Auburn special teamers that the return would actually go left, as it would on a punt return. In a heartbeat every

Tiger blocker sprinted to the left sideline to form a wall, and the Alabama players—most of whom had watched the kick fall short rather than run toward the ball—were slow to react.

Davis blazed down the sideline, untouched, and then collapsed in the end zone, winning the game for Auburn, 34–28, on the play that became known as the Kick Six. The Tiger student section bull-rushed a fence, pushed past security, trampled a flowerbed, and charged onto the field, some jumping on the dog pile atop Davis, who couldn't breathe under the mass of sweat-soaked humanity. "It looked like Bourbon Street out there," said Auburn special teams coach Scott Fountain.

Dozens of students cannonballed into the prickly-leafed holly bushes that ringed the stadium. Others used pocketknives and keys to carve up slices of the field for keepsakes. More than one thousand fans broke off twigs from the holly bushes. And at the 37-yard line on the Auburn side of the field after the final play a fan dumped the ashes of a loved one, which the stadium maintenance crew found the following day.

Saban emerged from the chaos on the field and was still irate over that RPO that tied the score at 28–28. He made a decision then and there: His offense needed to change to keep up with the times. "The RPO pass that Nick Marshall hit before the Kick Six changed everything for Alabama," said Gary Danielson, the color analyst for CBS who called the game. "Nick said, 'OK, if this is how things are going to be called, we're going to have to change, too. If that's going to be the rule and they're not going to call the linemen downfield for blocking, I'm going to do it, too.' That is when the philosophical switch occurred. And that led to the hiring of Lane Kiffin and the opening up of the Alabama offense."

"After that play, Coach Saban basically said, 'I can't defend that,'" said Barrett Jones, a former Alabama offensive lineman who is now an ESPN college football analyst. "When the offensive linemen show run for three or four seconds and the quarterback gets to the edge, it forces the defensive back to run up at the quarterback or stay with the wide receiver. Saban just said, 'I've got to a run a style of offense like that.'"

The play also changed Alabama's defensive philosophy. When Alabama won the national championship in 2011, the defense was on the field for about eight hundred plays—and faced only five run-pass option plays. But by the end of 2013, the RPO had become a common offensive play. How did Saban and the Tide respond? They changed the type of defender they wanted.

"Go back to the Alabama defense of 2009 and the average weight of the front seven was about 270 pounds," said Phil Savage, the former general manager of the Cleveland Browns and the Alabama radio color analyst from 2009 to 2018. "Coach Saban knew that he had to get lighter up front because of the spread offense and the RPOs. In 2009, for instance, they had Terrence Cody as a defensive tackle and he weighed about 365 pounds. Well, a guy like Cody isn't even on the recruiting radar by the end of 2013 because they need more speed up front to chase down those running quarterbacks. Saban is always adjusting and adapting. He got that from Bill Belichick, who won his first Super Bowl with Tom Brady in an I-formation offense and then he started winning Super Bowls with a spread offense. Saban is the same way. He won his first national title in 2009 with a big defense and a running game. By the end of 2013 he realized he needed to change both his offense and his defense."

The Play That Changed Nick Saban

‹🏈›   ‹🏈›   ‹🏈›

Lane Kiffin and Nick Saban knew one another. At age thirty-one in 2007, Kiffin—the son of longtime NFL coach Monte Kiffin—became the head coach of the Oakland Raiders, making him the youngest NFL head coach in the modern era, which dates to 1946. He lasted less than two years, fired after compiling a 5-15 record. He then moved to the University of Tennessee, but left after a single season to become the head coach at USC. After a 62–41 loss to Arizona State, he was fired in September of 2013. Athletic director Pat Haden delivered the news as he pulled Kiffin off the team bus on the tarmac at Los Angeles International Airport.

Kiffin had sought Saban's counsel when he was USC's head coach. Before the start of the '13 season, Kiffin flew to Tuscaloosa and had a list of thirty-two questions for Saban, ranging from how to organize practices to how to discipline players. Saban patiently answered every question posed to him by Kiffin who, like Saban, was represented by agent Jimmy Sexton. Though the two coaches were separated by twenty-four years and had little in common off the field, they admired each other's football acumen.

Days after losing in the 2013 Iron Bowl, Saban invited Kiffin back to Tuscaloosa to observe practice as the Tide prepared to face Oklahoma in the Sugar Bowl. For eight days, Kiffin evaluated the Alabama offense. After his first day at practice, he ate dinner at Saban's house and they spent three hours discussing what he had seen. Then, after every practice, the two would huddle for about fifteen minutes to compare notes and ideas. Saban never announced to the other staffers why Kiffin was there, but the message was clear: Saban wasn't happy with his offense. In one meeting with the staff, Kiffin leveled a frank assessment of Alabama's offense: It was too predictable on third downs.

After Oklahoma beat Alabama in the Sugar Bowl 45–31 on January 2, 2014, offensive coordinator Doug Nussmeier left for Michigan. Saban then hired Kiffin, who moved into a $2,400-a-month condo in a complex filled with college students. Kiffin was in Tuscaloosa to do two things: Fix Saban's offense and his own image—the first of several disgraced former head coaches who would join Saban's staff during the next five years to rehabilitate their images and learn the Alabama way.

"At the time we had no idea why Coach Saban would hire Lane," said Barrett Jones. "It was totally bizarre. Lane didn't fit Coach Saban's system and he had a lot of baggage. But Saban saw that he needed to change things on offense. He's always inviting coaches to come to Tuscaloosa and asking them where they think the game is moving. He has a mentality of 'I have a lot to learn.' This is why he's been able to sustain his success. Some coaches have success for a short time but then the opposition figures them out and their run is over. But Saban is always trying to see where college football is moving and he'll adapt as fast as he can. And that's really why Kiffin was there."

❖   ❖   ❖

Lane Kiffin went to work, installing a West Coast, wide-open attack for the 2014 season that featured quick passes to Amari Cooper and RPOs with quarterback Blake Sims, a converted running back. A freethinker and free spirit, Kiffin didn't enjoy the daily 7:30 a.m. staff meetings or Saban's obsession with detail—

a psychologist who worked with the Alabama staff characterized Kiffin as a "conceptual thinker" while Saban and the majority of the other assistant coaches were described as "structural" and "practical thinkers"—but he relished the freedom that Saban gave him to overhaul the offense.

Kiffin operated the offense at a faster tempo—Alabama went from averaging 63.5 plays per game in 2013 to 72.7 in Kiffin's first season—and created more open space on the field by mixing in outside flash passes with down-the-field vertical throws. This was a radically new offensive attack for Saban, who only three years earlier had criticized up-tempo offenses because he believed it endangered the players.

"Is this what we want football to be?" Saban said in September 2012 after Alabama's 33–14 victory over Ole Miss, a team that employed a hurry-up, no-huddle, pass-heavy offensive scheme. "I think that the way people are going no-huddle right now that at some point in time, we should look at how fast we allow the game to go in terms of player safety." Saban then explained that his defenders couldn't get lined up correctly before the ball was snapped and this led to increased chances of injury.

But less than two years later, the Alabama offense often looked a lot like that Rebel offense in 2012—four wide receivers, no huddle, shotgun snaps. In Kiffin's up-tempo offense in 2014, wide receiver Amari Cooper set an Alabama record with 124 catches. Saban's team was now doing to others what they had done to him, playing "speed ball"—his words—and using an athletic quarterback as a duel threat. Kiffin's priority, endorsed by Saban, was to get the ball into the hands of his best player, Cooper, as much as possible.

Alabama earned the top seed in the College Football Playoff but lost to Ohio State, 42–35, in the semifinals. Despite the defeat, the offense piled up more than 400 yards, but it was ultimately undone by three Blake Sims interceptions. Nonetheless, the wheels of Nick Saban's offensive evolution were now in motion—and gaining speed. The Alabama offense under Saban would never be the same.

CHAPTER 12

The Fall Surprise

1971

On New Year's Day, 1971, the Alabama players and coaches boarded a plane in Houston. Bryant settled into his seat in the middle of the cabin—he normally sat in the back row—and pulled a yellow legal pad and fountain pen from his briefcase. He began to sketch and scribble and dream. Even before the bird had reached cruising altitude, Bryant's notepad was full of one thing: the future of Alabama football. Bryant was sketching out a tectonic shift in his offensive philosophy—one that would eventually cause an earthquake to rumble across the college football landscape.

The previous night in the Astro-Bluebonnet Bowl the Crimson Tide and Oklahoma had played to a 24–24 tie in the Astrodome. The Sooners rushed for 349 yards and routinely confused the Tide defense by running the Wishbone offense—a formation that featured three backs behind the quarterback lined up in an inverted V behind quarterback Jack Mildren. He was a sleight-of-hand magician; he'd fake pitches, or hand the ball to the fullback for up-the-middle dives, or turn left or right and give the ball to tailbacks on misdirection runs, or keep the ball and run wide to either side for a keeper or an option play. The Tide defenders could not quickly identify with certainty who had the ball and who didn't. To Bryant, it seemed as though his defense was playing a game of three-card monte. Oklahoma had been running the offense for only half the season—the Sooner coaches had learned the Wishbone from the staff at Texas—and Bryant marveled at both its calculated deception and its artful finesse. The Wishbone offense proved a conundrum for his defense to solve, a riddle that stirred his imagination and now had him sketching the Wishbone against defensive alignments on the plane back to Alabama.

For most of the flight, Bryant continued to draw and diagram, his X's and O's and squiggly lines filling up page after page of the yellow legal pad. The seeds of change—radical change—were being planted on those pages.

He had to do something.

Alabama had finished the 1970 season with a 6-5-1 record, including a 24–0 loss to Tennessee and a 33–28 defeat to Auburn. Bryant's teams were always small and fast, but in 1964 the NCAA repealed its rules on the "one-platoon system." This meant offenses and defenses could substitute as many players as they pleased after every dead-ball whistle. (In 1954 the NCAA had passed a set of rules that allowed only one player to be replaced between plays, which effectively ended the "two-platoon system" used by the likes of Army's Earl "Red" Blaik.)

While teams across the country took advantage of the rule change to bring in fresher players, Bryant was slow to adapt. Suddenly, his leaner, fitter, smaller players no longer had an advantage over bigger, stronger opponents; now the teams they faced could bring in waves of larger, rested players. The result: Bryant's once-famed defenses started getting pushed around at the point of attack and surrendered more touchdowns in single games than his defenses of the early '60s gave up in an entire season. After Tennessee walloped the Tide, 41–14, in 1969, Volunteers linebacker Steve Kiner told Bryant, "Gee, coach, they don't seem to have the same pride in wearing that red jersey anymore."

Bryant knew his team had to get bigger. In the past he had left the majority of recruiting responsibilities to his assistants, but now, in 1969, that changed. He gave up his day-to-day duties as athletic director—a position he'd held since taking the job in '58—except for overseeing football affairs, and turned the position over to Sam Bailey. This freed up more time for recruiting, and Bryant began giving the thumbs-up or -down to every high school player his assistants brought to his attention. He also issued a directive to them: *I want big players.* So by the time the 1971 season kicked off, his roster was filled with the likes of offensive linemen John Hannah (who weighed 273 pounds) and Jim Patterson (252 pounds).

In the spring of '71, atop his steel tower, Bryant watched his team practice daily for several weeks. Near the end of spring ball he vowed to make another change—one he would keep secret until the Tide traveled to Los Angeles to face USC in the season opener. After studying his roster, Bryant believed that the drop-back passing game that had been so successful with Joe Namath and Ken Stabler would no longer work in the SEC. He had a stable of talented running backs—Johnny Musso, Joe LaBue, and Ellis Beck—and the most powerful offensive line of his tenure in Tuscaloosa. He had a fleet-footed quarterback named Terry Davis, who struggled to throw but loved to run. Finally Bryant—after a "helluva big gut check," he said—made up his mind: He would install the Wishbone at Alabama.

When spring practice ended, Bryant flew to Austin, Texas, where Longhorns coach Darrell Royal—a longtime friend—had perfected the art of running the Wishbone. In that formation the fullback is positioned three yards directly behind the quarterback, and the two halfbacks are set back a few yards behind and to the left and right of the fullback. Bryant had decided that this was the formation that was going to propel Alabama back to national prominence.

Royal picked up Bryant and an assistant at the Austin airport, and the two longtime friends then drove to a hotel. Royal had offered Bryant the use of an office in the Longhorn athletic department, but Bryant declined. He feared that a reporter would see him and start asking questions. Bryant carried a projector and film into his hotel suite, where the coaches began watching the flickering black-and-white images that the Texas staff had put together detailing the nuances of the Wishbone.

For hours, Royal reviewed the film with Bryant and his assistant. Throughout the day and deep into the night, Royal and Bryant watched reels of tape on the projector, the Texas coach explaining every intricacy of the offense, from blocking techniques to play calls in different down-and-distance situations to the type of running backs that would make the offense flourish. Bryant was riveted, believing he had found the solution to his offensive problems. He flew back to Tuscaloosa armed with suitcases packed full with films and playbooks.

Once home, Bryant continued to immerse himself in the offense. In August, Royal and a few Texas coaches flew to Tuscaloosa to speak at a coaching clinic for high school and college coaches. During the evenings Bryant and Royal sat on Bryant's front porch, sipping cocktails and talking more about the Wishbone. Once the clinic was over, Bryant gathered his assistant coaches at the Stafford Hotel. He had a surprise for them: The Longhorn assistants were there to debrief them on the Wishbone offense. Bryant was concerned that an enterprising reporter might see the Texas coaches, which was why the clandestine meeting was held at a hotel and not at the Crimson Tide football office.

A *Birmingham News* reporter, unaware that the Texas staff was secretly teaching the Alabama coaches the offense, asked Royal about the Wishbone. "You've got to have confidence in it before you go into it," Royal said. "Some teams try and then, the first time something went wrong, they went back to something they had confidence in. The same thing happened when the Split-T came out. A lot of teams junked it because they didn't have the patience to stay with the basic attack."

Four days before the start of fall practice, Bryant called in his assistants for a meeting. "Men, we are going to sink or swim with the Wishbone," he said. "And we're not going to just fool around with it for a few days and toss it out. This is it."

On August 15, the players reported to Bryant Hall, where they were assigned rooms. That evening Bryant met with his varsity players in the projection room. "We have gotten away from championship football," Bryant said. "We had gotten to the point where we had a number of blue-chip athletes who were good enough to make plays, and we would win ball games. But I know that's not the way to win championships. You can't win on athletic ability alone. You've got to have that mix of players who are disciplined, have a work ethic, and a desire to be something. We have come to this. What I have done is taken myself out to Texas and have learned the Wishbone offense from Darrell Royal and his team. We have decided we are going to run the Wishbone offense. We have taken what they have taught us, and we have affected it and tweaked it. We think that we have the best Wishbone offense in the country. That's what we are going to line and play Southern Cal with."

Bryant walked to the chalkboard and, for the first time, began diagramming the offense for his players. He emphasized the need for a fullback who could both run and block; the need for a quarterback who was smart enough to read defenses and determine whether he should hand the ball to his fullback, keep the ball himself, or run an option to the side of the field where the defense was most vulnerable; and the need for talented tailbacks who could break tackles and had enough speed to get to the edge of the field. Several players remember Bryant being as animated and excited as they had ever seen him as he spoke.

"After going over the Wishbone, Coach Bryant called Johnny Musso to the chalkboard and asked him to repeat everything he had just said," said Bill Oliver, an assistant coach on the team. "Coach Bryant often did this with assistants during meetings, but now he was doing it with a player. And Musso, who was really smart and Coach Bryant knew it, nailed it. He got everything right almost verbatim. That gave the other players confidence that they could learn the offense relatively quickly."

Bryant told his players not to discuss the switch with anyone—not parents, not friends, not girlfriends. Before the first fall practice, Bryant ordered that a canvas tarp be placed around the field. He also asked that a security officer patrol throughout the adjacent area to keep any scouts from USC or reporters from spying on practice. When reporters were allowed to watch practice, the offense went back to the I-formation. Like any good general, Bryant understood how valuable the element of surprise is to win a battle—and football games.

Bryant once explained why he so admired the Wishbone. "It's the best formation I've ever seen," he said. "In the first place, the fullback is always in the same spot, and it's very easy for the quarterback to get the ball to him. In the old Split-T, with the irregular line splits, the quarterback was reaching out a lot of the time...

"Two, in the old Split-T, when the quarterback moved out to option on the defensive end, he had to pitch the ball blind or blind behind him to the trailing halfback. With the Wishbone, the halfbacks are lined up a little deeper and closer to the fullback....the halfback winds up about four yards wider when the quarterback makes his pitch, and the quarterback can see him. It's so much easier."

On the first day of fall practice, five players quit the team, not willing to endure the hard labor of Bryant's practices. "I really think they lost their guts, if they ever had any," Bryant told reporters. "Anyway, I'm glad they quit now rather than wait until they got into a game."

A week before the team traveled to the West Coast for the season opener against USC, thirty-eight sports reporters from the South visited Tuscaloosa on what was known as the SEC Skywriters Tour. Bryant again reminded his players not to say anything about the Wishbone. The coach was so concerned about the secret leaking out that he asked police to closely monitor the perimeter of the practice field and tell him if there were any "spies" from USC. One local reporter from the *Tuscaloosa News* had an inkling that the switch to the Wishbone was coming. When he privately asked Bryant about it, Bryant put his arm around the reporter and said, "I wouldn't ever tell you what to write. But the way I feel, you're either with us or against us."

The reporter never mentioned the word "Wishbone" in any of his preseason stories.

♦   ♦   ♦

A day before Alabama kicked off against USC, Bryant was drawing on a Chesterfield in his Los Angeles hotel room when the phone rang. "You think McKay knows?" asked Darrell Royal, who had become Bryant's unexpected mentor in the off-season.

"Naw," said Bryant. "I don't think he has any idea."

But McKay did in fact have an inclination that Bryant could use the Wishbone—he just had no idea that Bryant, on the eve of his fifty-eighth birthday, would employ it on every offensive snap. In pregame warm-ups Bryant ordered his players to run the old offense, still not wanting to tip his hand. Then it happened: After receiving the opening kickoff, the Tide lined up in the Wishbone and swiftly moved down the field against the confused USC defense. Less than three minutes into the game, Musso scored on a 13-yard touchdown run. By halftime the Tide, an eleven-point underdog, had built a 17–0 lead, mostly because the Trojan defenders didn't know where to line up. Alabama held on to beat USC 17–10 in the biggest upset of Bryant's career.

The Alabama players and coaches returned to Tuscaloosa the day after the game. Reaching their house around midnight, Bryant and his wife Mary Harmon were astonished at what they found in their pool—a twenty-foot float festooned with flowers congratulating Bryant on his two hundredth career victory. In the span of one year, Bryant had integrated his team and reshaped the identity of his team. The Bear was coming back.

• • •

With the Alabama Wishbone confounding opposing defenses—it was astonishing how often defenders tackled runners who didn't have the ball in their hands—the Crimson Tide cruised to the 1971 SEC championship, including a 31–7 victory over Auburn in the first-ever matchup of undefeated teams in the Iron Bowl. The second-ranked Tide went down to No. 1 Nebraska, 38–6, in the Orange Bowl, but after losing ten games in the previous two seasons, it was clear that the Second Act of Bryant's coaching career was starting to bloom like a springtime garden in the South.

"I didn't realize he had gone anywhere," said Bill Battle, a former Bryant player who'd become the head coach of Tennessee, which Alabama defeated 32–15 on October 16 at Legion Field. "Coach Bryant is just back to coaching his kind of game—jaw-to-jaw, hard-nosed football. And now he has the players for it."

CHAPTER 13

The Search for Answers

2015

N ick Saban picked up the phone.

Still reeling from the 42–35 upset of his top-ranked team by Ohio State in the College Football Playoff semifinal game in the Sugar Bowl on January 1, 2015, he called new Houston coach Tom Herman. Just a month earlier he had been the offensive coordinator for the Buckeyes team that had shredded the Alabama defense, and now Saban had a favor to ask: Could he send some of his Crimson Tide offensive staff members to the Cougars campus to learn how to implement elements of the spread offense that Herman was installing in Houston? Herman said he would be happy to open up his playbook.

Lane Kiffin and a few other Alabama coaches flew to Houston. Herman explained how certain motions in a spread offense—most notably, the "jet" motion—confused undisciplined defenders, tricking them into reading the wrong key and miss-ing their assignment. Kiffin particularly wanted to learn how to run a no-huddle spread offense without having to sacrifice a bruising run game. Saban and Kiffin knew their offense in 2015 would be centered around running back Derrick Henry, yet Alabama also wanted to keep using the spread that had been so successful a year earlier during Kiffin's first season as offensive coordinator.

After spring practice ended, Saban invited Herman and his offensive staff to Tuscaloosa for another skull session. Saban was still dissecting how his defense surrendered six touchdowns to Ohio State in the Sugar Bowl—the most TDs an opposing team had ever scored on a Saban defense since he'd been at Alabama. Saban wanted to know what his team needed to do better when playing against spread offenses. The Tide had already started changing the standards of height and weight at each position in their recruiting but, according to one former Alabama coach, the meeting with the Houston staff was critical because Cougar coaches repeatedly emphasized one major theme: The Bama defense needed to be much faster, especially at the safety position.

"Our defense got exposed against Ohio State because we just weren't fast enough at certain positions," said the coach. "Our corners weren't fast enough to keep up with their receivers and our safeties weren't fast enough. Ohio State ran vertical routes all night and beat us over the top. They got us on our heels and that opened up the running game for Ezekiel Elliott. What they did to us wasn't a fluke and Nick knew it."

Saban and Herman met one-on-one for thirty minutes in Saban's office. Saban peppered Herman with questions: How fast do you practice? How do you create a fast-paced spread with a powerful running game? How do you defend against the spread? What type of safety is best against the spread? Do you mix man and zone coverage when going against the spread? Herman realized when he walked out of the meeting that he hadn't asked Saban a single question. He had seen a side of Saban that was rarely revealed in public: A coach searching for answers.

Before the start of the 2015 season, Saban made changes to both his defense and offense. He needed slimmer, faster players in the defensive line, linebackers who could cover tight ends running down the middle of the field, and safeties who could cover like cornerbacks. In preseason camp Saban moved cornerback Eddie Jackson, who had been repeatedly beaten in the Ohio State game, to safety. This meant when Alabama played nickel or dime packages on defense to counter spread offenses, all five or six defensive backs were former cornerbacks. No player in the secondary weighed more than two hundred pounds, a dramatic departure from earlier seasons.

Alabama's recruiting changed as well. A high school safety who weighed 215 pounds was turned into a linebacker in Tuscaloosa; a linebacker who tipped the scales at 220 would be transformed into a defensive end. The alterations in the height-weight standard at each position were made with one goal in mind: to be faster on all three levels of the defense.

An end at Alabama from 1933 to '35, Bryant helped the Crimson Tide win the 1934 national championship. Bryant often described himself as the "other end" on the team—the one who played opposite future NFL Hall of Famer Don Hutson. *Courtesy of the Paul W. Bryant Museum*

In the early 1960s, as Bryant was building his empire in Tuscaloosa, the 6'4" coach with wide shoulders and a quick temper always commanded the attention of his players. Country-strong even then, he demonstrated different drills and techniques and—every so often—would toss a player to the ground as if he were nothing more than a water boy. *Courtesy of the Paul W. Bryant Museum*

This is the enduring image of Paul W. Bryant: leaning against a goalpost, watching his boys go through their pregame routine. On January 1, 1972, Bryant cut the familiar pose before Alabama faced Nebraska in the Orange Bowl in Miami. *Courtesy of the Paul W. Bryant Museum*

The legendary 33-step tower was Bryant's perch in the sky, the place where he typically watched practice. Armed with a bullhorn, he could bring the action below him to an immediate stop when he shouted down from his metallic mountaintop in his thick Southern drawl. *Courtesy of the Paul W. Bryant Museum*

At age 68, the Bear prowled the sideline with his customary intensity during the 1981 Iron Bowl, played at Legion Field in Birmingham. After falling behind early, Alabama defeated Auburn 28–17, delivering Bryant his historic 315th victory. "Did you hear?" a popular joke began in Alabama. "The Bear got hurt this morning. He was out walking his duck and a motorboat ran over him." *Courtesy of the Paul W. Bryant Museum*

Minutes after Bryant became the winningest coach in college football history by capturing his 315th career victory, he received a phone call from President Ronald Reagan. The smile on Bryant's face was more out of relief than joy—the journey to topping Amos Alonzo Stagg's mark took a hard toll on the Bear. *Courtesy of the Paul W. Bryant Museum*

Bryant earned his last victory ride when the final whistle blew on his brilliant career. Players hoisted Bryant onto their shoulders after Alabama defeated Illinois 21–15 in the Liberty Bowl on December 29, 1982. Twenty-eight days later, the Bear would be gone. *Courtesy of the Paul W. Bryant Museum*

The Saban dynasty began on January 7, 2010, with a 37–21 victory over Texas in the Rose Bowl—Saban's first national title at Alabama. A month earlier Mark Ingram (right of Saban) had become the first Heisman Trophy winner in school history. *Courtesy of Getty Images*

Saban led his players through a crush of fans lined along the Walk of Champions outside Bryant-Denny Stadium before facing Auburn on November 29, 2008. Alabama's 36–0 victory in this Iron Bowl ended a six-game losing streak to their in-state rival and signaled a shift in the balance of football power in the South. *Courtesy of Getty Images*

Like Bryant, Saban is continually evolving and adapting. He hired offensive coordinator Lane Kiffin (left of Saban) in January 2014 to do one thing: transform his offense from smash-mouth to spread. The radical makeover, which many pundits questioned at the time, led to multiple national titles. *Courtesy of Getty Images*

The maternal figure over the entire Alabama program, Terry Saban—aka Miss Terry—has been by her husband's side since their first high school date, when Saban took his future wife to see *Gone With the Wind*. Here they share a light moment before the 2017 Iron Bowl. *Courtesy of Getty Images*

The fundamental success of college football's top coach of the twenty-first century can be distilled into two words: hard work. Here he is at his office desk in April 2018. *Courtesy of Getty Images*

A former high school quarterback, Saban can still throw a beautiful spiral, as he displayed during the spring of 2018. Unlike Bryant late in his career, who preferred to watch practice from his tower, Saban is always on the practice field with his players, interacting, critiquing, and coaching—always coaching. *Courtesy of Getty Images*

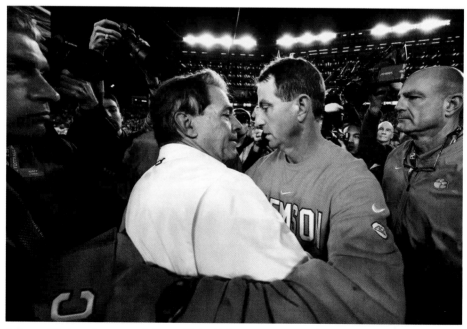

After suffering the worst defeat of his Alabama career—a loss to Clemson, 44–16, on January 7, 2019, in the national title game—Saban embraced Tigers coach Dabo Swinney at midfield. "See you next year," Swinney told Saban. Days later, Saban overhauled his coaching staff with one goal in mind: winning a record seventh national title in the 2019 season. *Courtesy of Getty Images*

Kiffin employed the up-tempo spread offense early in the 2015 season in victories over Wisconsin and Middle Tennessee. Saban played two quarterbacks, Cooper Bateman and Jake Coker, and he was hoping that one would emerge and "win over the team." But as the third game of the season against Ole Miss approached, neither player had seized the starting job. Practice reps were split between Bateman and Coker, which had a negative effect on the offense. Bateman was a runner in the mold of Blake Sims; the six-five, 230-pound Coker was more like a traditional drop-back passer. The lack of an anointed No. 1 QB hurt the offense—its identity changed depending on who was behind center.

The problems came to a head against Ole Miss in a night game at Bryant-Denny. Alabama fumbled the opening kickoff, committed five total turnovers, and lost, 43–37. But Coker showed he could be a running threat in Kiffin's offense—he rushed for 59 yards on 7 carries—and the two-quarterback experiment was over. With talk swirling in the media that the Alabama dynasty was dead, Saban named Coker the starter the following week against Louisiana-Monroe.

Saban was most concerned about the five total interceptions the two quarterbacks had thrown in the early part of the season. "Everybody is telling them to take what the defense gives, go the check down if it's not open," Saban said. "The most important thing is the ball, the ball, the ball. If every offensive possession ends in a kick—a punt, a field goal, or an extra point—I'm good with that. So you tell me what part of that is going to make you force the ball?"

On the Thursday before the Louisiana-Monroe game, Saban walked into Baumhower's restaurant in Tuscaloosa for his weekly live radio show in front of a crowd. Saban is normally relaxed during the show, shaking hands and signing autographs during commercial breaks or chatting with Miss Terry, who always attends and sits close to the stage. On this night a caller named Joe from Hartselle, Alabama, asked Saban why he had abandoned "old-school smashmouth Alabama football." At first Saban said, "I like that kind of ball." But then he turned into something of a football professor, explaining how the rest of the SEC West had changed in recent years. He noted that the teams were faster and Alabama could no longer beat its opponents by running the ball between the tackles and occasionally throwing the deep play-action pass. He said that Alabama needed to embrace the same offensive principles of Auburn, Ole Miss, and Texas A&M—teams that used hurry-up spread attacks and exploited the perimeter of the field. "If you don't do some of that," Saban said, "you're not taking advantage of the rules."

Saban promised that Alabama wouldn't stop running the ball. In fact, after the loss to Ole Miss, the Saban-Kiffin brain trust made running back Derrick Henry the lifeblood of the offense, which would open up play-action deep passes to receivers Calvin Ridley and ArDarius Stewart. Kiffin also utilized quick throws to the receivers when one of them was isolated one-on-one with a safety. Virtually everything Kiffin had learned from the Houston coaches during the off-season was incorporated into the playbook.

A turning point for Coker came against Texas A&M on October 17. Facing a third-and-six, Coker delivered a vicious forearm shiver to defender Nick Harvey at the end of a lumbering sixteen-yard run. The Alabama sideline erupted at the sight of the hit. "Anytime he does that, that gets guys on the team hyped up," said linebacker Reggie Ragland. "The guys in the locker room love it."

Added Saban, "It's the personality of the player. Jake's a tough, competitive guy. He's a big, physical guy. He's getting better and better every week. I don't want to take his aggressiveness away because we're fearful something bad is going to happen. I just don't coach that way."

In the SEC championship game against Florida, the Tide trailed 7–2 in the second quarter when Kiffin and Saban made an adjustment that would alter the game. The Gators didn't consider Coker a credible running threat, so the Florida defensive ends were penetrating up the field and zeroing in on Henry. On the sideline the coaches told Coker to call a run-pass option play and they wanted him to keep the ball and run—something Coker hadn't done all season on an RPO. On the play Coker gained seventeen yards, changing the complexion of the game. Now viewing the Alabama quarterback as a threat to keep the ball and run, the Florida defensive ends stopped crashing into the backfield. Henry rushed for 189 yards on 44 carries and the Tide won the game, 29–15.

Saban was especially pleased after the game. The season had been a grind—he knew this wasn't his most talented team—and he sounded like a proud father when he said, "They wanted to do something special. And probably more than any other time I've ever coached, I wanted to see these guys succeed."

After beating Michigan State, 38–0, in the national semifinal—the Spartan safeties consistently cheated up toward the line of scrimmage, and Kiffin responded by having Coker throw deep balls (he completed 25 of 30 for 286 yards and 2 touchdowns)—Alabama faced Clemson for the national championship in Glendale, Arizona. On the morning of the game Saban met with kicker Adam Griffith in a conference room at the team hotel. In his dozens of hours of film study during the week, Saban had noticed that when Clemson expected a kickoff to be directed deep and to one corner of the field, the entire Tiger return unit shifted to that side of the field. Saban explained to Griffith that if he saw Clemson line up like this early in the game that it could create the opportunity for a pop onside kick late.

On the first four Alabama kickoffs, the Tigers lined up the way Saban wanted—all shifted to the right side of the field, leaving about twelve yards of open space on the opposite side. But each time Saban opted against trying the onside kick. Like a gambler holding a royal flush, Saban didn't want to show his hand until he absolutely had to. Then the moment of the game—and the season—arrived.

They were tied at 24 in the fourth quarter, and as his defense struggled to contain Clemson quarterback Deshaun Watson, Saban believed the time was right. Normally risk averse, Saban made a gutsy call—even though the target of the play, cornerback Marlon Humphrey, had dropped the ball in the team's walk-through practice before the game and even though surprise onside kicks in college football, according to various analytics, are successful only about 40 percent of the time. "Desperate times call for desperate measures," said center Ryan Kelly.

Griffith approached the tee slower than normal, but that didn't alert any of the Clemson players. He pooched the ball toward the right sideline in a perfect arc. With no Tiger defender within three yards of him, Humphrey caught the ball in stride at the 50-yard line. The successful trick prompted a blue-moon-rare, I-got-you grin from Saban on the sideline as Clemson coach Dabo Swinney screamed at the referees, even though nothing about the play was illegal. It was as if Swinney realized that he had been hoodwinked. Two plays later Coker connected with tight end O. J. Howard down the left sideline for a 51-yard touchdown. Alabama ended the night with 16 possessions; the Tigers had 15. The onside kick was the key play in Alabama's 45–40 win.

The victory delivered Saban his fifth national championship. He now trailed Bear Bryant by one. Saban was asked about Bryant after the game, but he didn't want to talk about history or his chasing of the Bear. Slowly walking toward the team bus ninety minutes after the game, Saban shook hands with dozens of still-cheering fans, prolonging the night, clearly relishing the outcome of the game and the long season past. Of all his national championships, this one was different. Title number five was won because of one play that was rooted in one thing:

Nick Saban's obsessive film study.

CHAPTER 14

The Gut Check

1972 TO 1979

They met when he was the new coach at Alabama. Bear Bryant enjoyed socializing and drinking at the Tuscaloosa Country Club, and soon after he was named the Tide's coach in 1958 he was introduced to a bartender at the club named Billy Varner, a young African-American man. The coach loved to talk with Billy— especially after downing a round or two of Jack Daniels and Coke doubles—and the two became friends.

A few years later Varner became a bartender at Indian Hills Country Club. Bryant, who lived on the third fairway, sometimes spent his off-season afternoons playing cards and cutting up—and drinking—with his buddies. Varner served Bryant and his entourage, and the coach and the bartender grew closer. Because of his own rise from poverty, Bryant could relate to African-Americans and many of their struggles. He so enjoyed the company of Varner he made him his personal aide. For the rest of Bryant's life, Varner was never far from the coach's shadow.

Varner had a front row seat for Bryant's second run of glory years at Alabama—national titles in 1973, 1978, and 1979. The man under the houndstooth fedora rose to mythical proportions, even in the eyes of some reporters. He sometimes drank too much in social settings, but those occasions never appeared in the light of print because in those times journalists didn't write about the frailties of iconic sports figures, especially about a hero's tendency to overindulge in Alabama, where more than half the counties didn't allow the sale of booze and where many considered drinking a sin. Some of Bryant's friends said that he drank to escape, to get away from the burden of being the Bear. But that was seen only by his inner circle. When one of his assistant coaches told Bryant in June 1970 that former Green Bay Packers coach Vince Lombardi had died of colon cancer at age fifty-six, Bryant spoke of the regrets in his life—namely, that he didn't spend more time with his family.

Bryant tried to change that. After the Tide beat Florida, 38–0, in Gainesville in September 1971, the team drove in buses to the airport. Their plane was delayed, and Bryant could tell that his boys were anxious to return to Tuscaloosa. Bryant told them, "When we get back, if you don't have anything better to do, bring your wives or your dates and come over to our house. We got a new pool with AstroTurf all around, and Mary Harmon will cook up something."

Bryant didn't believe more than a handful of players would take him up on his offer. But then, as Bryant sat in his living room with a drink in his hand and listening to a college football game on the radio, nearly half of the team arrived. At first, the players and their significant others lounged around the pool in the warm fall night. Then one player walked inside and sat on the floor close to his coach. Then another. And another. Soon, every player in attendance was in the room with Bryant, sitting close to the Bear—their father figure.

Later in his life, Bryant would close his eyes and recall this particular night in vivid, microscopic detail—the closeness of it, the warmth of it, the joy of it.

🏈   🏈   🏈

In the days leading up to Alabama's final game of the 1973 season—a showdown with Notre Dame in the Sugar Bowl—Bryant admitted that he was now taking three sleeping pills a night. The stress of the job rarely left him. The UPI already had named the Tide national champions after Alabama finished the regular season 11–0 and was ranked No. 1 in the country—the UPI began crowning its champion after the bowl season in 1974—but Bryant was still a hornet's nest of nerves before what he called "the biggest game in the South's history."

Bryant rarely ventured into the French Quarter during Alabama's prep time in New Orleans, preferring instead to remain in his suite in the Fontainebleau. His Wishbone attack had been wildly successful during the 1973 season—Alabama outscored its regular season opponents 431 to 65—and Bryant had twelve players rush for at least 115 yards. Against LSU on November 22, Bryant shuttled in more than seventy players during the 21–7 victory. After the game Tigers coach Charley McClendon marveled at the size of Bryant's offensive line. Sipping a beer in the locker room, McClendon said, "Dagburn it! The program says that 'Bama center is 223 pounds. Why, his one damn leg weighs 223 pounds. It just doesn't seem proper that 'Bama gets all those good folks who like to play. But I'll tell you something, the best one of 'em all is old Bear himself."

Facing Notre Dame at the old Tulane Stadium, Bryant leaned against the goalpost during pregame warm-ups, his houndstooth hat on, inspecting his players. He had said before kickoff that this was a game that fans had been looking forward to for years, and the contest lived up to the hype: It was jawbone-to-jawbone football at its finest. Notre Dame prevailed 24–23. Minutes after the final whistle, as Bryant was leaving the field, he saw a sign taped up on the west side lower deck of the rusting stadium that read: "God Made Notre Dame No. 1."

Years later, another Alabama coach would atone for this crushing loss to the Fighting Irish in a national championship game.

In 1974, at age sixty-one, Bryant coauthored a book with *Sports Illustrated*'s John Underwood. In the penultimate chapter, Bryant wrote, "I'm more fired up than I was twenty years ago. I have been fortunate, I've had honors. But if I couldn't stay in it I'd probably croak in a week. I don't have as much fun as I used to because I'm not as close to the kids, not coaching as much...I don't work as hard. I'm not as tied up. I don't bleed inside like I used to. I take more time to enjoy it, and I get a lot of that attention I craved so much as a kid."

Underwood—*SI*'s top college football writer—and Bryant had

grown uniquely close. In the mid-1960s the two had collaborated on a series of stories for *SI*, written in Bryant's voice, and Bryant had come to trust Underwood. They eventually agreed to write a book together, but it took several years to complete due to Bryant's busy schedule. Underwood seized on any chance he got to spend to time with the Bear—on a vacation with the Bryants to the Florida Keys, at the Bryant's home-away-from-home on Lake Martin in central Alabama—but Underwood's most memorable experience with Bryant took place in Las Vegas. Bryant liked to lose himself in the thrill of possibility, especially in games of chance.

During one trip to Sin City in the early '70s, Underwood stood next to Bryant inside a casino at a craps table. Bryant, enjoying the complimentary drinks, was winning big. Then suddenly there was a ruckus: Bryant, with one hand, grabbed a man standing to his left, lifted him up, and slammed his face onto the table, directly into a pile of chips. Underwood then noticed that in the right hand of the man who had just been face-planted was Bryant's wallet. He had tried to pickpocket Bryant.

The next day Underwood traveled with Bryant to Malibu, California, for a speech that Bryant was slated to deliver at Pepperdine University. Underwood was concerned: The coach looked especially worn out from the previous night and pale. But Bryant walked onto the stage and, invigorated by the crowd, began to captivate the audience with his words and stories. Then, near the end of the speech, Bryant's voice suddenly dropped a few octaves. Then he said, "I don't know how to say this, but is there a doctor in the house?"

The coach slumped to the floor. Underwood rode with Bryant in the ambulance. Bryant handed the writer his wallet and said, "John, take care of this." Inspecting its contents, Underwood discovered it bulging with $100 bills—his winnings from the craps table. It was reported in newspapers the next day that Bryant had experienced a heart attack; in reality, he was suffering from a bout of extreme exhaustion. Underwood later told reporters that Bryant's problem wasn't that he drank too much; it was that he drank too fast, given how many hours he logged at the office.

But Underwood always marveled at Bryant's ability to enjoy himself. After the 1974 season, Bryant and Underwood were scheduled to meet in New York the night before a Hall of Fame banquet. Underwood's flight was delayed, and by the time he reached his hotel he figured Bryant had already called it a night—even though the coach had left a message for Underwood at the front desk to meet him at Patsy's restaurant. Underwood was in bed when the phone rang.

"Where the hell are you?" Bryant asked.

"It's raining. It's cold. I'm in bed," Underwood said.

"Frank Sinatra is at my table," Bryant replied. "You better get on over here."

"Yeah, sure," said Underwood, believing Bryant was joking. "I wouldn't want to miss Old Blue Eyes. Is Bing with him?"

"OK, dammit," said Bryant. "Hold on."

Bryant handed the phone to another person. Underwood immediately recognized the silky voice. "Hello John? This is Francis Albert Sinatra. The Bear says for you to get your ass over here."

Throughout the mid-1970s, Bryant delegated more and more responsibilities to his assistants, allowing them more latitude to coach the players during practice. Bryant still put in grueling days—he often worked eighteen hours at the office—but he turned his attention more to game planning, making personnel decisions on who played and who didn't, and to putting out the brush fires that always accompanied overseeing a college football team. He watched practices more from his tower, but he still could put the fear of God in his assistants and players if they heard him coming down those snaking metal steps and yelling that something wasn't to his liking.

Bryant assigned most of the off-season recruiting duties to his assistants. So instead of crisscrossing the South in search of high school talent, he did the one thing with his grandchildren that he didn't do with his own children: He spent time with them. Bryant enjoyed taking them fishing on Lake Martin. As he'd done as a kid growing up in Arkansas, Bryant used a cane pole with a cricket on a hook. His grandchildren thought Bryant was the most doting grandfather in Alabama; they had no idea that he'd been gone for most of his own children's childhoods.

But he tried to make up for that. In the spring of 1977 he took one of his grandkids, Marc Tyson, on a trip to see the Yankees in New York, the Red Sox at Fenway Stadium, and the Reds in Cincinnati. Before each game, Bryant introduced the wide-eyed Marc to all the top players in the clubhouses. In Cincinnati, Pete Rose gushed on and on about having the chance to meet the great Bear Bryant.

On the field Alabama had become a ruthless power. From 1974 to 1977, the Tide went 42-6, winning three SEC titles over that span. Players around the nation wanted to come to Tuscaloosa to play for the legend, even if Bryant spent more time coaching his coaches rather than the players. Bryant's rosters of the mid-1970s were no longer filled with smaller, tough-minded overachieving players. No, now his teams were loaded with more blue-chippers than any college football team in America.

◉   ◉   ◉

On the morning before the Sugar Bowl, on January 1, 1979, Bryant had his breakfast delivered to him in his suite on the top floor of a high-rise hotel that overlooked the Crescent City: an egg-and-bacon sandwich and coffee in a polystyrene cup. Bryant was thirty-six hours away from playing for his fifth national title against undefeated and top-ranked Penn State. The Tide's only loss of the season had been to USC (24–14) in late September, and now the team was 10-1 and ranked second in the nation.

As usual before games, Bryant worried in his hotel suite—specifically about his defense. He told a reporter that the defense had played very well at times but also had struggled at various points in the season, and that this kind of inconsistency was "not recommended" when going against a team with the offensive talent of Penn State, which had won nineteen straight games.

With less than seven minutes left in the '79 Sugar Bowl, Penn State had the ball first-and-goal at Alabama's 8-yard line, trailing 14–7. On first down, Nittany Lion running back Mike Guman gained two yards. On second down, Penn State quarterback Chuck Fusina completed a pass to tight end Scott Fitzkee, who was pushed out-of-bounds by cornerback Don McNeal at the one. Before third down, Alabama linebacker Barry Krauss, the defense's captain, called the defensive play: Double-X Pinch. This sent every defender crashing into the middle to stop a run up the gut. The risky call paid off: From his linebacker spot, Rich Wingo stopped fullback Matt Suhey just short of the goal line.

Penn State then called a time-out. On the Alabama sideline, defensive coordinator Ken Donahue again called Pinch. Across the field, Penn State coach Joe Paterno wanted Fusina to fake a run and then pass the ball to his tight end in the end zone. But his assistants persuaded him to send Guman up the middle again.

In the Tide huddle, the players told each other, "This is Alabama football. This is all about what Coach Bryant has taught us." Murray Legg yelled, "Gut check! Gut check."

As Fusina walked to the line, defensive tackle Marty Lyons shouted at him above the din of the crowd: "You'd better pass!" The ball was snapped, and Fusina handed to Guman. Lyons penetrated into the backfield, collapsing the line, and Wingo smashed into Suhey, the lead blocker. When Guman attempted to leap over the pile, Krauss met him face mask to face mask, driving him backward with a hit so violent it left Krauss momentarily paralyzed. Legg, streaking in from his safety spot, then pushed Guman backward and onto the ground, six inches short of the goal line. The Tide held and won 14–7, delivering Bryant his fifth national championship.

At the precise moment that Krauss and Guman collided, *SI* photographer Walter Iooss Jr. snapped an iconic shot that would make the cover of that week's issue, a picture whose spirit and upward thrust of angles faintly echoed the famous photo of the flag-raising at Iwo Jima. So powerful was the image that Daniel Moore, then a twenty-five-year-old graphic designer in Birmingham, made a painting of the scene. It's no stretch to say that to this day *Goal Line Stand* is the most popular piece of artwork in Alabama; prints of it hang in countless dens, offices, restaurants, and bars throughout the state.

"That painting hit home because that single image symbolized Bear Bryant's philosophy," said Moore. "It was gut-check time for the players, and they made a stand."

The play, which lasted less than three seconds from snap to whistle, has had a lasting influence on the lives of the key participants. For Krauss, who played eleven years in the NFL, it earned him a reputation for performing in the clutch. "That play got my life going in the right direction," he said. "I've got that Daniel Moore painting in my den, and when I look at it I'm reminded that when our moment arrived, we made the most of it."

The play followed Krauss for four decades, shadowing him everywhere he went, reminding him of the defining hour of his youth. At least once a week in a restaurant or grocery store or movie theater, a stranger would approach Krauss and ask him about that New Year's night in 1979 when he made the biggest tackle of the Bear Bryant era at Alabama. "People always tell me where they were when we made the goal line stand," said Krauss. "My favorite is the guy whose mother was in labor with him during those four plays. He told me he's felt a special connection to me ever since, that he was always Barry Krauss when he played in backyard football games."

For Wingo and Legg, who each have spent time working in real estate in Birmingham, the play has morphed into parable. "I ask my kids, 'Will you be ready when your opportunity comes?'" said Legg. "Every time I see that painting, that's what I'm reminded of."

Said Wingo, who spent five seasons in the NFL with the Packers, "I use that play as a teaching tool all the time."

For Lyons, who played eleven seasons with the Jets, the play represented trust and friendship. "Football is a team game," said Lyons. "Penn State would have scored if every guy on our defense didn't do his job. And all these years later I'm still in frequent touch with guys from that team. That play made us as close as brothers."

And what about Guman, the running back who came up inches short? After spending nine years in the NFL with the Rams, he settled in Allentown, Pennsylvania, where he and his wife raised five children. For three decades he received copies of *SI* with that fourth-down photo on the cover. "It's mostly Alabama fans who want me to sign it and send it back," said Guman. "I'm happy to do it, because that play helped mold me into who I am today. You've got to get up when you get down. I've learned that you can overcome defeat."

Guman has evidence to back up that assertion. His five children won a combined ten high school state championships in basketball and volleyball, each title making their father's memory of the stand a little less painful. Guman believed it was cosmic justice. "I came up short," Guman said, "but my kids haven't. And you know what? It's worked out just fine."

For Joe Paterno, the loss would haunt him for years. He allowed his assistants to overrule his desire to throw a pass on the fourth-down play. Bryant always trusted his instincts; at his moment of reckoning, Paterno didn't—and paid for it.

Bryant had considered quitting coaching after the 1977 season, but then Charley Thornton found something in the NCAA record book and relayed it to him. Thornton, Bryant's publicity director, discovered that the winningest coach in college football history was Amos Alonzo Stagg, whose career began in 1890. Stagg spent fifty-seven years coaching at Springfield, Chicago, and Pacific, and amassed a record of 314-199-35.

The Number, as it become known, ballooned into a big topic during the 1979 season. After beating Penn State, Bryant was only thirty-one wins short of tying Stagg. Alabama opened the season with a 30–6 victory over Georgia Tech—thirty wins short. On the day before the next game, against Baylor, played at Legion Field, Bryant and the Alabama team stayed at the Holiday Inn in Bessemer, Alabama. That night one of Bryant's former players, Gaylon McCollough, knocked on the door of Bryant's hotel suite.

Bryant ushered McCollough, who was now a plastic surgeon in Birmingham, into his suite. Bryant had pulled the desk into the middle of the room, and McCollough noticed three yellow legal pads sitting under the circle of lamplight. The two talked for a few minutes until finally McCollough asked, "Coach, I can't stand it. Why three legal pads?"

"Shit, I've never told anyone this before," Bryant said. "The first legal pad is what I'm going to say if we lose the game. The middle one is what I'm going to say if we tie the game. And the one on the right is what I'm going to say if we win."

McCollough was flabbergasted: He always thought that Bryant's postgame speeches to his players were extemporaneous, spur-of-the-moment oratories. But now he knew why Bryant's words had always flown so seamlessly from his lips—his speeches had been prepared and rehearsed. McCollough learned a lesson that day from his coach: It's always easier to face a situation in life if you've already considered all the possible outcomes.

The next afternoon at Legion Field, in front of 77,512 fans, Alabama beat Baylor 45–0 in the first ever matchup between the schools—twenty-nine wins short of Stagg. Entering the regular season finale against Auburn, the Tide was 10-0 and ranked No. 1 in the country. Bryant was only twenty-one wins away from Stagg.

Before the Iron Bowl, Bryant told a reporter that "I'da as soon go back to plowin' than go to a bowl game if we lose to Auburn." This incensed Auburn fans, interpreting it as a swipe at the school's agricultural heritage. When Bryant walked onto Legion Field before the game, Tiger fans chanted, "Plow, Bear, Plow." Displaying his sense of humor at age sixty-six, Bryant instructed Charley Thornton to put his hands up high behind his back and then Bryant, with a grin, grabbed his wrists and pretended to steer him as if behind a plow.

Despite fumbling five times, the Tide defeated its archrival, 25–18. A month later Alabama faced Arkansas in the Cotton Bowl on January 1, 1980. The cameras caught Bryant walking along the sideline before the game. He looked older than his sixty-six years—his face was sun-baked, crinkly, and leathery—and his gait was slow. Many coaches across the country asked themselves how this old-looking man could preside over the top program in the nation, how he could be so good after thirty-five years of coaching.

Arkansas players and coaches didn't ask—they knew after Alabama drilled the Razorbacks, 24–9, the Tide's twenty-first straight victory. Bryant captured his sixth national title. "The only feeling better than playing for the national title in New Orleans on January 1," said defensive lineman Byron Braggs after the game, "is being in Tuscaloosa on January 2 to celebrate winning it." And celebrate they did: Bryant gathered with friends and family in his home to toast what would be his final national championship.

Now he was eighteen wins short of tying Stagg's record.

CHAPTER 15

Tying the Bear

2016 TO 2018

He jogged around the practice field with a sense of urgency, the sixty-six-year-old coach who showed no signs of slowing down. On this raw, late December afternoon in 2017 the former defensive back at Kent State oversaw his cornerbacks run through agility drills. Then the one-time high school quarterback began rifling passes at his defensive backs, imploring them to make the interception. He spent most of his time during this practice with his DBs, but Saban also moved from position group to position group, critiquing technique, imploring every player to maintain intensity, focus, and resolve. This wasn't Bear Bryant sitting on a folding chair and watching practice from atop his tower late in his coaching career—thirty-eight years earlier, Bryant had won his final national championship, in '79, at exactly Saban's age now. No, this was Saban in his final hours of Crimson Tide practices before facing the Georgia Bulldogs in Atlanta for the 2017 national championship.

A few days later, on the evening of January 8, 2018, at Mercedes-Benz Stadium, Saban had a decision to make. Up to now, his starting quarterback, Jalen Hurts, was 25-2 as a starter. He was the reigning Offensive Player of the Year in the SEC and had guided Alabama to the playoffs in back-to-back seasons. But now Hurts was struggling in the national title game against Georgia. In the first half he had completed only 3 of 8 passes for 21 yards. The Tide trailed 13–0 at halftime.

In the locker room Saban gathered his quarterbacks. He had a history of taking gambles in national championship matchups—the risky, late-game onside kick against Clemson had propelled Alabama to the '15 title—and now Saban told his quarterbacks he was going to make another bold move. In a matter-of-fact voice he said, "Tua, you're going to start the second half, and we'll see how it goes from there. We'll rotate if we need to." That declaration put Hurts on the bench in favor of true freshman Tua Tagovailoa, who had only played sparingly in blowouts during the season.

After making the pronouncement, Saban turned and led his team back onto the field for the second half. The coach wasn't overly concerned about making the switch; he knew exactly what Tagovailoa was capable of—and he also knew that Georgia coach Kirby Smart hadn't game-planned to stop the season-long backup who for months had been the talk of the Mal Moore Athletic Facility.

In the winter of 2014 Saban had dispatched Lane Kiffin to Hawaii to check out young Tagovailoa. After watching the left-hander throw in drills at a passing camp—Kiffin swore he didn't have one off-the-mark pass in about fifty attempts—Kiffin fired off an email to Saban back in Tuscaloosa: "This kid is Steve Young."

Sitting in his office, Saban studied hours of high school tape on Tagovailoa. His throwing accuracy was unlike anything Saban had seen in the last decade. Tagovailoa had a unique ability to feel and elude the rush, with Saban describing the skill as "athletic intuition." Saban then phoned the family in Hawaii and offered a scholarship. Tagovailoa's mother, Diane, took the call while driving a car; she had to pull to the side of the road, overcome with emotion.

The entire Tagovailoa family—father, mother, brother, and two sisters—traveled four thousand miles to Alabama and moved into a house in Alabaster, sixty miles from Tuscaloosa. As soon as Tagovailoa stepped on campus, he wowed coaches and teammates with his throwing ability. Hurts had led Alabama to the 2015 national title game—a 35–31 loss to Clemson—but several coaches implored Saban to give Tagovailoa more playing time as the '17 season unfolded. "The whole building knew that Tua should be the starter," said one coach. "Sometimes Coach Saban is reluctant to make a big change. That's not who he is."

But Saban was forced to finally insert Tagovailoa in the national title game, because of Hurts's ineffectiveness. Saban also put in several fellow freshmen with whom Tagovailoa had repeatedly run plays during practice and was comfortable with—running back Najee Harris and wide receivers DeVonta Smith, Jerry Jeudy, and Henry Ruggs III.

Tying the Bear

In the third quarter Tagovailoa's inexperience was revealed: He threw an interception on a play that everyone else on the offense believed was a run call. He jogged to the sideline, threw an arm around Saban, and said, "It's going to be OK, Coach." Saban scowled, shaking his head in frustration.

And it *was* OK. Tagovailoa led a furious comeback. Tied at 20, the game went to overtime. After a Georgia field goal on the Bulldogs' opening possession, the Tide had the ball on its own 25-yard line, first-and-ten. Tagovailoa dropped back to pass. With a Georgia defender approaching, Tagovailoa retreated, trying to escape. But he took a sixteen-yard sack. On the sideline Saban stomped and grimaced. Tagovailoa, unfazed at the prospect of second-and-twenty-six, then dropped back again. After looking to the right side of the field, he lofted a high-arcing rainbow of a pass deep down the left side. The ball fell into the arms of DeVonta Smith, hitting him in stride for the forty-one-yard touchdown pass—the longest touchdown throw during an overtime football game in college history.

As the confetti fell, Tagovailoa huddled with his family in a stadium corner, his eyes welling with tears. Jalen Hurts smiled and congratulated his replacement. In the locker room Saban approached his young quarterback, telling him in harsh language that he should not have ever—*ever!*—taken that sack on first down in overtime. Tua joked that he needed more room to make the throw. "That shit ain't funny," Saban barked, still coaching moments after he'd won his sixth national title, tying him with Bear Bryant for the most ever won by one coach.

That night in the team hotel Tagovailoa gathered with his family, savoring the moment, reliving the final play, sitting in a circle and praying together. Close by in another room Jalen Hurts huddled with his family, hugging his mother and father, crying together, wondering if now was the time to transfer to another school.

🏈　　🏈　　🏈

The 2018 college football off-season was dominated by one question: Would Jalen Hurts stay or go?

In April his father, Averion Hurts, who coaches high school football at Channelview High outside Houston, told *Bleacher Report*, "[Jalen] would be the biggest free agent in college football history." In August at Alabama's media day Hurts said, "No one came up to me the whole spring, coaches included, no one asked me how I felt. No one asked me what was on my mind. Nobody asked me what my future held."

Saban had a delicate, gossamer-like situation to manage. In September he announced that Tagovailoa would start and Hurts would be the backup. A new redshirt rule allowed Hurts to play in four games and still transfer at season's end while not burning a year of eligibility. Saban consistently met with both quarterbacks, telling them the team would ultimately need the skills and wills of both to defend the national championship. And at press conferences he referred to Hurts as being "like a son" to him and he grew testy with any reporter who questioned whether or not Hurts would leave the program.

The coaches stressed to Hurts, according to another Alabama player, that his time would come. "From the day he didn't start," said running back Josh Jacobs, "he always said there would be a time when he had to make a play."

Tying the Bear

That moment arrived in the 2018 SEC title game—back in Atlanta, back against the team that had sent him to the bench in the national championship game eleven months earlier. When Tagovailoa went down with an ankle injury early in the fourth quarter against Georgia, Saban summoned Hurts from the bench. Alabama was trailing 28–21. With the ball on his own 29-yard line and facing third-and-twelve, Hurts hit tight end Irv Smith for a thirteen-yard gain. The throw illustrated how much Hurts had improved since the previous time he was in that stadium: Now he stood tall in the pocket, kept his eyes glued downfield, and threw with exquisite anticipation and accuracy to Smith. Minutes later, on a third-and-five play, he delivered a twenty-three-yard bullet to freshman Jaylen Waddle. And then he unleashed a perfect strike to Jerry Jeudy in the right corner of the end zone for a touchdown— the kind of pass he never could have thrown a year earlier.

After a failed fake punt by Georgia, Hurts led the team back out onto the field again. With time running out in the fourth quarter, Hurts completed two passes for thirty-five yards and then took off on a ten-yard touchdown run. On the sideline Saban smiled like a proud father and hugged his backup quarterback when he reached the sideline. After the 35–28 win, Saban put his arm up and around Hurts's shoulders and said to an ESPN reporter, "I've probably never been more proud of a player than Jalen. It's unprecedented to have a guy that won as many as games as he won over a two-year period, start as a freshman, only to lose a couple games this whole time that he was a starter, and then all of a sudden he's not the quarterback. How do you manage that? How do you handle that? You got to have a tremendous amount of character and class to put team first, knowing your situation is not what it used to be, and for a guy that's a great competitor, that takes a lot. It's not easy to do."

As Saban spoke, his voice cracked. Several longtime Alabama observers remarked that they had never seen the coach so emotional. He had just won his eighth SEC championship. And for the fourth consecutive year, Saban and Alabama were heading back to the College Football Playoff.

CHAPTER 16

The Bear in Winter

1980 TO 1983

In August 1980 Bear Bryant checked into a hospital. He was diagnosed with fluid in his lungs. Doctors told him to cut back on his drinking and smoking, which he did. Released a week later and twenty pounds lighter, he began walking two miles a day. His friends offered to go with him on his strolls around Tuscaloosa, but Bryant preferred to be alone—his only quiet time to think and ponder his place in the world. He could sneak in a cigarette without anyone telling him it was bad for him. Ever the perfectionist, Bryant measured his walks with an odometer hooked to a belt loop on his pants. He also started swimming laps in his heated backyard pool.

Yet Bryant looked different after his hospital stay. His cheeks were sunken, his skin was sallow, and his face had countless lines, like a ball of aluminum foil. Even his speech seemed to lose pace, lacking its characteristic force. He took eleven pills a day and told friends, "I don't know what any of 'em are for." That fall a headline in a Texas paper read, "The Old Gray Bear Isn't What He Used to Be." The Tide finished the '80 season 10-2 and ranked sixth in the nation. Bryant was now nine games away from breaking Stagg's record.

After the 1980 season ended, as Bryant was shooting a Ford commercial, a producer said, "Coach, you look awful. You need a face lift to make your neck look skinnier." Bryant soon talked to Gaylon McCollough, a former player who was a plastic surgeon with a practice in Birmingham.

"I need to get some shit done to my neck," Bryant said. "Can you help me?"

McCollough agreed. But Bryant didn't want anyone to discover that he would undergo a face and neck lift. The two came up with a plan. Bryant had been telling friends and fans that he had wanted to take a trip to North Africa, where he had spent fourteen months in 1943–44 during World War II as a Navy lieutenant junior grade, overseeing aircraft maintenance and serving as a physical fitness instructor. Bryant never saw combat, but he longed to return to his outpost in Africa. "You can tell people that you're going back to Africa," McCollough told Bryant. "You can stay in one of our villas behind our clinic. No one will know you are there while you recuperate."

The day before surgery, McCollough gave Bryant a "scrub suit"—a surgeon's cap and a white lab coat—and sunglasses. The getup would conceal Bryant's identity. "I think I look like a doctor," Bryant said. "I probably would have made a good surgeon."

His identity disguised, Bryant reported for surgery the next day.

McCollough performed a face and neck tuck. For the next ten days, Bryant recovered in seclusion in a villa behind the clinic. Only his wife and Billy Varner were with Bryant, and the coach grew reflective and lonely. But he and McCollough talked for hours every afternoon. Bryant was particularly concerned about one question: Had he performed enough good acts in his life to earn a spot in heaven?

"I'm worried about heaven," Bryant confided to McCollough. "I just don't know if I can get in."

"Coach," said McCollough, "if you weigh the good you've done versus the bad, there is no question in my mind that there is a place for you. You've touched so many lives and so many people love you. You'll be in heaven. You'll be fine."

Still, the question would haunt Bryant until his final breath.

On the first day of two-a-days in August 1981 Bryant—his face now tighter, his neck now skinnier—sat in the back of Billy Varner's Buick LeSabre at 5:45 a.m., the moon still hanging in the sky. Bryant was beginning his twenty-fourth season at Alabama. Forty-four of his assistants had gone on to become head coaches. He'd sent hundreds of players to the NFL. But Bryant still relished the grind of practice. As he sat in the car, the milk trucks were out, the first sliver of dawn was breaking, and there was a sense of optimism in the back seat. "I do love the football, the contact with my players," he said. "I still get a thrill outtta jes goin' to practice. Jes steppin' out there. I do. That's my hobby."

Bryant strolled into his office, put on a baseball cap, met

with his players, then walked through a guarded tunnel that connected the building where his office was to the practice field. Once outside, Bryant put out his cigarette, hopped into a golf cart, and zoomed toward his tower, a smile on his wrinkled face. A train whistled by in the distance, and Bryant climbed up the thirty-three steps of the tower. He took a seat in his chair and grabbed his bullhorn. Looking down on his players—there were more than 120 on the field—he'd yell into his bullhorn at various times, "You can't run any faster than that, get your ass outta here" or "Nice catch." Throughout the entire practice, Bryant looked invigorated.

The '81 season began and the wins piled up. After beating Ole Miss 38–7 in early October for win 310, a fan watched Bryant leave the now-named Bryant-Denny Stadium in Varner's LeSabre, which was chaperoned by two police officers on motorcycles. "They'll sure never be another Bear," the fan said. A reporter from the *Crimson White*, the school newspaper, replied, "Not unless there is another Civil War." To the believers, Bryant represented one thing: winning.

As Bryant approached his historic 315th victory in 1981, which would propel him past Amos Alonzo Stagg as college football's winningest coach, more and more reporters and photographers from around the country showed up in Tuscaloosa, wanting Bryant's time, trying to figure out who the "real" Bear Bryant was. Bryant grew weary of the attention, even telling his longtime PR man Charley Thornton that he wished Thornton had never unearthed Stagg's record.

Bryant's quest for 315 became a cottage industry in Alabama. The number was emblazoned on buttons, bumper stickers, cushions, commemorative coins, and calendars. Statues were made of Bryant, as were paintings and sculptures. Bryant was uncomfortable with all the fuss—he would even be followed into public bathrooms by adoring fans—and by the time Alabama faced Auburn in the Iron Bowl on November 28 he was ready for it to end, ready to finally win number 315 so everyone could move on.

On the morning of game day, yard signs sprouted all around Legion Field that read: 315. Fans had the number painted on their faces in red lipstick and donned buttons that read: "I Was There When Bear Won 315." The tailgating Alabama fans shared a popular joke: "Did you hear? The Bear got hurt this morning. He was out walking his duck and a motorboat ran over him."

Trailing 17–14 at the start of the fourth quarter, the Tide rallied: Quarterback Walter Lewis threw a thirty-eight-yard touchdown pass to split end Jesse Bendross; then, following an Auburn punt, running back Linnie Patrick broke six tackles on a thirty-two-yard run to the Tigers 17-yard line. Two plays later, Patrick ran into the end zone, sealing a 28–17 win for Alabama.

Bryant wasn't carried off the field—he gave his players strict instructions not to do that—and he handed his houndstooth hat to a policeman, so it wouldn't be stolen. Bryant made his way through the mob on the field to a media trailer behind the south end zone, his facial expression never changing, remaining serious and stern. When he reached the trailer, Auburn coach Pat Dye, one of Bryant's former assistants, was just finishing his press conference. After Bryant entered, the two hugged.

"I want you to know, Pat, that Jimmy Carter called me on the telephone in the locker room," Bryant said.

Dye asked if President Ronald Reagan had called.

"I'm talking about Governor Carter," Bryant said. "You're from Georgia. I figured you'd appreciate that more."

"I'm not a politician, Coach," Dye said. "But what about President Reagan? Did he call you?"

"Why, he sure did call me," Bryant said. "I don't guess he's ever called you, has he?"

Bryant laughed and then took his seat at the podium. Number 315 had been conquered.

In January 1981, Bruce Arians drove his little Pontiac Astro into Tuscaloosa to talk to Bryant. Arians, twenty-eight, had spent the previous three years as an assistant at Mississippi State where, as the passing game coordinator, he helped the Bulldogs upset Alabama 6–3 the previous fall.

Arians walked into Bryant's office and immediately took a seat on the sofa, sinking like everyone else into the cushion. Bryant sat behind his massive oak desk, a string of smoke rising from a Chesterfield in the ashtray, silently inspecting Arians for a few moments. Then Bryant said in his bass-thumping drawl, "I hear you have a way with young black players. Is that true?"

Bryant knew that Arians had grown up with African-Americans in Yorktown, Pennsylvania, and that many of his best friends were black. "Well, Coach," Arians said, "I don't know about that. I don't care what color the kids are. Hell, they can be green, red, white, or gold for all I care. But I do know that I'm going to cuss them out if they screw up."

"I don't allow cussing," Bryant said. "It's a dollar a swear word."

"Shit, looks like I won't be getting a paycheck," Arians replied.

At that moment Arians had figured he had blown his chance at the job. But a few days later Bryant offered Arians a position as the running back coach—the first big break in Arians's coaching career. (Years later Arians would be named AP NFL coach of the year in 2012 with the Indianapolis Colts and in 2014 with the Arizona Cardinals.)

Beginning with his first day in Tuscaloosa, Arians watched Bryant closely, as if he was more his mentor than his grizzled boss. Bryant knew everybody's name in the building—from the janitors to the cafeteria workers to the secretaries—and he was aware of backstories. If a coach's secretary was having a bad day, Arians saw that Bryant would detect it and stop at her desk to offer a few encouraging words, suddenly brightening her afternoon. "It was magic the way Coach Bryant dealt with people, even at the end of his career," Arians said. "He could read others better than anyone. The importance of connecting with everyone in the program was one of the first valuable lessons I learned from him."

Arians continued:

Coach Bryant normally watched practice from his tower overlooking the field. Our running backs stretched right under the tower, and if we heard that chain jingle it meant Coach was coming down to chew some ass. One day I thought I was about to get ripped a new one. Before practice I was going over film with my players when I heard a knock on the door. It was Miss Linda, Bryant's secretary, and she wanted to know if we were going to practice today. "Yes we are," I said. I then looked at my watch: Practice was scheduled to begin in a few minutes.

Man, we ran like hell out of that meeting room. The players quickly got dressed and we hustled onto the practice field. We didn't get a chance to stretch; the horn blew to signal the start of practice as we bolted out of the locker room.

The kids knew we were in trouble. I was in trouble. And we proceeded to have the best practice of the season, because all of us were on edge and our adrenaline was pumping. After practice was over, we stayed on the field doing drills. I remember running around with a blocking dummy and my players hitting me. Most of the coaches went inside, but some of the older coaches stayed around to witness this ass chewing that I was about to get.

Then Bryant came down from his tower and rolled up to us in a golf cart. My players couldn't wait to see me get my tail whipped. Coach came up to me. "Shit, ya'll ought to be late more often," he said. "That was the best damn practice ya'll had all year." Then he drove off. I learned a lesson: A head coach who is a little bit feared is a good thing.

On December 15, 1982, Bryant walked into a press conference in Tuscaloosa, which aired on radio and TV across Alabama. Bryant had been up all night worrying about what he was going to say— words that would cause people driving to work to pull over onto the shoulders of roads, words that would bring the state to a standstill.

Bryant sat at a table filled with microphones and read a prepared statement. "There comes a time in every profession when we need to hang it up, and that time has come for me as head coach at the University of Alabama," Bryant said. "I'm a tired old man, but I'll never get tired of football."

In the days leading up to the 1982 Liberty Bowl in Memphis against Illinois the Tide assistants hardly slept, putting in extra hours at the office to make sure they sent Bryant out a winner. "We can't lose this game," Arians repeatedly said to the other assistants. "We just can't. They won't let us back into the state if we don't win. We can't let down Coach."

Days before his final game, *Sports Illustrated* writer John Underwood phoned the sixty-nine-year-old Bryant to ask him why he was hanging up his famous houndstooth hat. "Because four damn losses is too damn many," Bryant said, noting how many games Alabama had lost that season. "I'm up to my ass in alligators, John. These new young coaches just have too much energy for me. We need someone younger."

"So you really are tired?" Underwood asked.

"Naw," said Bryant. "To tell you the truth, I feel great. I got so many things I've been wantin' to do for so long, and now I'm gonna get to 'em."

"Like what?" Underwood said.

"I'm not sure just yet," Bryant replied.

In late December Underwood ended his *SI* tribute story to Bryant—who had once predicted that he'd "croak in a week" if he quit coaching—with the sentence: "All things considered, Bear Bryant didn't sound like a man who had croaking on his mind."

⬤   ⬤   ⬤

On the morning of the Liberty Bowl, on December 29, 1982, a dozen reporters from across the country were invited into Bryant's Memphis hotel suite for a casual pregame discussion. They found him sitting on a sofa, outfitted in his customary red sports coat and gray slacks, a string of smoke rising from the red-orange ember of his Chesterfield. Bryant told stories from his career, his life and times. As he spoke, he looked worn out.

A few hours later the Alabama coaches gathered for a pregame meeting at the hotel. But at the time the meeting was to begin, Bryant didn't appear. "Bear was never late for anything," said Arians. "We knew he wasn't feeling well, so we began to worry."

One of Bryant's aides eventually found the coach alone in a hotel ballroom, the lights off, seated at the head of a table. His eyes stared vacantly into the silence. The end of something was near.

An estimated audience of 50 million tuned into the game—millions around the globe watched via the Armed Forces Network—to see Bryant patrol the sideline one last time on a bitterly cold night in Memphis. Alabama beat Illinois, 21–15. In the locker room after his final victory, Bryant hugged every one of his players and coaches. Arians remembers Bryant looking unusually tired as he walked out of a football stadium for the final time.

After his final press conference as Alabama's head coach, Bryant headed out of the interview tent and climbed into an automobile. A cluster of Crimson Tide fans, standing nearby, watched his every move, with many yelling, "We'll miss you, Bear! Thanks for the memories."

Seeing the fans, Bryant opened the car door, stood up, and uttered his final words to his adoring fans, "Y'all keep cheering for Alabama, y'all hear?" Bryant got back into the car and disappeared into the black Memphis night. The brilliant sun of his football career had set.

●   ●   ●

Twenty-seven days after his last game, Bryant experienced severe chest pains while at the home of a friend in Tuscaloosa and was driven to Druid City Hospital, where he was wheeled into the intensive care unit. By the next morning, though, he was feeling better and his family expected him to be released. Around noon he was sitting upright in his bed with a yellow notepad in his hands, writing down reminders of things he wanted to do, words he wanted to say to those who mattered most to him. Ray Perkins, his replacement, stopped by to check in with his mentor; Bryant upbraided him for not being out on the recruiting trail. Then, while in his bed eating lunch, Bryant suffered a massive heart attack at 12:24 CT on January 26, 1983. Doctors frantically tried to revive him, but at 1:30 p.m., the pronouncement call was made: The Bear was dead twenty-eight days after coaching his final game.

"I don't think the pressures of his retirement contributed to his heart attack," said Dr. William Hill, Bryant's cardiologist. "He had been free of pressures lately. He was looking forward to hunting trips, recreational trips. The coach was fully sixty-nine years old—certainly not a young man."

The news of Bryant's death traveled quickly throughout Tuscaloosa and across Alabama. Grown men openly wept, like they'd just lost their most cherished family member. Farmers, steel workers, lawyers, and stay-at-home moms stopped what they were doing, as if the realization that Bryant was gone took away the collective breath of the entire state in one seismic gut punch. Bryant's passing was a lead story on all the national networks. "The Bear is dead," said NBC's Tom Brokaw. Local broadcasters labored to summon the strength to not break down on camera; some were more successful than others. Schoolteachers all across the state, many teary-eyed, stopped their classes to break the news to their students. That night President Ronald Reagan called Mary Harmon, Bryant's widow, to offer condolences, to tell her that the nation was now mourning with her.

"Today we Americans lost a hero who always seemed larger than life," Reagan said. "Bear Bryant gave the country the gift of a life unsurpassed. In making the impossible seem easy, he lived what we strive to be."

The day after he died nearly six thousand students and friends attended a service at Memorial Coliseum; later thousands more visited Hayes Funeral Home to touch the casket that was covered in crimson and white carnations. Many were overcome with emotion at the sight of the closed casket. Two days after his passing, Bryant's funeral was held at the First United Methodist Church in Tuscaloosa, but the tiny church couldn't accommodate the surge of well-wishers who had flown in from around the country to say good-bye to Bryant. Every head coach from the SEC was present, as was Nebraska's Bob Devaney and former Ohio State coach Woody Hayes. Hundreds of working reporters and former players arrived in town from as far as New York and Chicago. To enable everyone to see the short service, closed-circuit television cameras were installed and the service was relayed to monitors in two nearby churches.

"We give thanks to God for Paul Bryant," Rev. Joe Elmore said. "We give thanks to God for [Bryant's] long years of influence on young people, challenging them to excellence, discipline, confidence, and hard work. We give thanks for his ability to teach and motivate people—to teach them important lessons for life."

After the final prayer was uttered at First United Methodist, eight Alabama players carried Bryant's casket down the steps of the church. As his body was placed in a white hearse, more than two hundred photographers frantically clicked away, their flashbulbs popping like lightning through the gray afternoon.

The funeral procession stretched three miles and consisted of nearly three hundred cars, including six buses filled with former and present-day players and coaches. As the procession rolled down Tenth Street in Tuscaloosa, thousands of locals stood four, five, and six deep to see Bryant one last time, waving at the hearse in respectful silence. The procession slowed when it passed Bryant-Denny Stadium—named after him in 1975—as if to give the coach a final look at the soaring cathedral where he made so many dreams come true, the place where his legend was forged and his legacy rests. Church bells tolled and flags hung at half-staff as the hearse moved through Tuscaloosa. And then the procession pulled onto Interstate 20/59 and headed east for Birmingham.

All along the fifty-five miles from Tuscaloosa to Elmwood Cemetery in Birmingham the interstate was lined with people, young and old, Yankees and Southerners, all compelled to stand in the chill of the winter afternoon and cry and grieve and tell stories about Paul William Bryant. To Alabamians, this was a state funeral, every bit as significant as a president being laid to rest in Arlington National Cemetery. The *Birmingham News* estimated that 250,000 people had witnessed the procession, which meant that one of every twelve residents of Alabama had bid farewell to Bryant in person.

The procession turned into the cemetery, where flowers from all the living presidents—Ronald Reagan, Jimmy Carter, Gerald Ford, and Richard Nixon—awaited the casket. About eight thousand mourners followed the hearse through the gates of Elmwood.

The procession ended at the gravesite, which was under a canopy. Eight Alabama players from Bryant's most recent team carried a Southern Pine casket draped with red and white carnations to the opening of red clay in the ground. The Lord's Prayer and the Twenty-Third Psalm were recited.

Then the Bear was gone.

CHAPTER 17

Chasing the Bear

2018 TO 2019

He donned the No. 17 black practice jersey and walked into the indoor practice field just off Paul W. Bryant Drive in Tuscaloosa. It had been eight months since the four-star quarterback had announced in a Twitter post: "I felt that same calling that my Great Grandfather had when he was asked to come home. Alabama is home and that's where I want to spend my college career."

On December 15, 2018, Paul Bryant Tyson made his practice debut for the Crimson Tide. Reporters were on hand to document the moment for posterity, to write about the return of a Bryant to T-Town, even though Tyson had just graduated from high school and enrolled at Alabama a day earlier. He wouldn't be eligible to participate in the upcoming College Football Playoff.

He threw passes to a teammate as quarterbacks coach Dan Enos stood nearby, analyzing his young player's throwing motion and footwork. Enos stopped Tyson a few times to demonstrate how he wanted him to change his release point and how he wanted him to make his drops in the pocket; Tyson nodded his head and did as he instructed. At age seventeen, the heir of the Bear was a work in progress.

Tyson moved into Bryant Hall, the name of the dorm where, back in the '60s, his great-grandfather worked with players deep into the night, often sleeping in a dorm room. Bryant wrote letters to his freshmen players before they reported for their first summer camp at Alabama. On the December day that his great-grandson made his Crimson Tide debut, Bryant's words still echoed through the mists of time, describing the culture of toughness and winning— and hatred of losing—that are the bedrock of the football process and program in Tuscaloosa:

"You will be expected to report to football practice on August 17," Bryant wrote to one player in the 1970s:

We will expect you to arrive in the afternoon and our first meal will be served that evening at the dorm.

On the 18th, you will take your physical, including the mile run, get your room and locker assignments and participate in Photographer's Day in the afternoon. Our first practice will be on the morning of the 19th.

I am expecting you to report in top physical condition, clean-cut, smiling, bright-eyed, bushy-tailed and raring to go. Also, I am expecting you to be prepared to run, hit, pitch, kick, catch, sweat, smell and enjoy it. There are no easy ways but there are ways to enjoy the journey and we must find them.

I am also expecting you to work hard, eat well, sleep well, play well, display a winning attitude at all times, be a leader and help me sell the squad on what it takes to enjoy the journey.

I hope you will share your problems with me whether it be at home, at the dorm, in your school work, with teammates, with coaches, with training regulations, self-discipline, or even flying a kite. If you do that, I will try to help you and, if I can't, I'll recommend you get a job, join the Army, or join the Foreign Legion, but in any event, to reside in another state.

Nothing's too good for winners. I want to love you, pat you, pet you, brag on you and see you hoot, run and shout and laugh, pray, hug, kiss and win with humility. If we lose, I want all of us to be unhappy, no one to have any fun, and expect only what is reserved for losers but take it with dignity while planning to come back.

Please remember us to your family and make your personal plans on how you are going to reach your goal—the NATIONAL CHAMPIONSHIP.

Sincerely, Paul Bryant

With a Bryant again on campus, the spirit of the Bear was stronger than ever in Tuscaloosa.

◆　　◆　　◆

"There are many similarities between Coach Bryant and Coach Saban," said Bill Battle, an end on Bryant's teams from 1960 to 1962 and the athletic director at Alabama from 2013 to 2017, during

Saban's tenure. "They both believe in field position football, in out-conditioning the opponent, and out-preparing the opponent. But they have very different personalities. Coach Bryant was more outgoing and spent more time communicating with people. He was folksy and people really related to him. Nick is much more businesslike. He loves to coach players and he loves to recruit. Coach Bryant enjoyed interacting with the outside world more than Nick."

"Coach Bryant and Coach Saban don't look alike or talk alike, but between the ears they are identical twins," said Gaylon McCollough, a center on Bryant's teams in the early 1960s who became one of his doctors and most trusted friends late in life. "Saban's Process is exactly the same as Bryant's Winning Theory that he taught us. Coach Bryant always told us, 'On the first kickoff, you pick out one of them boys and you hit them between the numbers as hard as you can to the ground. Then put out your hand, help him up, and say, "I'll be back for more."' That's the kind of attitude you see out of Saban's teams as well."

"I've read and learned a lot about Bear Bryant and he reminds me so much of Coach Saban," said Barrett Jones, an offensive lineman who played for Saban from 2008 to 2012. "Neither would be described as a 'players coach' and both were discipline-minded coaches. They both inspired fear and awe among their players."

"Coach Bryant had a great run from 1961 to '66 and then things kind of lapsed," said Scott Hunter, who played quarterback at Alabama from 1966 to 1970. "At that point he could have faded into history and not won any more championships. But instead Coach Bryant reconstructed himself and changed. He started recruiting black players and changed his offense to the Wishbone.

Coach Saban has also changed. He saw that college football was becoming a high scoring game. He knew he needed to score forty-five points a game to win championships. So instead of having a game manager at quarterback, he goes out and recruits guys who can throw it all over the field. It's been a sea change. But like Bryant, he recognized that if he didn't change the game would have passed him by."

⬤　⬤　⬤

Nick Saban walked along the sideline of Levi Stadium in Santa Clara, California. It was January 7, 2019, and the clock was ticking late in the fourth quarter of the national championship game against Clemson. The Tigers had scored thirty consecutive points and held a 44–16 lead. Outwardly, Saban didn't look mad. He hadn't thrown and broken his headset, as he had done in the national semifinal game against Oklahoma nine days earlier while holding a 28–10 lead in the second quarter after his offense had committed a penalty. And now he wasn't yelling at assistants or players. He looked calm, almost resigned, slowly pacing the sideline with his arms folded, deep in thought.

Clemson ran a few more offensive plays to end the game, handing Saban the worst defeat of his career at Alabama—and denying him the chance to overtake Bryant and win a record seven national titles. He walked to midfield and shook the hand of Tiger coach Dabo Swinney, who had played wide receiver at Alabama and began his coaching career in Tuscaloosa. "See you next year," Swinney said to Saban. Then Saban shook a few more hands and walked to the portal that would take him to the Alabama locker room. He kissed and hugged Miss Terry, briefly spoke to his players, then met the media in a small auditorium. Through it all, he never raised his voice.

"I just have a feeling that I didn't do a very good job for our team, with our team, giving them the best opportunity to be successful," he said. "I always feel that way, even sometimes when we win, I think there's things we could do better or that I could have done better. But particularly in this case, we never really ever got comfortable with what we needed to do to win this game."

After meeting with the media, Saban headed back to the team locker room, where he changed into a suit. He then ambled toward the idling team bus, his face a portrait of determination. Taking his front row seat, he looked at notes and was already trying to determine how everything had gone so horribly wrong on this midwinter night: how his defense had given up 482 yards, why his players in the secondary were so confused by Clemson's formations, and why his quarterback never looked comfortable facing the Tiger defense. Only minutes after the loss, Saban's autopsy of the game had begun.

"It's awfully important to win with humility. It's also important to lose," Bear Bryant once said. "I hate to lose worse than anyone, but if you never lose, you won't know how to act. If you lose with humility, then you can come back."

On January 8, the team flew across the country to Tuscaloosa. The next morning Saban called a 9 a.m. coach's meeting—late by

Saban's standard, but he wanted to give his coaches extra time to sleep off the jet lag.

In the meeting, according to sources, Saban berated his coaches, saying the entire staff—himself included—had failed their players. For the first time since he arrived at Alabama, Saban acknowledged that he and his assistants had been outcoached, outworked, and outclassed in a national title game. Within days seven Crimson Tide assistant coaches no longer had offices in the Mal Moore Athletic Facility—some left by choice; others were shown the door by the head coach. Saban had lost six assistants before the 2017 season and still advanced to the national championship game. Now he was on the verge of the biggest staff rebuild of his coaching career.

The brain drain on the Tide staff was nothing new. Since Saban had taken over at Alabama a decade earlier, thirty-two different co-ordinators and position coaches had left his staff. And ten of those coaches—almost one-third—went on to become head coaches. But even with the coaching turnover, the machine that Saban built kept humming with unrelenting efficiency. Since Saban arrived in 2007, Alabama has had twenty-nine first-round draft picks and only thirteen losses. And in eight of the last nine years, Saban had hauled in what was widely considered the No. 1 recruiting class in the country—a trend that continued in February 2019.

Why hasn't the constant churning of assistants hurt Saban and the Crimson Tide in recruiting? "When you sign up to play for Alabama you're not signing up to play for the assistant coach who recruited you," said former offensive lineman Barrett Jones, who won the Outland Trophy in 2011. "You come to play for Coach Saban. He's the draw. He's the program. He's the reason why guys come, pure and simple. You want to be around that greatness. You want to be around to see what it looks like to be a winner. As long as Coach Saban is there, it won't matter how much turnover there is on his staff. He'll still win recruiting national titles just because he knows how to identify talent, he knows how to make you feel wanted, and players know that he's better than any coach in America in preparing you for the NFL."

●   ●   ●

On the evening of February 6, 2019, a few hours after signing his final prospect in yet another top-ranked recruiting class on National Signing Day, Saban strolled out of the Mal Moore Athletic Facility and slid into the passenger's seat of his silver Mercedes. The driver was Cedric Burns, who is Saban's personal assistant and who has worked at Alabama since the last years of the Bear Bryant era, when he was a janitor in Bryant Hall.

Led by two police officers on motorcycles with blue lights flashing, Burns drove Saban down Bear Bryant Drive. Dusk was settling over Tuscaloosa, and in the distance stood the towering Bryant-Denny Stadium, framed by the last blush of sunlight that swept across the winter sky. Burns and Saban then pulled onto Stadium Drive.

Outside his passenger window, Saban could see the bronze statue of Bear Bryant. Then the car drove close to his own likeness outside the stadium. Fans were taking pictures of both statues—they are annually the two most photographed structures, man-made or natural, in the state of Alabama—and Saban glanced at the fans as the Mercedes slowed to a stop. Dressed in a Crimson-colored blazer and gray slacks, Saban climbed the front stadium steps and entered Gate 1 of Bryant-Denny.

He rode an elevator to the fifth floor, where hundreds of Alabama fans awaited him in a 12,600-foot lounge area above the north end zone. Saban strode onto an elevated stage and introduced his seven new assistants, including offensive coordinator and quarterbacks coach Steve Sarkisian, who raved about the "bloodlines" of Bear Bryant's great-grandson Paul Tyson and his potential. As each coach spoke, Saban stood off to the side, checking his watch, fidgeting, looking like a man who had places to be, people to call, problems to solve.

Then Saban stepped back onto the stage. "I never felt like after the LSU game this year that we kept improving," Saban said. "We had a lot of guys that put their own outcome ahead of what we were trying to do as a team, and I also think we lost our humility a little bit as a team, which creates a blatant disregard for doing things the right way and paying attention to detail. You think you're above and beyond doing the right stuff to win. This affected how we practiced and how we prepared for games. We didn't play well defensively and we got our asses embarrassed against Clemson. I'm not happy about that. We're going to get all this stuff fixed.

"You have to have talent on your team. You got to have everybody giving great effort. But you also have to have everyone focused on the right stuff. If you start focusing on outcomes, you get very distracted—where are you going to in the NFL draft, where are you going to be picked in the draft—all of these things keep you from preparing the way you need to prepare. Eventually, if you don't pay attention to detail it will catch up to you. That's the goal for our team.

"If you came here to hear some kind of speech about how we're rubbing on everyone's neck and we're happy about how we ended the season, that ain't happening. Not happening."

After speaking for forty-five minutes, Saban walked out of the stadium, once again passing the statues. Now he rode through the dark streets of Tuscaloosa in his silver Mercedes, its low beams shooting streams of light into the cool Southern night, through the town that has been his home for more than a decade.

He met his assistants at a downtown restaurant called 5, which specializes in Southern cuisine. Inside a private room off to the side of the main dining area, in the dim light, there was no prolonged toasting of their top-ranked recruiting class, no discussing the potential of the 2019 team, no talk of distant horizons or faraway dreams. Saban and his coaches lingered over one thing most of the evening, the one thing that Nick Saban and Bear Bryant continually focused on as coaches at Alabama:

What they were going to do tomorrow to get better.

Acknowledgments

This book never would have been possible without Seth Wickersham, a senior writer at *ESPN: The Magazine* and a friend. Seth messaged me in late 2018, telling me he had spoken to a book editor in New York City who was interested in a project on Alabama football. That started the boulder rolling down the hill for what you now hold in your hands. Thank you, Seth.

I never met Bear Bryant, but he did speak to me through the words he wrote with author John Underwood in their book, *Bear*, published in 1974 by Little, Brown and Company. This autobiography was an essential resource in piecing together Bryant's life and re-creating the touchstone moments of his career.

I've had several one-on-one interviews with Coach Nick Saban over the years, beginning in the late 2000s when I was a senior writer at *Sports Illustrated*. Coach Saban has always been patient with me, treated me with respect, and even liked to joke around—a far cry from the national perception of him. These interviews provided the backbone for the narrative on Coach Saban in this book.

I'm in debt to the scores of folks who spoke to me about Coach Bryant and Coach Saban, some on the record, some on the condition of anonymity. These interviews provided colorful background details on both coaches and insight into what made each man tick. I started covering Alabama football for *SI* about a decade ago, and the hundreds of interviews I conducted over the span with players and coaches were instrumental in creating this narrative. I also incorporated published material that originally appeared in my books *The Storm and the Tide* and *The Quarterback Whisperer* (co-written with Bruce Arians).

Over the years reporters from around the nation have written thorough examinations on both coaches, but I want to acknowledge ten writers whose works I especially leaned on in crafting this book: Keith Dunnavant, Allen Barra, Todd Stoddard, John David Briley, Al Browning, Mark Kriegel, Phil Savage, Monte Burke, Mickey Herskowitz, and Andy Staples.

My literary agent, Scott Waxman, has been with me for more than twenty years. Scott helped shape the idea for this project in its earliest stages and fine-tuned the book proposal. This project never would have gotten off the ground without Scott.

My editor at Grand Central Publishing, Sean Desmond, is simply one of the best in the business. He believed in this book from the first email. His big-picture ideas for the narrative were always pitch-perfect, and his deft edits greatly improved the final product. Rachel Kambury at Grand Central shepherded the manuscript through the editing process and always had all the answers to my questions. I'm lucky to be surrounded by such a talented team.

My stepfather, Gordon Bratz, a retired Army colonel and a former professor at West Point, edited an early draft of the manuscript. His pen improved nearly every paragraph. I had a high-ranking member of Alabama's athletic department fact-check

Acknowledgments

the narrative—this person wishes to remain anonymous—and this longtime Crimson Tide official made sure that I was as accurate as possible in telling the stories of Bryant and Saban.

Finally, none of this would have been possible without my wife, April. We have three small children. When I had to spend long days and late nights in my office making calls and tapping the keyboard, April was always there to take care of our little ones and make sure our house was in order. She is the national champion of this family.

Notes

1. BRYANT AND SABAN: ON THE SAME TEAM AT LAST

3   **Bryant had planned:** Al Browning, *I Remember Paul "Bear" Bryant* (Nashville: Cumberland House, 2001), 276.

2. MAMMA CALLED

8   **"The only reason I'm going back":** Paul W. Bryant and John Underwood, *Bear: The Hard Life and Good Times of Alabama's Coach Bryant* (Boston: Little, Brown, 1975), 160.

8   **"All my life":** Bryant and Underwood, *Bear,* 160.

8   **Anyone who cursed:** Tom Stoddard, *Turnaround: The Untold Story of Bear Bryant's First Year as Head Coach at Alabama* (Montgomery, AL: Black Belt Press, 1996), 28.

9   **Grantland Rice told a friend:** Stoddard, *Turnaround,* 32.

10   **At his introductory press conference:** Mickey Herskowitz, *The Legend of Bear Bryant* (Austin, TX: Eakin Press, 1993), 123.

12   **"Get out! Get out!":** Keith Dunnavant, *Coach: The Life of Paul "Bear" Bryant* (New York: Simon & Schuster, 1996), 138.

13   **"We are going to do two things":** Allen Barra, *The Last Coach: A Life of Paul "Bear" Bryant* (New York: W. W. Norton, 2005), 212.

13   **He redid the football offices:** Bryant and Underwood, *Bear,* 164.

NOTES

16 **And they did what was called a grass drill:** Stoddard, *Turnaround*, 78.

16 **Trash cans that reeked:** Dunnavant, *Coach*, 139.

16 **Players would stand under the shower heads:** Barra, *The Last Coach*, 215.

17 **"Nobody makes money":** Stoddard, *Turnaround*, 85.

17 **Right guard Billy Rains:** Stoddard, *Turnaround*, 111.

18 **Bryant penned a letter to his players on July 15:** Stoddard, *Turnaround*, 115–116.

19 **"Look around at the guys":** Dunnavant, *Coach*, 141.

20 **At 6:00 a.m. he held:** Stoddard, *Turnaround*, 121–122.

20 **"Hello Coach":** Stoddard, *Turnaround*, 131.

22 **A temporary wooden grandstand:** C. J. Schexnayder, "Alabama vs. LSU," SB Nation (website), November 4, 2011.

23 **"How you gonna win":** Bryant and Underwood, *Bear*, 167.

3. THE SECRET MISSION

30 **Chuck Moore was astonished:** Mal M. Moore with Steve Townsend, *Crimson Heart: Let Me Tell You My Story* (Tuscaloosa, AL: The Mal and Charlotte Moore Crimson Heart Foundation, 2014), 215.

30 **"Uncle Mal":** Moore, *Crimson Heart*, 215.

36 **"Mal, you must think":** Moore, *Crimson Heart*, 230.

42 **"Pendry to light into McElroy":** Phil Savage with Ray Glier, *4th and Goal Every Day* (New York: St. Martin's Griffin, 2017), 85.

44 **Each player was timed:** Henry Bushnell, "How Nick Saban Revived Alabama Football," Yahoo! Sports (website), November 28, 2018.

4. THE BEAR BUILDS

52   **He bemoaned:** Alexander Wolff, "The Great Bear Hunt," *Sports Illustrated,* August 30, 1993.

52   **"Most of us were country boys":** Wolff, "The Great Bear Hunt."

54   **"It was embarrassing":** Dunnavant, *Coach,* 149.

55   **never stay blocked:** C. J. Schexnayder, "Coach Bryant's Defensive Theory for the Alabama Crimson Tide," *Roll 'Bama Roll* (blog), SB Nation (website), November 24, 2011.

55   **Oklahoma coach Bud Wilkinson:** Dunnavant, *Coach,* 150.

55   **Bryant had five objectives:** Schexnayder, "Coach Bryant's Defensive Theory."

57   **"The Tide belongs to all Alabama":** Barra, *The Last Coach,* 227.

58   **"Now Billy":** Barra, *The Last Coach,* 228.

5. THE RISING OF SABAN'S TIDE

68   **Sometimes she would recite:** Monte Burke, *Saban: The Making of a Coach* (New York: Simon & Schuster, 2015), 256.

68   **"About twenty-five years ago":** Burke, *Saban,* 257.

6. BE BRAVE

79   **"There are several basic rules":** Dunnavant, *Coach,* 151.

80   **"You can't do that, Doc!":** Bryant and Underwood, *Bear,* 170–171.

80   **"What's going on, Pat?":** Bryant and Underwood, *Bear,* 176.

83   **Then Joe Sheehan:** Barra, *The Last Coach,* 245.

84   **Monroe never recovered:** Dunnavant, *Coach,* 18.

NOTES

84 **"I was a mamma's boy"**: Bryant and Underwood, *Bear,* 20.

85 **He wasn't sure whether to use a knife or spoon**: Bryant and Underwood, *Bear,* 20.

85 **"I am going to whip you for that"**: Bryant and Underwood, *Bear,* 23.

86 **Paul and his mother often wouldn't pull up to the schoolhouse:** Dunnavant, *Coach,* 20.

87 **"Why don't you go in there?"**: Bryant and Underwood, *Bear,* 26.

89 **"Yes sir, I guess I do"**: Bryant and Underwood, *Bear,* 28.

89 **The core of his future football beliefs**: Dunnavant, *Coach,* 26.

91 **They were waiting for Wade**: Lewis Bowling, *Wallace Wade* (Durham, NC: Carolina Academic Press, 2006), 68–69.

92 **"I've never heard of Alabama"**: Eli Gold, *Crimson Nation* (Nashville: Rutledge Hill Press, 2005), 45.

93 **It had been branded with the stigma**: Bowling, *Wallace Wade,* 76.

95 **"And they told me Southern boys could fight"**: Warren St. John, *Rammer Jammer Yellow Hammer* (New York: Broadway Books, 2005), 35.

95 **"I never imagined anything could be that exciting"**: Barra, *The Last Coach,* 4.

7. "THIS IS THE BEGINNING"

113 **"Is this what you want?"**: Nick Saban with Brian Curtis, *How Good Do You Want to Be?* (New York: Ballantine Books, 2005), 71.

8. THE FOUNDING FOOTBALL DOCUMENT

127 **"Stud"**: Mark Kriegel, *Namath* (New York: Penguin Group, 2004), 73.

Notes

128   **Namath had all summer to study:** Kriegel, *Namath,* 67.

129   **"Alabama?":** Kriegel, *Namath, 67.*

129   **Rose marched upstairs:** Kriegel, *Namath,* 68.

131   **"It's not your job to pitch":** Kriegel, *Namath,* 76.

133   **"Who is he trying to kid?":** Morton Sharnik, "A Rough Day for the Bear," *Sports Illustrated,* November 26, 1962.

135   **Namath's "finest hour":** Kriegel, *Namath,* 101.

136   **Now Bryant felt as if he'd somehow failed Namath:** Bryant and Underwood, *Bear,* 201.

136   **"Sir," Namath said, "I don't want you to do that":** Kriegel, *Namath,* 102–103.

137   **"Joe, what happened?":** Barra, *The Last Coach,* 314.

138   **"Namath was terrific":** Kriegel, *Namath,* 107.

139   **"He moves like a human now":** Barra, *The Last Coach,* 317.

140   **"I want to look you in the eye":** Bryant and Underwood, *Bear,* 207.

141   **He liked to review the performance of different stocks:** Dunnavant, *Coach,* 194.

144   **"Normally when I'm on the field I don't want anybody around me":** William Greider and David DuPree, "Sports and Integration," *Washington Post,* May 21, 1978.

10. A SECRET PLAN

182   **"Shoot, Coach":** Bryant and Underwood, *Bear,* 282.

182   **"Well, you've done so much for the university":** John Hammontree, "The Story of the Man Who Gave Bear Bryant His Job Back," *AL.com,* August 9, 2016.

NOTES

183 **"I can't get anybody as good as me":** Bryant and Underwood, *Bear,* 283.

184 **"I can get a job":** Dunnavant, *Coach,* 270.

185 **"If any of you don't like it":** John David Briley, *Career in Crisis,* (Macon, GA: Mercer University Press, 2006), 9.

185 **"Four years ago":** Briley, *Career in Crisis,* 10.

186 **"It might be a little early":** Pat Putnum, "He Cried All the Way to the Bank," *Sports Illustrated,* September 21, 1970.

188 **"John," Bryant said, "I can't thank you enough":** Barra, *The Last Coach,* 370.

189 **"If you come here and if there are ever any problems":** Ray Melick, "Turning the Tide for Black Athletes," *Chicago Tribune,* September 10, 1995.

189 **"I admire your courage, young man":** Keith Dunnavant, *The Missing Ring* (New York: St. Martin's Griffin, 2007), 275.

190 **Simmons told his parents he wanted to transfer:** Briley, *Career in Crisis,* 55–56.

191 **"Mrs. Mitchell, John and I have talked":** Bryant and Underwood, *Bear,* 303.

192 **She overheard him ask the coach:** Melick, "Turning the Tide for Black Athletes."

11. THE PLAY THAT CHANGED NICK SABAN

201 **A psychologist who worked:** Pete Thamel, "Reimagined, Remastered, Unleashed: Is New Lane Kiffin Ready to Succeed as Head Coach?" *Sports Illustrated,* December 29, 2016.

12. THE FALL SURPRISE

204 **Bryant continued to draw and diagram:** Briley, *Career in Crisis,* 87.

Notes

205 **"Gee, coach, they don't seem to have the same pride":** Pat Putnum, "Pride in the Red Jersey," *Sports Illustrated,* October 11, 1971.

205 **He also issued a directive:** Putnam, "Pride in the Red Jersey."

207 **During the evenings Bryant and Royal:** Putnam, "Pride in the Red Jersey."

207 **"You've got to have confidence in it":** Briley, *Career in Crisis,* 92.

208 **"We have gotten away from championship football":** Briley, *Career in Crisis,* 95.

209 **"I really think they lost their guts":** Briley, *Career in Crisis,* 99.

13. THE SEARCH FOR ANSWERS

213 **Saban and Herman met:** Andy Staples, "This One Is Special," *Sports Illustrated,* January 18, 2016.

216 **On this night a caller named Joe:** Staples, "This One is Special."

14. THE GUT CHECK

220 **He was introduced to a bartender at the club named Billy:** Wright Thompson, "The Last Ride of Bear and Billy," ESPN (website), May 24, 2012.

221 **"When we get back":** Bryant and Underwood, *Bear,* 319–320.

223 **"Dagburn it!":** Ray Kennedy, "'Bama Takes Charge," *Sports Illustrated,* December 3, 1973.

224 **Suddenly there was a ruckus:** Browning, *I Remember Paul "Bear" Bryant,* 268.

224 **"I don't know how to say this":** Browning, *I Remember Paul "Bear" Bryant,* 269.

225 **Underwood later told reporters:** Barra, *The Last Coach,* 414.

NOTES

225 **"Where the hell are you?":** John Underwood, "After Many a Splendid Season, The Bear Hangs Up His Hat," *Sports Illustrated*, December 27, 1982.

226 **In the spring of 1977 he took one of his grandkids:** Barra, *The Last Coach*, 420.

227 **this kind of inconsistency was "not recommended":** John Underwood, "The Rising of the Tide," *Sports Illustrated*, January 8, 1979.

15. TYING THE BEAR

236 **"This kid is Steve Young":** Greg Bishop, "Tua Tagovailoa Still Has Much to Prove: For His Name and His Culture," *Sports Illustrated*, December 26, 2018.

237 **"It's going to be OK, Coach":** Bishop, "Tua Tagovailoa Still Has Much to Prove."

16. THE BEAR IN WINTER

242 **He took eleven pills a day and told friends, "I don't know what any of 'em are for":** Herskowitz, *The Legend of Bear Bryant*, 215.

243 **"I do love the football, the contact with my players":** Frank Deford, "I Do Love the Football," *Sports Illustrated*, November 23, 1981.

244 **"You can't run any faster than that":** Deford, "I Do Love the Football."

244 **"They'll sure never be another Bear":** Deford, "I Do Love the Football."

245 **"Did you hear? The Bear got hurt this morning":** Herskowitz, *The Legend of Bear Bryant*, 11.

249 **"Because four damn losses is too damn many":** Underwood, "After Many a Splendid Season."

250 **They found him sitting on a sofa:** Dunnavant, *Coach*, 15.

250   **One of Bryant's aides eventually found the coach:** Dunnavant, **Coach,** 16.

251   **"Y'all keep cheering for Alabama":** Browning, *I Remember Paul "Bear" Bryant,* xxviii.

17. CHASING THE BEAR

256   **"You will be expected to report to football practice on August 17":** Roy Exum, "Bear Bryant's Summertime Letter," *Chattanoogan,* May 8, 2012.

Index

Index

INDEX

Index

Index

Index

San Francisco 49ers, 155
Savage, Phil, 99–100, 123
Schnellenberger, Howard, 126,
    128–29, 182
Scottsboro (AL) High School, 80
SEC Skywriters Tour, 210
segregation. *See also* integration, 126,
    144, 191
Sexton, Jimmy, 32, 33, 40
Sharpe, Jimmy, 14
Sheehan, Joe, 83
Shula, Don, 183
Shula, Mike, 25–26, 29–30, 40–41,
    48, 63
Sibley, Harper, 181
Simmons, Jim, 190
Sims, Blake, 200
Sinatra, Francis ("Frank"), 225
Skelton, Bobby, 57, 59–60
Sloan, Steve, 141
Smalley, Earl, 181
Smart, Kirby, 146, 170, 235
Smelley, Brad, 68
Smith, Andre, 75
Smith, DeVonta, 236–37
Smith, Drucilla, 87
Smith, Irv, Jr., 102, 239
Sports Illustrated, 54, 64, 143, 228,
    249, 265
Square, Damion, 69
St. Paul's High School (Mobile), 46
Stabler, Ken, 141, 206
Stagg, Amos Alonzo, 231–33, 242,
    244
Stallings, Gene, 27–28, 33, 106,
    163–64
Starr, Bart, 7
Stewart, ArDarius, 216
Sugar Bowl, Alabama appearances,
    77, 82, 136, 143, 158, 173, 199–200,
    222–23, 227–28
Suhey, Matt, 228
Sunseri, Sal, 66–67, 157–58
Super Bowl, 31–32, 47, 73, 143, 198
SuperPrep (magazine), 102

Swinney, Dabo, 219, 259
Syracuse University, 122, 148

Tagovailoa, Diane, 236
Tagovailoa, Tua, 235–39
Tangerine Bowl, 119
Tebow, Tim, 29, 77, 102–03
Tennessee, 46–48
Tennessee Volunteers, 12, 43, 56, 76,
    139, 186, 199, 204–05
Texas A&M
    1957 Gator Bowl loss, 12
    2009 championship loss to
        Alabama, 173
    2010 championship loss to
        Alabama, 145
    2012 victory over Alabama, 170–71
    2013 victory over Alabama, 193–98
    2015 victory over Alabama, 214–16
    Bryant coaching record, 18
    Bryant departure from, 6, 8, 11–12
    Cotton Bowl loss to Alabama, 19
    Junction training camps, 7–8, 21,
        82–83
    Orange Bowl win over Alabama,
        140
    playing ability of Johnny Manziel,
        170, .193–94
Texas Christian University, 28
Texas Longhorns
    2009 loss to Alabama, 103–08
    running the Wishbone offense,
        203–04
    teaching the Wishbone to
        Alabama, 206–09
Thomas, Frank, 9, 19, 106
Thornton, Charley, 231, 244
315 wins (aka The Number), 231–33,
    244–46
Tinker, Carson, 165, 167
Tuberville, Tommy, 76
Tucker, Jerome, 189
Tulane University, 56, 131
Turnipseed, Thad, 165
Tuscaloosa, AL

287

INDEX

Index

About the Author

LARS ANDERSON is a *New York Times* best-selling author of nine books, including *The Mannings*, *The Storm and the Tide*, *Carlisle vs. Army*, and *The All Americans*. A twenty-year veteran of *Sports Illustrated* and a former senior writer at *Bleacher Report*, Anderson is an instructor of journalism at the University of Alabama. He lives in Birmingham, Alabama, with his wife, April, and their three children.

Twitter handle: @LarsAnderson71